RICHARD II AND THE IRISH KINGS

Richard II
and
the Irish Kings

DARREN MCGETTIGAN

FOUR COURTS PRESS

Typeset in 12.5pt on 16.5pt Garamond PremierPro by
Carrigboy Typesetting Services
FOUR COURTS PRESS LTD
7 Malpas Street, Dublin 8, Ireland
www.fourcourtspress.ie
and in North America for
FOUR COURTS PRESS
c/o ISBS, 920 NE 58th Avenue, Suite 300, Portland, OR 97213

ISBN 978-1-84682-602-3

Printed by TJ International
Padstow, Cornwall, England

To my parents,

Eamonn and May

For Art MacMurchadha Caomhánach

EOGHAN MACCRAITH

Ór corcra ar chlar a mbrannaibh
Ór ceard ar a gcath-bharraibh
Ór tar sréin glan-nuaidhe a ngreagh
le féinn lann-uaine Laighean.

Bright gold is on their chessboard,
Wrought gold on their helmets,
Goldwork on the shining bridles
Of the steeds of Leinster's green-lanced host.

Ní leas-ainm Laighnigh an óir
D'fhéinn Laighean um cheann gcomhóil
Feinnidh um an ól ní ibh
Éin-digh nach a hór ibhthir.

Leinstermen of the gold
is no false name for them at banquet;
At carouse no hero
quaffs drink but from gold.

Contents

Abbreviations   8

List of illustrations   9

Acknowledgments   11

Introduction   15

1. Richard II and his western island   31

2. Fourteenth-century Gaelic Ireland – a new Sparta   61

3. Richard's first expedition to Ireland, 1394–5   93

4. Richard and the Ó Néill kings of Tyrone   121

5. Richard's second expedition to Ireland, June–July 1399   165

6. 'Now for our Irish wars'   195

Bibliography   203

Index   217

Abbreviations

AC	Annals of Connacht
AFM	Annals of the Four Masters
ALC	Annals of Loch Cé
ASI	Annals of Saints' Island
AU	Annals of Ulster
CIHM	Chronicle of Ireland by Henry Marleburrough
DIB	*Dictionary of Irish biography*
IHS	*Irish Historical Studies*
JRSAI	*Journal of the Royal Society of Antiquaries*
NHI	*New history of Ireland*
ODNB	*Oxford dictionary of national biography*
PRIA	*Proceedings of the Royal Irish Academy*
UJA	*Ulster Journal of Archaeology*

Illustrations

FIGURES

Maps

1	The island of Ireland 1394	37
2	Leinster 1394	43
3	Ulster 1394	51
4	Wales 1399	183

Genealogies

1	The English royal family	23
2	Richard II's immediate family	33
3	The Ó Néill kings of Tyrone	62
4	The MacMurchadha Caomhánach kings of Leinster	97

PLATES
(between pages 128 and 129)

1 Richard II and his queen, Anne of Bohemia, from the illuminated 'R' of the Shrewsbury Charter (1389)

2 Interior of the left wing of the Wilton Diptych: Richard II presented by John the Baptist, Edward the Confessor and Edmund, king and martyr. Interior of the right wing of the Wilton Diptych: the Virgin and Child with eleven angels (c.1395–9)

3 Rock and castle of Dunamase

4 The rath of Tullaghoge and a crannog in Tyrone (1602)

5 Harry Avery's castle, Newtown-Stewart, Co. Tyrone

6 The O'Kane tomb, Dungiven priory, Co. Derry

7 A late-medieval Irish spur

8 A late-medieval Irish dagger with scabbard

9 The castle of Carlow

10 Shrine of the Book of Mulling

11 The Kavanagh Charter Horn

12 Thomas Mowbray, earl of Nottingham and marshal of England, with Richard II

13 Seal of Aodh Reamhar Ó Néill

14 Carrickfergus castle

15 The ecclesiastical settlement of Armagh, as it lay destroyed in 1602

16 Trim castle, Co. East Meath

17 Teach Midchuarda: plan of the banqueting hall at Tara

18 Tower of St Mary Magdalene, Drogheda, Co. Louth

19 The Seven Churches, Glendalough, Co. Wicklow

20 A duel with daggers

21 Richard II knighting Henry of Monmouth, the future King Henry V

22 Relief ships arriving on the Leinster coastline

23 Art MacMurchadha parleys with Sir Thomas Despenser, the earl of Gloucester

24 Jean Creton and John Montagu, the earl of Salisbury, arrive at Conway in Wales

25 Richard II's fleet returns to Britain

26 Richard II is captured by Henry Percy, the earl of Northumberland

Acknowledgments

First and foremost I would very much like to thank my family –
my parents Eamonn and May, my brothers Paul (and Cliana) and
William (who again did some proofreading for me), my sisters
Teresa and Anna, my niece Solas and nephew Daniel and my aunt
Ann – for their continued love and support of my history career.
I would also like to thank my wider family in Co. Wicklow and
Co. Donegal, especially my grand-aunt Kathleen McGettigan and
my cousin Frank McGettigan (who again provided some
photographs for one of my books), for their continued support of
my research and publications. I would like to take the opportunity
of the publication of this book to remember my relatives who have
sadly passed away since my last book was published. These include
my grand-uncle and grand-aunt John and Bridget McGettigan, my
grand-uncle Fr Oliver McGettigan, my grand-aunt Madge
Sherman, my Donegal cousins Cathal Bonner and Neal McGettigan
and my aunt in New Zealand, Josephine Hunter-Walsh.

I would also like to thank my friends for their continued
friendship and support: Terry Clavin, who did some proofreading
and editing for me, Joe and Estefania McNabb (and Thomas and
Hugo), Gavin Slattery, Emmett and Emer O'Byrne (and all their

children), Paul McGuill and Denis Teevan. Since the publication of my last book I have been working as a tutor and occasional lecturer in the School of History at University College Dublin. For their kind support of my teaching at UCD, I would like to thank my fellow tutors and lecturers, Kate Breslin and Emma Lyons in the Secretary's Office, all my students and especially Dr Tadhg Ó hAnnracháin, head of school. Thanks also are due to Michael Merrigan, Seamus O'Reilly, Dr Gianpiero Cavalerri and Edmund Gilbert of the Irish DNA Atlas Project, who co-opted me as historical advisor onto their very exciting project.

There are many people from libraries and institutions all over Europe that I wish to thank for their assistance in sourcing the illustrations for this book. In Ireland, I would like to thank Finbarr Connolly of the Rights and Reproductions Section of the National Museum of Ireland, Berni Metcalfe and James Harte of the Manuscript Department of the National Library of Ireland, Sharon Sutton of the Digital Resources and Imaging Services Office at Trinity College Dublin, Fr Paul Finnerty of the Limerick Diocesan Office and Naomi O'Nolan and Aoife O'Shaughnessy of the Hunt Museum, Limerick. From institutions abroad I would like to express my grateful appreciation to Jackie Brown, permissions manager, and Martin Mintz and Chris Rawlings of the Picture Library at the British Library, Sharon Davies of the Shropshire Archives, Daragh Kenny of the Picture Library at the National Gallery (London), and Luca Pes of the Bayerische Verwaltung der staatlichen Schlösser, Gärten und Seen, München. I also wish to thank Ciaran McLarnan and Mark Cranwell of the Department of the Environment of Northern Ireland for facilitating my access to the O'Kane tomb in the priory at Dungiven.

ACKNOWLEDGMENTS

This book has its origins in the early 1990s with the wonderful undergraduate history course taught by professor (and later, president of UCD) Dr Art Cosgrove. Art gave a very memorable series of lectures comparing late-medieval Ireland, England, Scotland and Wales. I remember promising myself that one day I would write a book about Richard II's encounters with the Irish kings during his two expeditions to Ireland in the 1390s. Perhaps the book is a little late but I do hope readers will think that it was worth the effort. Four Courts Press have again shown themselves to be great supporters of my research and I would like to express my appreciation to all the staff, especially Martin Fanning and Sam Tranum, for seeing another one of my books through to publication.

Finally, I would very much like to acknowledge my appreciation of the National University of Ireland, which very kindly awarded me a grant towards publication of the wonderful illustrations that appear in this book.

Introduction: the forgotten kings

Occasionally historians make the assertion, sometimes unwarranted, that they are writing about a forgotten aspect of history. I believe that I am not mistaken, however, in stating that Art MacMurchadha Caomhánach, the king of the Irish of the Leinster mountains (1375–1416/17), and Niall Mór and Niall Óg Ó Néill, rulers of the Irish kingdom of Tyrone and high-kings of Ulster (1364–97 and 1397–1403, respectively), are not very well known in Ireland today, outside the world of historians who specialize in late-medieval Irish history. These three men were successful, ambitious and capable kings, who achieved a great deal of real substance. In fact, they were by far the most successful Irish kings of the late-medieval period. Their maturity and willingness to compromise when necessary compare favourably with their warlike Irish counterparts of the sixteenth century. Art MacMurchadha and the Ó Néill kings bequeathed intact and expanded kingdoms to their successors, and it is not their fault that their fifteenth-century successors failed to build on these solid foundations. Although many Irish people may be aware of the English king Richard II (1377–99), any awareness is possibly because of Shakespeare's play, written centuries later. Most may not be aware that Richard led very large armies to Ireland twice at the close of the fourteenth century, in 1394–5 and 1399, and that the king's second sojourn to his western island cost Richard his crown, and ultimately his life.

The account written by the French chronicler Jean Creton, during the second expedition, of the parley he witnessed between Art MacMurchadha and Thomas Despenser, the earl of Gloucester, that occurred in the summer of 1399, is one of the most dramatic and famous records to have been preserved concerning late-medieval Ireland. Richard's march or *chevauchée*, through the mountain ranges and forests of south Leinster had not gone well, and the English king and his generals had just decided to return with their hungry army to Dublin. It was at this moment that Art MacMurchadha, who had isolated and harassed the English soldiers for the previous eleven days with his horsemen and kerne, sent a friar to request a parley. The earl of Gloucester and the entire rearguard of the English army, 'two hundred lancers, and a thousand archers', were sent to meet with the Irish king, somewhere in the mountains and woods of south-east Co. Wicklow.[1] Creton tagged along 'as one desirous of seeing the honour, condition, force, and power of Macmore'.[2] The king of Leinster appeared very dramatically on a fine white horse that Creton states cost him four hundred cows. 'Between two woods, at some distance from the sea', MacMurchadha left his warriors and galloped down to meet Despenser 'near a little brook', casting 'a great long dart ... with

---

1 J. Webb, 'Translation of a French metrical history of the deposition of King Richard the Second, written by a contemporary, and comprising the period from his last expedition into Ireland to his death', *Archaeologia*, 20:1 (1823), 37–9; hereafter cited as, Creton, 'A French metrical history'.   2 Ibid., 39.

much skill' as he did so.[3] They spoke together for a while, but the talks failed, and according to Creton, Art said 'nothing venture nothing have' to the earl of Gloucester as both departed from the little stream and returned to their men (see figure 23).[4]

When told the details of the negotiations, Creton records that King Richard's face 'grew pale with anger', and that 'he sware in great wrath by Saint Edward, that, no, never would he depart from Ireland, till, alive or dead, he had him [Art] in his power'.[5] By the end of the year, however, it was Richard who had been deposed and was a prisoner of his enemies. Art went on to have a highly successful career as king of the Irish of south Leinster until his own death sometime in 1416 or possibly very early 1417. The fact that a contemporary coloured drawing of the parley between MacMurchadha and the earl of Gloucester was made to accompany Creton's chronicle has only served to increase the importance and drama of the event.

A similarly dramatic account of a pilgrimage made in 1397 by a Catalan viscount, Raymon de Perellós, to St Patrick's Purgatory in Lough Derg in Ulster has also been preserved.[6] The Catalan visited the court of Niall Óg Ó Néill, the king of Tyrone, at Christmas 1397, and later wrote a remarkable account of the customs, manner of dress, food and general way of life of the Irish people of Tyrone whom he encountered. As a result, we are unusually well informed about this group of late-medieval Irish kings.

---

3 Ibid., 40.   4 Ibid., pp 41–3.   5 Ibid., pp 43–4.   6 D. Carpenter, 'The pilgrim from Catalonia/Aragon: Ramon de Perellós, 1397' in M. Haren and Y. de Pontfarcy (eds), *The medieval pilgrimage to St Patrick's Purgatory*, pp 99–119.

THE SOURCES

A French chronicler, Jean Froissart (*c.*1337–*c.*1410), wrote an account of Richard II's first expedition to Ireland in 1394–5, although Froissart never visited the island himself. Born in Valenciennes in the County of Hainault, Froissart was a Burgundian who travelled to England in 1361 to serve Queen Philippa. The queen, also a native of Hainault, was married to the English king, Edward III. Froissart remained in the service of Queen Philippa until her death in 1369, during which time he visited both Scotland and Wales. He was also present in English Bordeaux in 1367, where he witnessed the birth of Prince Richard.[7] After 1369 Froissart spent most of his time back in Flanders, where he became a priest. He returned to England in 1395, where he met with King Richard, who had just returned to England from his first expedition to Ireland.[8] Froissart was interested in the kingdoms and principalities to the west and north of England, and, while on a journey to Leeds castle to meet the English king, he interrogated an English knight, Sir William de Lisle, about his experiences in Ireland while on the expedition with the king. De Lisle had taken the opportunity to visit St Patrick's Purgatory while in Ireland. Froissart records in his chronicle that he met Richard in his chamber in Leeds castle and presented the English king with an expensive and beautifully decorated book, which he states greatly pleased the king.[9]

While in the service of Queen Philippa (before 1369), Froissart had accompanied the king's son, Lionel, duke of Clarence, on an embassy into Italy.[10] When he encountered at court the English

---

7 G. Brereton (ed.), *Jean Froissart: Chronicles* (London, 1978), pp 9–11; hereafter cited as Froissart, *Chronicles*. 8 Ibid., pp 11–15. 9 Ibid., pp 405–8. 10 Ibid.,

squire Henry Cristall (or Crystede), who had been captured in his youth by the Irish and eventually freed by the duke of Clarence, Froissart interrogated the man for information about his exotic early life among the Irish. Cristall recounted that he had been captured as a young knight while fighting for the English earl of Ormond, by a Leinster Irishman called Brin Costerec. According to Cristall, his horse had bolted during a skirmish, and Brin Costerec had leapt on and taken him prisoner by wrapping his arms around him. Cristall was probably still a young teenager at the time and perhaps the Irishman took pity on him. In any event Cristall, was not harmed. He ended up married to Brin Costerec's daughter 'and had two daughters with her'. He informed Froissart that he lived honourably among the Irish for seven years, until he was exchanged for his father-in-law, who was captured in 1361 by the duke of Clarence's soldiers. Brin Costerec had been riding the horse Cristall had been on when originally captured, which had been recognized by the earl of Ormond's men. When Cristall returned to the English, he did so with his Irish wife and youngest daughter, and they all went to live near Bristol.

The Cristall family continued to speak Irish among themselves, and, as a result, Henry appears to have been hired as chief interpreter for Richard's expedition to Ireland in 1394–5.[11] He recounted to Froissart that he had been asked by the English king to help train some Irish kings – this may have included Niall Óg Ó Néill, the king of Tyrone – in how to become proper Englishmen, in preparation for their knighthood ceremony.[12] Although there are problems with the exact date, place and attendance for this story, there is enough circumstantial evidence

p. 11.   11 Ibid., pp 411–13.   12 Ibid., pp 413–16.

to suggest that the squire Henry Cristall prepared at least some of the Irish kings he mentioned for some sort of knighthood ceremony performed by Richard. Although the account of his capture and life with the Irish appears garbled and some of the events it describes are hard precisely to locate and identify, Cristall probably was a real person and did live for an extended period somewhere in Irish Leinster.[13]

A second contemporary account is a '*viatge*' (Catalan/ Occitan for 'journey') written after 1397 by Ramon de Perellós, first viscount Perellós and second viscount of Roda (d. *c.*1419). Viscount de Perellós was a Catalan, a native of the Perpignan/ Rousillon region of the kingdom of Aragon. He was a soldier and ambassador by profession. He had been captured earlier in his life by the Moors in Granada in 1374. He was also a great personal friend of John I, the king of Aragon (1387–96). De Perellós happened to be on an embassy to Avignon when John I died unexpectedly. According to legend, the king of Aragon dropped dead from fright when he encountered a huge she-wolf while out hunting. As a result, Viscount de Perellós decided to make a pilgrimage to St Patrick's Purgatory in Lough Derg in the north of Ireland, apparently because he was worried about how his deceased friend was faring in the afterlife. St Patrick's Purgatory had the reputation in medieval Europe for being a gateway to purgatory.[14]

The viscount left Aragon on 8 September 1397 and was back on the Continent by March 1398. According to his *viatge*, the Catalan travelled to London first and then spent ten days with Richard, perhaps near Oxford. He recounts how he then travelled to Holyhead in Wales, where he took a ship for Ireland, but made

---

13 R. Hawkins, 'Henry Chrysted (fl. *c.*1340–*c.*1395)', *DIB* (Cambridge, 2009), ii, p. 505.   14 Carpenter, 'The pilgrim from Catalonia/Aragon: Ramon de Perellós,

landfall first on the Isle of Man before eventually reaching Dublin. De Perellós states that he met Roger Mortimer, the earl of March and Ulster, who was Richard's lieutenant in Ireland, and then John Colton, the archbishop of Armagh. Colton brought him to Drogheda and Dundalk and then gave the viscount two guides and a bodyguard of 100 men, who fled back to Dundalk after travelling only five leagues into Tyrone. Ramon was found by Eoin MacDomhnaill, the galloglass constable of Ulster, and escorted to meet Niall Óg Ó Néill. The Catalan then travelled on to make his pilgrimage at St Patrick's Purgatory, before returning to Tyrone to spend Christmas at the court of Ó Néill. He has left a truly remarkable account of the people and customs he encountered there. He spent New Year's Day 1398 with the countess of March, and then returned to France via England.[15] Although large parts of de Perellós' text are taken from earlier accounts of pilgrimages to Lough Derg, his account of his travels in Ulster and his experiences at the court of Ó Néill of Tyrone are regarded as valuable and accurate. The earliest versions of his text that survive today are in Catalan and the Pyrenean dialect Occitan.[16]

A third account comes from Jean Creton (fl. 1386–1420). The official title of the metrical history he wrote is 'La prinse et mort du roy Richart' or 'Book of the capture and death of king Richard II'. It is preserved in the British Library as BL, Harley MS 1319, and is mostly in verse with some prose sections. This manuscript has sixteen wonderful coloured miniatures depicting many aspects of Richard's 1399 expedition, including his envoy's meeting with Art MacMurchadha, and the English king's travels and capture in north Wales.[17] Creton appears to have been a *valet-de-chambre* at

1397', pp 99–103. **15** Ibid., pp 103–19. **16** Ibid., pp 102–3. **17** Jean Creton,

the court of the French king, Charles VI.[18] In the opening of the text he refers to himself as 'a French Gentleman of distinction' and states that in late April 1399, one of his knight friends asked him to accompany him on a visit to England.[19] Creton arrived in London just in time to join the stragglers who were leaving the city in order to join Richard II's expedition to Ireland.[20] The French chronicler caught up with the English monarch before the king reached the port of Milford Haven in south Wales.[21] Creton went on to accompany Richard to Ireland, where he appears to have lived in close contact with the English king, as he was present for many dramatic events and announcements. Although often in close proximity to the king, Creton appears not to have been taken into the king's confidence, and to have misinterpreted the character and role of Richard's cousin, Edward, duke of Aumerle. The duke arrived late in Ireland owing to important business in the border region with Scotland. Creton was sent back early to Wales with John Montagu, the third earl of Salisbury, perhaps for the Frenchman's own safety. This may have been necessary if Creton had alienated Aumerle with his suspicions that the duke was acting traitorously toward Richard. As a result, Creton was perfectly placed to record the capture and deposition of Richard II in north Wales by his cousin, Henry Bolingbroke, who became King Henry IV.

Creton's history is regarded as a crucial contemporary source, although historians agree that his sense of the passage of time is not good and that he was prone to misinterpreting the motives and

'La prinse et mort du roy Richart', BL, Harley MS 1319; http://www.bl.uk/ catalogues/illuminatedmanuscripts/ record.asp/ index.html, accessed 22 May 2015. 18 C. Given-Wilson, *Henry IV* (London, 2016), p. 133, n. 68. 19 Creton, 'A French metrical history', 13. 20 Ibid. 21 Ibid., 13–23.

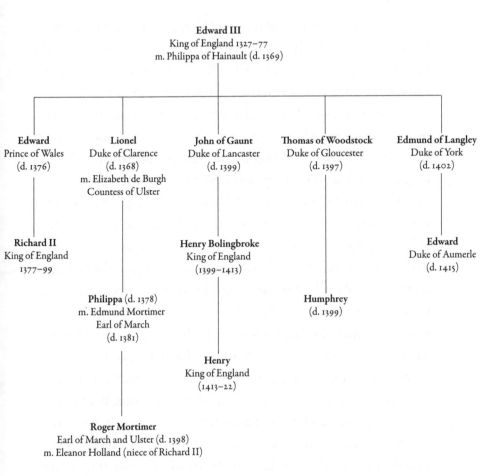

1. The English royal family.

actions of some of the crucial participants in the dramatic events he witnessed.[22] On the plus side, Creton always places events in their correct chronological order, and he is a regarded as a truthful witness. It is his interpretations that modern historians sometimes take issue with. Creton was commissioned to write his history

22 N. Saul, *Richard II* (London, 1999), pp 409–16; D. Johnston, 'Richard II's departure from Ireland, July 1399', *English Historical Review*, 98: 389 (1983), 787–90.

c.1401–*c*.1405, after he had returned to France, by Philip the Bold, the duke of Burgundy.[23] It received the title 'A French metrical history of the deposition of King Richard the Second' from its early nineteenth-century translator and editor, John Webb.

A wide selection of good Irish primary sources survives for this period. These include contemporary bardic poems, one of which was written by an Irish Franciscan friar for one of the Ó Néill kings, and at least one other bardic poem composed to honour Art MacMurchadha Caomhánach.[24] There is also a large group of Irish annals written throughout the late-medieval and early modern periods, which contain good entries for the years 1300–1450. These include the late-medieval Annals of Connacht, the fifteenth-century Annals of Ulster, the Annals of Loch Cé, which date from the late sixteenth century, as well as the Annals of the Four Masters and the Annals of Clonmacnoise, which were written in the first half of the seventeenth century, but are based on earlier sources.[25] A fragment of a set of annals compiled while Richard II was in Ireland survives preserved in manuscript Rawlinson B.488 of the Bodleian Library, Oxford. These annals were largely written by Aughuistín Magraidhin, a canon of Oileán na Naomh or Saints' Island in Lough Ree, in the Irish midlands. Canon Magraidhin, who died in 1405, was known as 'an undisputed master of sacred and secular wisdom, including Latin learning, history, and many other sciences, *ollamh* of eloquence for Western Europe, and

---

23 Creton, 'La prinse et mort du roy Richart'. 24 C. Mhág Craith (ed.), *Dán na mBráthar Mionúr* (Dublin, 1967), i, pp 1–9; (Dublin, 1980), ii, pp 1–4; L. McKenna (ed.), *Aithdioghluim Dána*, i, pp 54–65; ii, pp 33–9; McKenna, 'To Art MacMurchadha Caomhánach', *Irish Monthly*, 56:655 (1928), 98–101. 25 T. O'Neill, *The Irish hand: scribes and their manuscripts from the earliest times to the seventeenth century with an exemplar of scripts* (Portlaoise, Co. Laois, 1984), pp 50–3; N. Evans, 'Annals and Chronicles' in S. Duffy (ed.), *Medieval Ireland: an*

compiler of this book and of many other books'.[26] These annals cover the years 1392–1407 and are a unique record as the fragment does not appear to have been used as a source for any of the later Irish annals.[27]

The Irish annals are complemented by a number of English annals written in Latin. These include the Annals of Ireland, compiled in Kilkenny city by the Franciscan friar, John Clyn. He was the guardian of the friary of Carrick in 1336, and was in the large English town of Kilkenny in 1348–9, where he witnessed first-hand the human devastation wrought by the Black Death. His annals then fall silent, and it is presumed that Clyn himself died of the plague during the early summer of 1349.[28] The Annales Hiberniae were compiled c.1537–9 by James Grace, another native of Co. Kilkenny. These run from 1162 to 1370 and are preserved in a later manuscript in the library of Trinity College Dublin.[29] The Annales Breves Hiberniae were written by Thaddeus Dowling, treasurer and chancellor of the diocese of Leighlin, sometime before 1628.[30] More Latin annals recording events in Ireland throughout the fourteenth century were written at the great Cistercian monastery of St Mary's, just north of the river Liffey in the English city of Dublin.[31] Henry Marleburrough's *Chronicle of Ireland*, which appears in Sir James Ware's *Ancient Irish histories*, is an English source that begins in 1285 and

encyclopedia (New York, 2005), p. 22. **26** Annals of Saints' Island, hereafter referred to as ASI, 1405. **27** S. Ó hInnse (ed.), *Miscellaneous Irish annals (AD 1114–1437)* (Dublin, 1947), pp xiv–xviii. **28** B. Williams (ed.), *The annals of Ireland by Friar John Clyn* (Dublin, 2007), pp 19–20; ibid., pp 252–3. **29** http://www.ucc.ie/celt/published/T100001/index.html, accessed 22 May 2015. **30** http://www.ucc.ie/celt/online/L100012/index.html, accessed 22 May 2015; A. McCormack, 'Thaddeus (Thady) Dowling', *DIB*, iii, pp 433–4. **31** J.T. Gilbert (ed.), *Chartularies of St Mary's Abbey, Dublin* (London, 1884), i, pp 281–366.

continues to the year 1421. It contains good records for the Leinster and east Ulster regions, and is particularly full for the years surrounding King Richard's two expeditions to Ireland in 1394–5 and 1399.[32]

A series of thirty-nine instruments and thirty-six letters, all written in Latin, connected with Richard II's first expedition to Ireland, survive copied into an exchequer roll belonging to the late-medieval English treasury.[33] Brought back to England from Ireland, they were personally given by Richard to the treasurer of England, John Waltham, the bishop of Salisbury (1388–95). Waltham was ordered by the king that the Irish records should be 'enrolled in his Exchequer and afterwards [that he] should place them in his Treasury for safe-keeping'.[34] On 25 June 1395, the instruments and letters were enrolled onto Exchequer Roll 18 for Richard's reign. The Latin instruments contain records of the submissions of eighty Irish kings and chieftains, as well as some gaelicized English lords, to Richard during his time in Ireland, and they date from March 1395 to April 1395.[35] Twenty-three of the Latin letters were written to Richard, mostly by Irish kings, chieftains and bishops, from January to April 1395. This collection of letters contains an important series written by the Ó Néill kings, Niall Mór and his son Niall Óg.[36] Ten of the original documents survive in the English chancery files, including one submission by the king of Irish Leinster, Art MacMurchadha Caomhánach.

---

32 J. Ware (ed.), *Ancient Irish histories: the works of Spencer, Campion, Hanmer and Marleburrough* (Dublin, 1809), ii.   33 E. Curtis, *Richard II in Ireland, 1394–5 and submissions of the Irish chiefs* (Oxford, 1927), pp v–vi.   34 Ibid., 'The instruments touching Ireland', p. 149.   35 Curtis, *Richard II in Ireland*, p. v; ibid., 'The instruments touching Ireland', pp 149–201.   36 E. Curtis, 'Letters sent to the king when in Ireland', pp 203–25.

Unfortunately, these ten documents were in very fragile condition when examined by the historian Edmund Curtis in 1927.[37]

Around 1927 Curtis also rediscovered a series of seven letters written in French, six of which were connected with Richard II's first expedition to Ireland in 1394–5 and one of which was from the English king's second expedition to the island in 1399.[38] The letters were preserved in a 'formulary' book meant to provide scribes and notaries with models for their compositions, which was found in the library of All Souls' College at Oxford University.[39] As Curtis pointed out, the letters are copies but 'The first copyist must, of course, have seen the originals'.[40] Five letters were dictated by Richard II himself, four around October 1394 and one in June 1399, and were sent to various recipients in England. One letter was written in 1394–5 by the king's Gascon knight, Janico Dartas, who sent it to Bishop Waltham in England. The author of another, also written around October 1394, is unknown. The content of many of the letters is extremely vivid and noteworthy, and they provide a great deal of detail about the arrival of Richard's first expedition in Ireland in October 1394. Various dramatic accounts of the fighting that occurred over the ensuing days, in the forests of Co. Carlow, between the king's soldiers and the warriors of Art MacMurchadha, are uniquely preserved in these letters.[41]

Another great repository for primary-source material dating from the reign of Richard II is the Calendar of Irish Chancery Letters, c.1244–1509, known as CIRCLE. A part of the Irish Chancery Rolls Project, CIRCLE had been online since 2011.

37 Ibid., *Richard II in Ireland*, p. 1; Chancery Miscell. Bundle 10, File 25, National Archives, Kew, London.   38 E. Curtis, 'Unpublished letters from Richard II in Ireland, 1394–5', *PRIA*, 37C: 14 (1927), 276–303.   39 Ibid., 276.   40 Ibid. 41 Ibid., 283–98.

One hundred and twenty-three Irish medieval chancery rolls were destroyed in the great Four Courts explosion and fire that obliterated the Irish Public Record Office at the beginning of the Irish Civil War in 1922. Jocelyn Otway-Ruthven, a professor of history at Trinity College Dublin from 1951 to 1980, had the clever idea of reconstituting as much as possible of the Irish chancery rolls from calendars, facsimiles and extracts copied from the original rolls by scholars and authors before 1922. CIRCLE contains a substantial portion of what once were the close rolls and patent rolls for the reign of Richard II, dating from 1377 to 1399.[42]

Finally, there is a great deal of primary-source material concerning the reign of Richard II and his two Irish expeditions preserved in English archives. These include detailed accounts in a surviving wardrobe book of the wages for his troops, as well as the English equivalents of the Irish close and patent rolls for Richard's reign, which happily have survived.[43] There are also various contemporary English and Welsh chronicles that record Richard's expeditions to Ireland as well as many of the events, some of them quite momentous, that occurred in Richard's English kingdom at this time. These include Knighton's Chronicle, written by an Augustinian monk from Leicester, which covers the years 1337–96 and was written towards the end of the fourteenth century.[44] Another example is the Chronicle of Adam Usk, a Welsh cleric (d.1430) and supporter of the Mortimer earls of March and Ulster.[45] His chronicle covers the years 1377–1421 and

42 http://www.chancery.tcd.ie/index.html, accessed 22 May, 2015. 43 Saul, *Richard II*, p. 279; D. Johnston, 'Richard II and the submissions of Gaelic Ireland', *IHS*, 22:85 (1980), 2; E 101/402/20, National Archives, Kew, London. 44 G.H. Mardin (ed.), *Knighton's chronicle, 1337–96* (Oxford, 1995), p. xv. 45 C. Given-Wilson (ed.), *The chronicle of Adam Usk, 1377–1421* (Oxford, 1997), pp xiii–xxxviii.

has some material relating to Ireland. Usk was also a supporter of Henry Bolingbroke, the man who deposed Richard after his return from Ireland in 1399. As a result, he encountered an imprisoned Richard in the Tower of London on 21 September 1399, soon after he had been deposed.[46]

46 *Chronicle of Adam Usk*, 1399, pp 62–5.

CHAPTER I

Richard II and his western island

The English king, Richard II, was born in the town of Bordeaux, then a part of English Gascony, in January 1367.[1] His father was the famous Black Prince, Edward of Woodstock, prince of Wales and the victor of the battle of Poitiers fought in 1356 when the king of France was captured by the English army.[2] Richard's mother was Joan, herself a princess, the daughter of Edmund, earl of Kent, who was the sixth son of King Edward I.[3] Richard's grandfather, Edward III, king of England from 1327 to 1377, was one of the most successful late-medieval English monarchs. The Black Prince died before becoming king in 1376, after years of ill health. Richard himself became king of England soon after, when his by now very elderly grandfather died in June 1377.[4] The ten-year-old boy was crowned on 16 July 1377.[5]

Richard won fame at fourteen for his calm, brave conduct during the great Peasants' Revolt that broke out in Essex and Kent

1 Saul, *Richard II*, pp 6 and 12.   2 Ibid., pp 9–10; the Black Prince also fought well under his father, King Edward III, in 1346, at the battle of Crécy: J. Bradbury, *The Routledge companion to medieval warfare* (Abingdon, 2004), pp 200 and 205.
3 Saul, *Richard II*, pp 10–12.   4 Ibid., pp 17–23.   5 Ibid., pp 24–6.

in May and June of 1381. The immediate cause of the revolt was the clumsy introduction by the government of the English kingdom of a poll tax that was regarded as unfair by substantial elements of the population. There had been a build-up of other grievances over the preceding years, which exploded into unrest that summer. The leaders of the revolt were Wat Tyler and the shadowy figure Jack Straw.[6] The rebels marched on London, got into the city on 13 June and went on the rampage. The prisons were broken open and the Savoy palace, which belonged to Richard's uncle John of Gaunt, became a particular target of the rebels and was completely destroyed. Richard negotiated with the rebels at Mile End on 14 June. The next day, in another parley with the rebels at Smithfield, the young king encountered Wat Tyler. Tyler was discourteous to the king and ended up being killed by the mayor of London, Sir William Walworth. Afterwards, Richard led the remaining rebels out of London, and they largely dispersed. Bloody retribution was later exacted from the surviving leadership of the revolt by the nobility and agents of the king, once they had recovered their composure. The personal role of the king in successfully defeating what was a highly dangerous revolt was emphasized by his supporters and many of the chroniclers writing at the time.[7]

When Richard grew to adulthood, he was not much of a warrior king. He favoured peace with the French and took a great interest in art and in how he was perceived as king (see figure 2).[8] He developed some odd and dangerous habits that created problems for the governance of his English kingdom. In particular,

6 *Chronicle of Adam Usk*, 1381, pp 2–5.   7 Saul, *Richard II*, pp 56–82.
8 C. Allmand, *The Hundred Years War: England and France at war, c.1300–c.1450* (Cambridge, 2001), pp 24–6; D. Gordon, L. Monnas and C. Elam (eds), *The regal image of Richard II and the Wilton Diptych* (London, 1997).

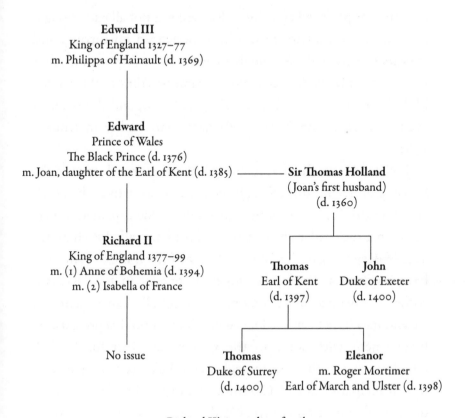

2. Richard II's immediate family.

he periodically became so attached to an individual or a very small group of favourites that he needlessly alienated the vast majority of the English nobility, who felt excluded from royal favour as a result. This character trait led to explosions of unrest and even deadly violence among the English higher nobility on a number of occasions during his reign. On occasion, Richard also lacked a sense of proportion, and he could be extremely vindictive towards enemies. In particular, in 1397 Richard was involved in the murder of his uncle, Thomas of Woodstock, the duke of Gloucester, who was killed in Calais. This darkened his reputation at the time, and the stain has persisted ever since.[9] Richard was not all bad, though. He was often kind to those who experienced misfortune and appears to have had a genuinely loving relationship with his first wife, Anne of Bohemia (see figure 1). Anne was the daughter of the Holy Roman emperor, Charles IV (1346–78), and the sister of Wenzel, king of the Romans. Richard married her in January 1382.[10]

Richard II was the first reigning English monarch to visit the lordship of Ireland since King John in 1210. Just why he had such an interest in it may never be fully known. One explanation may lie in what the modern historian Nigel Saul has called Richard II's 'idea of deepening his lordship within the British Isles'.[11] This may have involved a developing imperial concept in how Richard wished to organize his dominions. As a result, Richard's interest in Ireland may have been the logical development of his pre-existing involvement with some of the western areas of his English kingdom, such as the Chester region and Wales. Richard created a new principality out of Cheshire in 1397.[12] The king was the direct lord of over one-third of Wales, paid close attention to the country, and was quite popular among the Welsh.[13] Richard's first expedition to Ireland in 1394–5, therefore, might have made logical sense in the context of his other policies in western Britain. Still, the lordship of Ireland was normally far down the list of priorities of the late-medieval English kings. It usually came after the English possessions in France and Wales, and sometimes even

9 Saul, *Richard II*, pp 374 and 379. 10 Ibid., pp 86, 90 and 93. 11 Ibid., p. 270.
12 Ibid., pp 270, 291, 393–4; 'County of Chester erected into a principality', 21 Ric. II.c.9, *The statutes of the realm* (London, 1816/Reprinted 1963), ii, p. 100.
13 R.R. Davies, *The revolt of Owain Glyn Dŵr* (Oxford, 1995), pp 36 and 77–80; D. Johnston, 'Iolo Goch and the English: Welsh poetry and politics in the fourteenth century', *Cambridge Medieval Celtic Studies*, 12 (1986), 87.

the securing of the Scottish border. Seen in this context, Richard's interest in his western island was quite unusual, and many of his nobles and subjects seem to have thought so too.

Richard's preparations for his expedition to Ireland began well before the sudden death of his queen, Anne of Bohemia, at the manor of Sheen on 7 June 1394.[14] So the English king did not undertake his Irish campaign solely in an effort to assuage his personal grief, although no doubt keeping busy and the change of scene must have helped. There is also little evidence for support in Ireland for Pope Clement VII (the Avignon antipope) and certainly not enough to justify such a large English expedition. Peace with France during this period of Richard's reign was an important factor, as it freed up time and resources and allowed the English king and his advisors the opportunity for the Irish expedition. The ongoing Gaelic revival is often given as the major reason for Richard's sojourn to Ireland in 1394–5. The English of Ireland, however, had been telling the kings of England that their colony was about to fall to the Irish since 1311.[15] By 1390 the most successful Irish kings had already reached the limit of their power. When Richard II gathered his army and made his extensive preparations in early 1394, Dublin, for example, was not under siege by the Irish, and nor were Dundalk and Limerick. Although many English towns paid black rents to their Irish neighbours, none except for perhaps New Ross in Leinster, and the much smaller towns of the earldom of Ulster – Carrickfergus, Coleraine and Downpatrick – were actually under the immediate control of Irish kings. There was no sign in the early 1390s of the powerful

14 Saul, *Richard II*, p. 225; *Chronicle of Adam Usk*, 1394, pp 18–19. 15 J.F. Lydon, 'The Bruce invasion of Ireland: an examination of some problems' in S. Duffy (ed.), *Robert the Bruces's Irish wars: the invasions of Ireland, 1306–1329* (Stroud, 2002), p. 71.

Irish kings making a new high-king of Ireland from one of their number, as some of the Irish kings had done in the mid thirteenth century. Therefore, the real reasons for Richard's first expedition to Ireland must lie elsewhere. Nevertheless, when he landed in Ireland, he was faced by an able group of Irish warrior kings, who had known military success for decades, many of whom also had experience of high-level negotiations with the English.

THE ISLAND OF IRELAND, 1394

Although much better known than in earlier medieval times, the island of Ireland at the end of the fourteenth century was still an exotic place on the western edge of the late-medieval world. In 1394 there were really two Irelands. The first, the lordship of Ireland, was one of the many territories assembled in western Atlantic Europe by the kings of England over the centuries. The second was Gaelic Ireland, a strange land to late-medieval Europeans, a land of mountain, forest and bog, inhabited by native people viewed as savages by the English and other visitors to the island. The lordship of Ireland had grown out of the arrival of Anglo-Norman mercenaries invited into the kingdom of Leinster in the late twelfth century.[16] The large-scale migration of English people that followed transformed much of the island forever.[17] By 1394 the English colony was concentrated along the eastern seaboard of the island, stretching from Coleraine in Ulster to Kinsale in Munster, usually in fertile lowland areas with easy access to the ports of western England and Wales. The English of Ireland in 1394 were still generally a very distinct people to the Irish

16 J. Gillingham, *The Angevin Empire* (London, 2001), pp 27–9.   17 R. Frame, *Colonial Ireland, 1169–1369* (Dublin, 1981), pp 53, 69–79.

Map 1. The island of Ireland 1394.

inhabitants of the island, although there was an increasing level of gaelicization among a sizeable proportion of the English population in some areas of Ireland. (This had led to the passing of the Statute of Kilkenny in 1366.) English areas of Ireland, especially in the more fertile areas, were covered by a dense network of villages and small towns, connected by highways.[18] English farming practice included a high level of tillage and the English rode horses differently from the Irish, using saddles and stirrups.[19] In 1394 many of the English in Ireland still spoke various archaic dialects of English, two of which survived in south Co. Wexford and the Fingal region of north Co. Dublin into the early nineteenth century. The majority of the English in Ireland obeyed the English king's law and sent representatives from their towns and from among their nobility to the Irish parliament, as well as paying their taxes and contributing soldiers to official hostings.[20] The greater English nobles in Ireland also tended to visit the kingdom of England quite regularly, where they met the English kings and often married noble Englishwomen. All this served to make the English very distinct from the Irish population of Ireland. It must always be born in mind, however, that right from the very beginning of the arrival of the Anglo-Normans in Ireland, when Strongbow married Diarmait MacMurchadha's daughter Aoife in 1170, the island began to change them.[21]

The Irish inhabited most of the north, west and south-west, and also the mountainous, forested and bogland interior of Ireland. The late-medieval Irish were descended from the native pre-

18 M. Kelly, *A history of the Black Death in Ireland* (Stroud, 2001), pp 26–37.
19 S. Hughes, *Illustrating the past: archaeological discoveries on Irish road schemes* (Dublin, 2015), pp 82–91.   20 Frame, *Colonial Ireland, 1169–1369*, pp 92–110.
21 A.B. Scott and F.X. Martin (eds), *Expugnatio Hibernica: the conquest of Ireland, by Giraldus Cambrensis* (Dublin, 1978), pp 66–7.

invasion population of the island. Their customs, manner of dress and general way of life in the late fourteenth century made the Irish exotic and strange to most other Western Europeans of the time. In contrast to the English population of the island, by 1394 most of the Irish kings and chieftains recognized no authority in Ireland but their own. Much of Gaelic Ireland was heavily forested and the tree cover on the island appears to have been expanding throughout the later fourteenth century, owing to population loss caused by the Black Death of 1348–50.[22] There were very few settlements of any size – even large villages – in Gaelic Ireland, although ancient monasteries survived in some areas. The native wildlife in late-medieval Ireland was also quite exotic compared to that in more settled areas, such as the kingdom of England. Many types of Irish hawk were highly valued in late-medieval Europe for hunting, and, as a later English poet wrote, there was 'Great store of wolves in Ireland'.[23]

Over the centuries, the kings of England had shown little interest in their lordship of Ireland, especially after King Henry III. This was provided that the island was relatively quiet and that the by now prosperous English areas of settlement continued to be a lucrative source of revenue.[24] This ensured that Ireland was almost unique in a European context in that it had absentee rulers for most of the late-medieval period.[25] Although the lordship of Ireland shared this aspect of English overlordship with other territories ruled by the late-medieval English kings, in Ireland's case it led to the neglect of many aspects of government. One of the

22 Kelly, *A history of the Black Death in Ireland*, p. 11.   23 J. Small (ed.), *The image of Irelande with a discouerie of woodkerne, by John Derricke (1581)*, pp 39–40; D.C. O'Sullivan (ed.), *The natural history of Ireland by Philip O'Sullivan Beare* (Cork, 2009), pp 84–5, 96–105.   24 Frame, *Colonial Ireland, 1169–1369*, pp 61–3. 25 Curtis, *Richard II in Ireland, 1394–5*, pp 14–15.

most serious consequences of royal English neglect was that it allowed the English settlers to dominate the government of the island, to the exclusion of the descendants of the original inhabitants, the Gaelic Irish. The English kings over the years, and especially after the reign of Henry III, showed very little interest in the Irish. The assertion by one modern historian that no Irish king was ever 'transformed into a baron of the Crown with hereditary succession or [had ever] taken his seat among the peers of the Council' is only slightly exaggerated.[26]

By 1394, the lordship of Ireland had long ceased to be a wealthy possession of the English king. In fact, by the end of the fourteenth century the English colony was a needy drain on the financial and military resources of the king of England. It was an English king, Edward I (d. 1307), who probably financially destroyed the lordship of Ireland. It is estimated that from the time of King John in the early thirteenth century, the kings of England took almost £90,000 from Ireland, not taking into account many missing records, and the costly contributions that the lordship of Ireland made to the English kings' wars in troops, shipping and supplies.[27] Edward I alone was responsible for extracting over £52,000 of this from his Irish lordship.[28] In the end he not only bankrupted his Irish administration, but eventually precipitated an invasion of the island in 1315–18, sponsored by Robert Bruce, Edward's main opponent in the war for Scotland.[29] Edward I's successor, his son Edward II, is often blamed for the terrible impact that the Bruce invasion had on the lordship of Ireland. The real damage, however, had already been done by his father.

26 Ibid., p. 14.   27 J.F. Lydon, 'Select documents XXIV: Edward II and the Revenues of Ireland in 1311–12', *IHS*, 14 (1964–5), 39–57. 28 Frame, *Colonial Ireland, 1169–1369*, pp 66–7.   29 Lydon, 'The Bruce invasion of Ireland', pp 71–88.

The Bruce invasion of Ireland had coincided with a period of famine on the island, and had ushered in a very difficult era for the English colony. The impacts of war and famine had been compounded by many recorded instances of unusually bad weather and other natural disasters. Unfortunately for the English of Ireland in 1348–50, the nature of their settlements and way of life had provided nearly perfect conditions for the spread of the Black Death, a devastating outbreak of bubonic plague, part of a Europe-wide pandemic that had reached the island in those years. The English towns of Dublin, Cork, Drogheda, New Ross, Waterford, Youghal and Kilkenny were severely hit, as were the networks of villages, farms and abbeys in their hinterlands. This was especially true in the counties of Dublin, Tipperary, Kilkenny and Meath.[30] It has been estimated that 50 per cent of the English population of Ireland may have died during the Black Death of 1348–50.[31] The English colony in Ireland proved to be resilient and it survived.[32] Nevertheless, the colony was under pressure from constant attack by the Irish inhabitants of the island and found it difficult to recover. According to various annals and chronicles, throughout the fourteenth century there were serious 'cattle plagues' in Ireland, periods of severe storms, some very heavy snowfalls, major famines and various epidemics and outbreaks of smallpox and 'slaedan' – probably influenza. In the second half of the century, recurrent outbreaks of bubonic plague caused terrible mortality among the English – and later the Irish – populations of the island.[33]

30 Kelly, *A history of the Black Death in Ireland*, pp 28–38; R. Frame, 'Two kings in Leinster: the crown and the MicMhurchadha in the fourteenth century' in T.B. Barry, R. Frame and K. Simms (eds), *Colony and frontier in medieval Ireland* (London, 1995), p. 165; CIHM, 1348.   31 Kelly, *A history of the Black Death in Ireland*, p. 38.   32 Frame, *Colonial Ireland, 1169–1369*, p. 69.   33 AC, 1302, 1308, 1315, 1317, 1318, 1321, 1324, 1325, 1327, 1328, 1335, 1338, 1339, 1349, 1361, 1363, 1373; AU, 1314, 1315, 1318, 1321, 1324, 1325, 1336, 1346, 1360; ASI,

The region stretching from the small town of Dundalk south to Dublin was the most important English area on the island. A dense patchwork of English settlement stretched inland to cover most of the counties of Dublin, Meath, Louth and Kildare, as well as much of Co. Westmeath and some of north Co. Carlow. Dublin and Drogheda were big English towns and there was a network of smaller towns and villages across this entire region.[34] Foreign visitors to Ireland were impressed by the late-medieval city of Dublin. De Perellós, who visited Dublin in 1397, later wrote that it was 'quite a big city'.[35] Creton, who was in the city during the summer of 1399, noted that Dublin was 'a good city, standing upon the sea ... containing ... great abundance of merchandise and provisions'.[36] The main part of the city, including the walled old town, lay south of the river Liffey. Dublin had expanded greatly since the Anglo-Norman conquest in the late twelfth century, but the heart of the city was still predominantly centred on the area once covered by the pre-invasion Scandinavian town.[37] The descendants of the pre-Anglo-Norman population of Dublin lived to the north of the Liffey, in the suburb of Oxmantown.[38] At the end of the fourteenth century Dublin had two cathedrals: Christ Church, situated in the heart of the old town, and St Patrick's, which lay in a southern suburb outside the city walls. It was very

1392; Annales Hiberniae, 1310, 1317, 1330, 1332, 1337, 1348, 1361, 1370; Kelly, *A history of the Black Death in Ireland*, pp 39–40; Henry Marleburrough records 'great mortality' in coastal Ireland in 1348, 'a great mortalitie of men ... but few women' in 1361, a 'third great pestilence in Ireland' in 1370, and that 'the fourth great pestilence was in Ireland' in 1383; CIHM, 1348, 1361, 1370, 1383. 34 Some of the more important smaller English towns included Dundalk, Navan, Kells, Trim, with its great Anglo-Norman castle, Athboy, Mullingar, Kildare, Naas and Athy. 35 Carpenter, 'The pilgrim from Catalonia/Aragon', p. 108. 36 Creton, 'A French metrical history', 44. 37 H.B. Clarke, *Irish historic towns atlas, no. 11: Dublin, part 1, to 1610* (Dublin, 1995), pp 6–9. 38 Frame, *Colonial Ireland, 1169–1369*, p. 89.

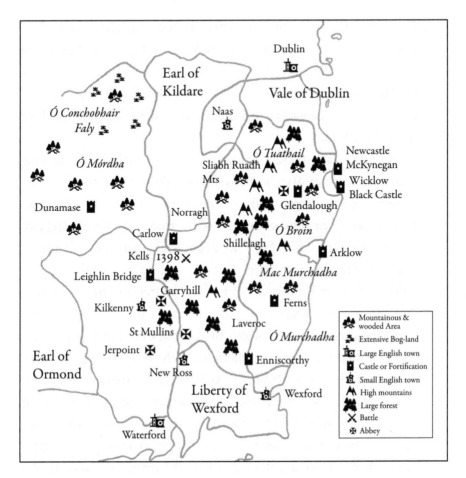

Map 2. Leinster 1394.

rare to have two cathedrals in one diocese, but there were examples
in late-medieval England: Bath and Wells, Coventry and Lichfield.
In 1362 the tower of St Patrick's was badly damaged in a fire; it was
rebuilt in 1372.[39] Other impressive religious buildings in Dublin
in the late fourteenth century included the Augustinian Abbey of
St Thomas the Martyr, just to the west of the town at Thomas

39 A. Gwynn and R.N. Hadcock, *Medieval religious houses: Ireland* (Dublin, 1970),
pp 70–4.

Court, St Mary's Abbey, north of the Liffey, which belonged to the Cistercian Order, and the Priory of St John the Baptist belonging to the Knights Hospitaller, which was situated a little to the west of Dublin at Kilmainham.[40] The buildings built by the Knights Hospitaller at Kilmainham 'were considered to be among the best in the kingdom'.[41]

Although late-medieval Dublin was a big place, with a thriving merchant community, the city's infrastructure seems to have been neglected by the English king's administration in Ireland. In 1380, Dublin castle, the symbolic centre of the rule of the king in Ireland, was in ruins and unusable.[42] In 1399, Richard II had to appoint two officials 'to purchase, purvey and take for the repair, construction and improvement of the k.[ing]'s castle of Dublin and the hall and other buildings in that castle'.[43] The English chronicles record that Dublin Bridge fell down in 1385, to the 'great damages and inconveniencies both to the k.[ing] and the citizens of his city of Dublin'.[44] Richard later provided money for its repair.[45] Dublin was fortunate to continue to thrive as a great trading city throughout the fourteenth century despite the silting up of the bed of the river Liffey. Although, as a port, it may have long suffered from a lack of depth in the river, the building of a weir at Islandbridge and the damming of the river Poddle, both of which occurred at the beginning of the thirteenth century, may have led to a 'dramatic change in the nature of the river'.[46] In 1358

40 Ibid., pp 130–1, 172–3.   41 Ibid., p. 335.   42 9. 29 June 1380, Close Roll 4 Richard II; Clarke, *Irish historic towns atlas, no. 11: Dublin*, pp 6 and 9.   43 6. 4 Mar. 1399, Close Roll 22 Richard II.   44 Holinshed's *Chronicles* (1577), 'The Historie of Irelande, 3.3'; The Holinshed Project, http://www.english.ox.ac.uk/index.html, accessed 28 Jan. 2014; 93. 9 Jan. 1386, Patent Roll 9 Richard II; P. Kewes, I.W. Archer and F. Heal (eds), *The Oxford handbook of Holinshed's Chronicles* (Oxford, 2013); CIHM, 1385.   45 Gilbert (ed.), *Chartularies of St Mary's Abbey, Dublin*, i, p. xliv.   46 A.R. Hayden, 'A rising tide doesn't lift all

King Edward III was warned about the potential danger to Dublin's trade posed by the silting up of the Liffey.[47] The small out-ports of Clontarf, Howth and Dalkey, in Dublin's immediate hinterland, however, were unaffected by the silting up of the river and provided alternative landing points for the city's merchants.[48] This saved Dublin's trade from going into decline.

A second major area of English settlement in the south of Ireland stretched from the coastal town of Wexford westwards to another coastal English town, Kinsale in Co. Cork. This region also included a large hinterland of dense English settlement, which in 1394 covered most of the southern portion of Co. Wexford, almost all of Cos. Kilkenny and Waterford, and much of south Co. Tipperary and the eastern half of Co. Cork. Within this large area were the major English towns of Waterford, Cork, Wexford, Kilkenny and New Ross, as well as a considerable network of smaller towns and villages.[49] There were also some more isolated and less heavily colonized English areas in the western and south-western parts of the island. The north of Co. Kerry and the majority of Co. Limerick formed one such region. This area was becoming quite gaelicized by 1394, but retained small English towns at Dingle, Traleee and Kilmallock, and one large town at Limerick. Another very gaelicized English region in 1394 was located in the east of Co. Galway and also covered almost all of Co. Mayo. This area had few English towns except for the large coastal town of Galway and the small town of Athenry in its hinterland.

boats: archaeological excavations at Meeting House Square, Temple Bar, Dublin' in S. Duffy (ed.), *Medieval Dublin XIV* (Dublin, 2015), p. 122. **47** Clarke, *Irish historic towns atlas, no. 11: Dublin*, p. 9; P. Wallace, *Viking Dublin: the Wood Quay excavations* (Sallins, 2016), pp 169–70. **48** S. Booker, 'The Knight's Tale' in S. Booker and C.N. Peters (eds), *Tales of medieval Dublin* (Dublin, 2014), p. 135. **49** Some of the more important smaller towns in this region included Callan, Clonmel, Carrick-on-Suir, Youghal and Kinsale.

There were some powerful and successful English noblemen on the island in 1394. Perhaps the best-known was Gerald Fitzgerald, the third earl of Desmond, who was called in Irish Gearóid Iarla (Gerald the Earl).[50] Lord of vast estates stretching from the town of Dingle in west Kerry, to Lough Gur in Co. Limerick, with considerable land and interests in north and east Co. Cork and in Co. Waterford, Gerald Fitzgerald was the most powerful overlord within the entire province of Munster. As his Irish name suggests, the third earl of Desmond 'was a leading example of the gaelicization of the Norman lords and was a noted composer of love poetry in the Irish language'.[51] Nevertheless, he struggled at times to maintain Fitzgerald supremacy over his Irish neighbours. In July 1370, in a major battle fought at Monasteranenagh in east Co. Limerick, the Annals of Ulster record that:

> Great defeat was inflicted by the king of Thomond, namely, by Brian Ó Briain, wherein were captured the earl of Desmond, that is Gerald and the chief foreigners of Munster likewise. And not often fell in one defeat before such a great tale of persons as fell and as were wounded of foreigners.[52]

Fitzgerald did his best to support the English administration in Ireland and he rallied to Richard II's side when the English king first came to Ireland in 1394.[53] When Earl Gerald died in 1398, the Annals of Ulster record that 'Ireland was full of lamentation for him'.[54]

---

50 D. Beresford and A. MacShamhráin, 'Gerald fitz Maurice ("Gearóid Iarla") FitzGerald', *DIB*, iii, pp 854–5.   51 D. Ó hÓgáin, *Myth, legend and romance: an encyclopaedia of the Irish folk tradition* (London, 1990), pp 227–30; 88. 8 Dec. 1388, Patent Roll 12 Richard II.   52 AU, 1366 (recte: 1370); AFM, 1369 (recte: 1370); CIHM, 1370.   53 147. 18 Jan. 1382, Close Roll 5 Richard II; 189. [12 Apr. 1382], Patent Roll 5 Richard II.   54 AU, 1398.

Another great English lord in Ireland at this time was James Butler (*c.*1360–1405), the third earl of Ormond. Earl James did much to concentrate Butler power in the Co. Kilkenny/south Co. Tipperary region, which was one of the major areas of English settlement in the southern part of Ireland. He purchased Kilkenny castle, one of the greatest Anglo-Norman fortresses in Ireland.[55] He also possessed the castle of Arklow on the south Leinster coastline and claimed an extensive hinterland in the area. The third earl of Ormond was a major figure in the administration of the English lordship of Ireland, and he was allowed to continue as justiciar by Richard II when the English king came to Ireland in 1394–5.[56] Still, he struggled at times to keep the upper hand in the unending conflict with his Irish neighbours. Irish lords bordered his lands to the east, the north and the north-west. In particular, Butler could not contain the extensive raiding of Murchadh 'na Raithnighe' ('of the Bracken' or 'of the Ferns') Ó Briain (d. 1383), and later his son Toirdhealbhach (d. 1399), who were based to the east of the river Shannon in the mountainous Arà region of north Munster. Earl James referred to Toirdhealbhach in 1392 as 'the most dangerous and chief malefactor of all the k.[ing]'s enemies'.[57] In the end, he had to resort to expensive bribery in an effort to curtail the attacks of these two warlike Ó Briain nobles.[58]

One of the less successful areas of English settlement in Ireland by 1394 was the south Leinster region. This district comprised the old lordship of Leinster, founded by the leader of the twelfth-century Anglo-Norman invasion, Richard de Clare, the famous Strongbow. The lordship had been consolidated by the even more famous William Marshal, who had married Strongbow's daughter

55 D. Beresford, 'James Butler, third earl of Ormond', *DIB*, ii, pp 125–6.   56 Ibid., p. 125.   57 21. 20 June 1392, Close Roll 16 Richard II.   58 Ibid.; 17. 24 Mar. 1378, Close Roll 1 Richard II; 44. 8 Apr. 1378, Close Roll 1 Richard II.

Isabel.[59] A substantial Irish population, the descendants of the pre-invasion inhabitants of the Irish kingdom of Leinster, continued to live in the English lordship under Strongbow and the Marshals. They were concentrated in isolated areas such as the centre of the Wicklow mountains, the forests of Co. Carlow, the wooded hills of Laois and the vast boglands of Offaly. The most prominent Irish family in the lordship of Leinster was the MacMurchadha dynasty, descendants of Diarmait MacMurchadha, the last pre-invasion Irish king of Leinster. It was Diarmait who had invited Strongbow to Ireland to serve as his mercenary.[60] Although the MacMurchadha family became closely tied to Strongbow through his marriage to Diarmait's daughter Aoife, and thus also to the subsequent Marshal lords of Leinster, the dynasty almost disappears from records soon after the Anglo-Norman invasion. It entered a period of obscurity that lasted for almost a century.[61] The male line of the Marshal family died out in 1245, and the lordship of Leinster was divided among William Marshal's five daughters in 1247.[62] The eldest, Matilda, Countess of Warren, received Co. Carlow and a section of Co. Wexford.[63] The division of the Marshal inheritance weakened the government of south Leinster, as there were no longer any ruling lords of Leinster to direct the

---

59 D. Crouch, *William Marshal: knighthood, war and chivalry, 1147–1219* (Harlow, 2002). 60 Scott and Martin (eds), *Expugnatio Hibernica: the conquest of Ireland.* 61 Curtis, Richard II in Ireland, 1394–5, p. 11; Frame, 'Two kings in Leinster: the crown and the MicMhurchadha in the fourteenth century', p. 155; E. O'Byrne, *War, politics and the Irish of Leinster, 1156–1606* (Dublin, 2003), pp 27–9; G.H. Orpen (ed.), *The song of Dermot and the earl* (Oxford, 1892), p. 161. 62 B. Colfer, 'Anglo-Norman settlement in county Wexford' in K. Whelan and W. Nolan (eds), *Wexford: history and society* (Dublin, 1987), p. 69; Frame, *Colonial Ireland, 1169–1369*, p. 63; Frame, 'Two kings in Leinster: the crown and the MicMhurchadha in the fourteenth century', p. 158; O'Byrne, *War, politics and the Irish of Leinster*, p. 265. 63 E. O'Toole, 'The parish of Ballon, County Carlow', *Journal of the County Kildare Archaeological Society*, 11:4 (July, 1933), 205.

affairs of the entire region. Some of the land Marshal's daughters inherited ended up in the hands of absentee noblemen, whose main landed interests were in the kingdom of England. Nevertheless, a good relationship seems to have continued between the MacMurchadha family and the Bigod earls of Norfolk, who inherited the lordship of Carlow.[64]

It was a period of severe weather in the Wicklow mountains around the year 1270 that upset the delicate balance between the English and Irish in this part of Ireland.[65] The bad weather led to a revolt of the Irish who lived in the many valleys of the mountain range, probably because they were starving. The Irish of the mountains began to raid neighbouring English areas and soon the fighting spread to include the MacMurchadha family, who re-emerge into Irish records in the forests of Co. Carlow. Roger Bigod, the earl of Norfolk and lord of the liberty of Carlow, attempted to restore peace to the region and was in Carlow in 1279. He gave robes, furs and wine to Muircheartach MacMurchadha, the leader of the family.[66] When Muircheartach MacMurchadha and his brother Art were murdered by the English at the port of Arklow in July 1282, relations between the Irish and the English in south Leinster were permanently damaged.[67] This damage was compounded in December 1306 when Roger Bigod died and the male line of the Bigod earls of Norfolk and lords of Carlow also failed. There were no more English lords of Carlow for most of the remainder of the fourteenth century.[68]

---

64 Curtis, *Richard II in Ireland, 1394–5*, p. 11. 65 O'Byrne, *War, politics and the Irish of Leinster, 1156–1606*, pp 58–9, 70. 66 R. Frame, 'The justiciar and the murder of the MacMurroughs in 1282' in R. Frame, *Ireland and Britain, 1170–1450* (London, 1998), p. 242; ibid., *Colonial Ireland, 1169–1369*, p. 65. 67 Frame, 'The justiciar and the murder of the MacMurroughs', pp 241–5. 68 Curtis, *Richard II in Ireland, 1394–5*, p. 11.

Although there continued to be some powerful English nobles in south Leinster, such as Maurice Fitzgerald, the fourth earl of Kildare (*c.*1321–1390), the English in many areas of the region suffered greatly at the hands of a resurgent Irish population.[69] Small districts such as the coastal region of Co. Wicklow and the eastern parts of the counties of Laois and Offaly were reclaimed by the Irish, and the English administration of the colony lost any control it had had over a vast area that included the Wicklow mountains and the heavily forested areas of the counties of Carlow, Wexford and Laois. One of the most famous incidents of the entire Gaelic revival occurred in the wooded hills of Laois. The chieftain Laoighseach Ó Mórdha, sometime before his death in 1342,

> violently expelled almost all of the English from their lands and inheritance, for in one evening he burnt eight of the English castles and destroyed the celebrated castle of Dunamase of Robert de Mortimer [see figure 3], and he usurped for himself the lordship of the neighbourhood making himself from a serf, a lord: from a subject, a *princeps* [prince].[70]

The growth in the power of the MacMurchadha and Ó Mórdha families posed a particular threat to the strategic highway that ran through Co. Carlow and south Co. Kildare, connecting the English Dublin region to the English areas of Co. Kilkenny and north and east Munster. Overland travel on this route became dangerous and was often blocked entirely by the Irish in wartime.[71]

---

69 D. Beresford, 'Maurice fitz Thomas FitzGerald (*c.*1321–90)', *DIB*, iii, pp 902–3. 70 *The annals of Ireland by Friar John Clyn*, 1342, pp 228–9. 71 Frame, 'Two kings in Leinster: the crown and the MicMhurchadha in the fourteenth century', p. 165; A. Cosgrove, *Late medieval Ireland, 1370–1541* (Dublin, 1981), pp 13 and 16.

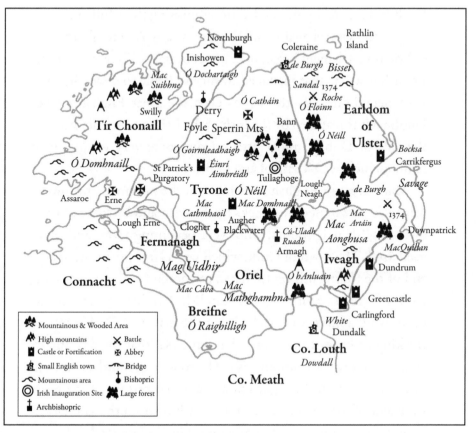

Map 3. Ulster 1394.

The MacMurchadha family assumed the leadership of the rebellious Irish of south Leinster at certain times and began to claim to be kings of Leinster again. The English administration in Ireland spent vast sums of money and sent large numbers of soldiers against them. Very difficult terrain and a population that rediscovered its warlike nature thwarted the many attempts by the English to pacify the mountains and forests of the region. Although on many occasions Irish chieftains were forced by successful English military expeditions to submit temporarily, the

English never really succeeded in reimposing their full authority over south Leinster again until the early 1600s. As a result, the area of English settlement began to contract dramatically, with even the English districts that managed to survive liable to attack by their Irish neighbours. By the 1390s even the great English city of Dublin felt threatened by the Irish of the Leinster mountains, with the vale of Dublin under attack from some very warlike Irish families, such as Ó Tuathail and Ó Broin.

Many areas of English settlement in the province of Munster were also threatened by attacks by the Irish and by some of their own English neighbours, who were becoming more and more gaelicized. The town of Cork, which was a large port towards the end of the fourteenth century, had to contend with an increasing level of violence among the English families settled in its hinterland. Things were so bad that the mayor of Cork wrote to the king's administration in Ireland in 1382 'that the city and its citizens are so greatly impoverished by robberies, murders, fire and other destructions brought upon them that certain of the more sufficient of the citizens intend to withdraw from the said city'.[72] In an effort to assist the townspeople, Gerald Fitzgerald, the earl of Desmond, 'went at his own expense to Cork, which was devastated by enemies and rebels', where he forced the unruly English Barrett family to surrender hostages to ensure their future good behaviour.[73] The citizens of the town later complained that not enough local foodstuffs were coming in due to the damage that had been done to the surrounding countryside.[74] The small town of Kinsale, a little to the south-west, was also in a bad way, owing to the fact that it was not walled. The residents were afraid to leave

72 195. 14 Jan. 1382, Patent Roll 5 Richard II.   73 147. 18 Jan. 1382, Close Roll 5 Richard II.   74 216. 24 Oct. 1386, Patent Roll 10 Richard II.   75 252. 23 May 1389, Patent Roll 12 Richard II.

the town in large numbers lest the Irish capture it in their absence.[75] By 1389 the king's administration in Ireland was aware of 'the immense cost they sustain and incur upon the enclosing of the same town with a stone wall in aid of the salvation of the neighbouring country in resistance of the malice of the said enemies and rebels'.[76]

The large English town of Limerick, situated on the river Shannon in north Munster, also suffered greatly owing to its location, right beside the Ó Briain kingdom of Thomond in Co. Clare. In 1391 the mayor of the town and the citizens wrote to the king to inform his administration 'how the city of Limerick is so destroyed by the continual invasions and destruction of Irish enemies and English rebels surrounding that city that no citizen dares to cross the gates of that city from any parts'.[77] As a result the townspeople of Limerick were granted the king's cocket 'of that city to have for a certain term specified in those letters, in aid of the repair and improvement of the walls of the city of Limerick'.[78] The town of Limerick experienced a disaster in the summer of 1370 in the aftermath of the defeat and capture of Gerald Fitzgerald, the earl of Desmond, at the battle of Monasteranenagh at the hands of Brian Ó Briain, the king of Thomond.[79] Ó Briain marched on the town and 'Limerick was broken down and quickly burned by the men of Thomond on that expedition and pledge-ship of young hostages of the town was made to Brian and to the Clann-Cuilen [the MacConmara family] likewise'.[80] Brian Ó Briain installed Síoda Óg MacConmara as his warden (governor) over the town.[81] The English townsmen, 'the foreigners of Limerick', however, murdered Síoda Óg MacConmara soon after

76 Ibid.   77 17. 10 Aug. 1391, Patent Roll 15 Richard II.   78 15. 10 Aug. 1391, Patent Roll 15 Richard II.   79 AU, 1366 (recte: 1370); AFM, 1369 (recte: 1370). 80 AU, 1366 (recte: 1370).   81 Ibid.

the king of Thomond and his warriors left the town to return to Thomond.[82] A chastened Ó Briain never again attempted to appoint an Irish warden over Limerick.

The English of the province of Munster credited Murchadh na Raithnighe Ó Briain, who died of the plague in 1383, with having wreaked the greatest havoc on their settlements during the latter half of the fourteenth century.[83] Murchadh na Raithnighe was a senior Ó Briain noble, whose family was living in the mountainous Ara region east of the river Shannon, having lost out in the competition for the kingship of Thomond in the early fourteenth century. A vivid account of the exploits of Murchadh na Raithnighe was recorded by the English planter and author Sir Edmund Spenser at the end of the sixteenth century and was included in *A view of the present state of Ireland*. This legend states:

> and there arose in that parte of Thomond, one of the O-Bryens, called Murrogh en ranagh, that is Morrys of the ffarne, or waste wylde places: who gathering unto him all the relickes of the discontented Irishe, aftsones surprised the said Castle of Clare, burnt and spoyled all the English there dwelling, and in short space possessed all the country beyond the river Shenan and near adjoining. Whence shortlie breaking forth like a sudden tempest, he overran all Mounster and Connaught, breaking downe all the holdes and fortresses of the Englishe, defacing and utterlie subverting all corporate Townes that were not stronglie walled: for those he had no means nor engines to overthrowe; neither indede would he stay at all about them, but speedily ran forwarde, counting his suddenness his most vantage, that he might overtake the

82 Ibid.   83 AFM, 1383.

Englishe before they could fortefie or gather them selves together.[84]

The range of Murchadh na Raithnighe and the number of English settlements that he is credited with destroying is astounding. Spenser wrote:

> So in short time he cleane wiped out many greate townes, as first Chegin, then Killalowe [Killaloe, Co. Clare], before called Clarry fort; afterward Tharles [Thurles, Co. Tipperary], Mourne, Buttevant [Co. Cork], and many others, viz. [gap in original text] whose names I can not remember, and of some of which there is now no memorie nor signe remayning.[85]

By the late 1500s Murchadh na Raithnighe should have been an obscure figure, little known except to Irish historians and genealogists. That his memory was still vividly alive and recorded by Spenser indicates that he probably was one of the major Irish leaders of the Gaelic revival in the north Munster region during the later fourteenth century.

Although the English colony had almost totally lost any control over the western province of Connacht and the many English families who settled there were highly gaelicized by 1394, this was not due to any major territorial reconquest by the Irish. In fact, the English of Connacht had rallied together in 1316 to inflict a crushing defeat on Feidhlim Ó Conchobhair, the last real Irish king of Connacht, who was killed along with much of his army at

---

84 Edmund Spenser, *A view of the present state of Ireland*: http://www.ucc.ie/celt/published/E500000-001/index.html, accessed 21 Jan. 2015.   85 Ibid.; E. Curtis (ed.), *Calendar of Ormond deeds* (Dublin, 1934), ii, p. 227; Frame, *Colonial Ireland, 1169–1369*, p. 80; AFM, 1382; 44. 8 Apr. 1378, Close Roll 1 Richard II.

the battle of Athenry.[86] Although most English families in the province – even the two most powerful, de Burgh and Bermingham – adopted Irish surnames, for example de Búrca and MacFheorais in these instances, they generally retained their local lordships and even began to build regional overlordships. Few large areas of Connacht were actually reconquered by the Irish. One exception was the Co. Sligo region, referred to as Lower Connacht in late-medieval times. The annals record that around the year 1371:

> Great depredations were committed by Ó Dubhda (Domhnall), in Tir Fhiachrach Muaidhe; the whole country was ravaged by him, and its castles were taken namely, the castles of Ardnarea and Castle-mic-Conor, and all the foreigners that were in them were driven out; and the country was after this parcelled out among his kinsmen and his own people.[87]

The reconquest of much of Lower Connacht left the unwalled English town of Sligo very isolated and practically defenceless against its Irish and increasingly gaelicized English neighbours. The Annals of Connacht record a major raid that was made on the town in 1398 by de Búrca of Mayo and the sons of Cathal Óg Ó Conchobhair. These annals state that 'They burnt and completely sacked the town'.[88] The Annals of the Four Masters place this event under 1396 and state (probably incorrectly) that it was Toirdhelbhach an Fhiona Ó Domhnaill the king of Tír Chonaill, who accompanied Tadhg, the son of Cathal Óg Ó Conchobhair, to Sligo to destroy the town. The Four Masters add that 'It was grievous that this town should have been burned for its buildings of stone and wood were splendid'.[89]

86 AC, 1316.   87 AFM, 1371.   88 AC, 1398.   89 AFM, 1396.

There was only one major area of heavy English settlement that fell to the Irish during the Gaelic revival and this was the earldom of Ulster. It covered an area roughly coterminous with Co. Antrim and Co. Down. Founded by the Anglo-Norman conquistador John de Courcey in the last years of the twelfth century, the earldom of Ulster eventually came into the possession of the Mortimer family, one of the great English noble houses, having passed through the hands of the de Lacy and de Burgh earls.[90] At the beginning of the fourteenth century the coastal areas of the earldom, stretching from Greencastle in south Co. Down as far north as the great Anglo-Norman castle at Carrickfergus, were heavily settled by the English. Both Carrickfergus and Downpatrick were important English towns.[91] A town had also been built by the earls of Ulster at Coleraine, at the mouth of the river Bann in north Co. Antrim. This town and the surrounding territory were still held by the English in 1394.[92] The interior of the earldom of Ulster, up along the valley of the river Lagan, was also heavily settled by the English by the early fourteenth century.[93]

There are a number of reasons why the earldom of Ulster was the one large English region to fall to the Irish during the fourteenth century. It bore the brunt of the invasion of Ireland by Edward and Robert Bruce. Edward Bruce based himself in the earldom and Carrickfergus castle endured a long siege from 1315–16 before it fell to the Scots.[94] Although Edward Bruce was eventually killed by the English at the battle of Faughart, fought near Dundalk in October 1318, the earldom of Ulster had

---

90 S. Flanders, *De Courcy: Anglo-Normans in Ireland, England and France in the eleventh and twelfth centuries* (Dublin, 2008). 91 T.E. McNeill, *Anglo-Norman Ulster: the history and archaeology of an Irish barony, 1177–1400* (Edinburgh, 1980), pp 7–16. 92 Ibid., pp 30–2. 93 Ibid., pp 85–93. 94 The earl of Ulster's castle at Northburgh in Inishowen was also captured by the Scots in 1315, CIHM, 1315.

unquestionably been damaged by its years under his rule.[95] Nevertheless, the earldom appears to have recovered quickly. It was the murder of William de Burgh, the young earl of Ulster, by some of the local English near Belfast in 1333 that did the real damage to English Ulster.[96] Many local English families who were involved in the murder of the Brown earl were decimated in retribution over the ensuing months.[97] No doubt the Black Death following on soon after in 1348–50 also affected English districts of the earldom severely.

As a result, English Ulster became vulnerable to attack by the Irish. This included Irish families who were native to the earldom such as MacAonghusa, MacArtáin and MacGiolla Mhuire. It also included the powerful Ó Néill kings of Tyrone, who over the course of the fourteenth century succeeded in overthrowing the power of the English in east Ulster and replacing it with their own province-wide authority.[98] It may even have been a branch of the Ó Néill family, the Clann Aodha Buidhe, who did most damage to English Ulster at a local level. Based east of Lough Neagh and the river Bann by the early fourteenth century, the Clann Aodha Buidhe lost out to the Ó Néill branch of Tyrone in the competition for the Ó Néill kingship. They are then recorded in the annals destroying the power of local Irish families east of the river Bann. For example, around the year 1356 Aodh Ó Néill of the Clann Aodha Buidhe killed Muircheartach Ó Floinn, heir to the king of Uí Tuirtre.[99] The death of Muircheartach's father Tomás Ó Floinn, king of Uí Tuirtre, 'eminent throughout Ireland

---

95 Duffy (ed.), *Robert the Bruce's Irish war*, 'Appendix A: the Brus: the history of Robert the Bruce, king of Scots', pp 163–78; Lydon, 'The Bruce invasion of Ireland', pp 71–88.   **96** Annales Hiberniae, 1333; CIHM, 1333.   **97** *The annals of Ireland by Friar John Clyn*, 1333, pp 210–11.   **98** McNeill, *Anglo-Norman Ulster*, p. 119.   **99** AU, 1356; AC, 1359.

for his bounty, valour and nobility', in 1368 is the final time that this family is recorded in the Irish annals.[100]

One of the last powerful English nobles in east Ulster, Sir Robert Savage, died in 1360.[101] A story about him (probably apocryphal), preserved in the English source the Annales Hiberniae, records an argument Sir Robert reputedly had with his son Henry regarding the defence of English east Ulster. The Annales Hiberniae record:

> Sir Robert had begun to build various castles in Ulster, and said to his son that in this way he should save it for himself and his children from the attacks of the Irish. His son Henry answered him 'where-ever there are brave men there is a castle, according to the saying, and there the children of Israel pitched their camp, I shall ever be amongst the brave, and therefore in a castle. I had rather', quoth he, 'have a castle of bones than of stones'. Being thus deterred his father, stopping the work he had begun, spent his substance in housekeeping, saying that his children would be sorry for it; which came to pass, for shortly after the Irish wasted the whole country because it was bare of castles.[102]

When Sir Robert Savage died in 1360 the Annales Hiberniae added:

> likewise died Sir Robert Savage, who with a few English had killed in one day three thousand Irish near Antrim; but he had before given every soldier a good drink of wine, and had

---

100 AC, 1368; McNeill, *Anglo-Norman Ulster*, p. 119. 101 AC, 1360; AU, 1357; McNeill, *Anglo-Norman Ulster*, pp 118–19; E. O'Byrne, 'Sir Robert Savage (*c.*1293–1360)', *DIB*, viii, p. 789. 102 Annales Hiberniae, 1352.

prepared a splendid feast against their return; he always kept a most splendid table; he was buried in the convent of the Friars Preacher of Coleraine [St Mary's Dominican priory], on the river Bann.[103]

By 1394 the English settlements in the Lagan valley in south Co. Antrim and north Co. Down had largely been destroyed by the Irish. This was also the case for many isolated English areas along the narrow coastal strip of south Co. Down that lay between the Mourne mountains and the sea. By 1394, Ó Néill of Clann Aodha Buidhe had taken control of most of the vast forests that lay east of the river Bann in what had been the Ó Floinn kingdom of Uí Tuirtre. The English still held the town of Coleraine and the surrounding areas known as *Twescard* (from the Irish word '*tuaisceart*' – 'the north') in 1394, as well as Carrickfergus, the Ards peninsula and Downpatrick, with its adjacent territory. The Savage family was still fighting for control of at least a sizeable portion of the earldom of Ulster. The Mortimer earls of Ulster and March also never gave up their ambitions for regaining their Irish earldom. Nevertheless, the achievement of the Irish in reconquering much of east Ulster from the English was a substantial one. It changed the dynamic of the province of Ulster, which became the one really large area on the entire island of Ireland that was dominated by one people, either English or Irish.

103 Ibid., 1360; Gwynn and Hadcock, *Medieval religious houses: Ireland*, p. 223.

CHAPTER 2

Fourteenth-century
Gaelic Ireland – a new Sparta

The vast majority of the Irish kingdoms were small and the chieftains themselves of limited importance. The kingdom of Tyrone, however, was a big territory, the last under native rule left on the island of Ireland. In 1394 this kingdom covered most of what today are the counties of Tyrone, Derry and Armagh. The centre of the medieval kingdom comprised the substantial Sperrin mountain range, which in late-medieval times was heavily forested. The most impressive wooded area was the great forest of Gleann Concadhain, north of Slieve Gallion mountain, which even as late as 1602 ran for 'ten mile broad and 20 mile long', along the banks of the Moyola river.[1] Although most of the forest was comprised of oaks, according to the early modern author Philip O'Sullivan

---

1 N. Everett, *The woods of Ireland: a history, 700–1800* (Dublin, 2014), p. 63; J. O'Donovan (ed.), 'A narration of the services done by the army employed to Lough Foyle, under the leading of me Sir Henry Docwra', *Miscellany of the Celtic Society* (Dublin, 1849), p. 264; M. Herity (ed.), *Ordnance Survey letters: Londonderry, Fermanagh, Armagh-Monaghan, Louth and Cavan-Leitrim* (Dublin, 2012), p. 78.

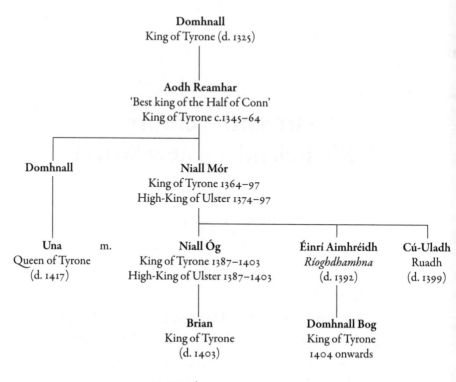

3. The Ó Néill kings of Tyrone.

Beare, 'There is no lack of pine, quite a high tree, mostly in the *Conkeinia* forest'.[2] The forests of the Sperrin mountains provided a safe place of retreat for the king of Tyrone and his followers. English armies entered at their peril.

The Ó Néill kings were inaugurated at the rath of Tullaghoge (see figure 4).[3] Their main house in the fourteenth century was at Fraochmhagh, which may have been a large crannog located at

---

2 O'Sullivan (ed.), *The natural history of Ireland*, pp 200–1.   3 P. Dineen (ed.), *Foras Feasa ar Eirinn* (London, 1908), iii, pp 12–13; G.A. Hayes-McCoy, 'The making of an O'Neill: a view of the ceremony at Tullaghoge, Co. Tyrone', *UJA*, 33 (1970), 89–94; the famous Leac na Ríogh (flag-stone of the kings), is not mentioned in the annals as part of the inauguration ceremony until the fifteenth

Augher in south-eastern Co. Tyrone (see figure 4).[4] Aodh
Reamhar Ó Néill, the father of Niall Mór, and king of Tyrone from
c.1345–1364, is reputed to have built 'sixty houses besides his own
mansion in *Fraochmhagh* ... in order to pay and reward poets and
practitioners of the lesser arts from all over Ireland'.[5] By 1394 the
heir apparent, Niall Óg Ó Néill, seems to have had a castle at
Dungannon, while his brother Éinrí Aimhréidh, probably the
second most powerful of the sons of Niall Mór Ó Néill, had a
castle in the hilly area of west Tyrone.[6] Other close family members
of Niall Mór and Niall Óg Ó Néill also had certain territories
within the late-medieval kingdom of Tyrone. Niall Mór's brother
and one-time rival Domhnall Ó Néill also had land in western
Tyrone. Niall Óg's brother Cú-Uladh Ruadh had estates in the east
of the kingdom, in the north-east of Co. Armagh.[7]

In 1394 the king of Tyrone's most important sub-chieftain, Ó
Catháin, the king of Oireacht Uí Chatháin (the territory of
O'Kane), was located north of the Sperrin mountains, where he
ruled the entire swathe of land between the rivers Bann and Foyle
(see figure 6).[8] The household lands of the king of Tyrone

century, AU, 1432; the stone inauguration chair destroyed by Lord Deputy
Mountjoy in 1602, however, may have been first constructed in that form in the late
fourteenth century, E. Fitzpatrick, *Royal inauguration in Gaelic Ireland, c.1100–
1600: a cultural landscape study* (Woodbridge, 2004), pp 143–4, 154. 4 K. Simms,
'Late medieval Tír Eoghain' in C. Dillon and H. Jefferies (eds), *Tyrone: history and
society* (Dublin, 2000), p. 146. 5 Ibid.; *Leabhar Cloinne Aodha Buidhe*, pp 32–3;
this king was also known as 'Aodh an Fhraochmhoighe'. 6 McKenna (ed.),
Aithdioghluim Dána, i, p. 57; ii, p. 34; 'Harry Avery's castle, Newtownstewart, Co.
Tyrone: excavations in 1950', *UJA*, 13:1–2 (1950), 91–2; Simms, 'Late medieval
Tyrone', p. 150. 7 Simms, 'Late medieval Tyrone', p. 147; AU, 1400, 1401; AFM,
1399, 1400. 8 AFM, 1376, note c; AU, 1371; in the early 1800s travellers going
south over the Sperrin mountains from Dungiven continued to be asked upon
arrival in Gleann Concadhain, 'What news from Kane's country?' (Herity (ed.),
Ordnance Survey letters: Londonderry, Fermanagh, Armagh-Monaghan, Louth and

stretched south and south-west from the rath at Tullaghoge. Some of these were the mensal lands of the Ó Néill king himself, farmed by his personal tenants. Others were held and farmed by the king's household families, who were referred to as the *lucht tighe*. Among the most prominent of the household families of Ó Néill were Ó hÁgáin, Ó Doibhlín, Ó Cuinn, Ó Mealláin and Ó Donnghaile.[9] Only the Ó Mealláin family are recorded in the annals during the fourteenth century, although the other families certainly served the king of Tyrone during this period.[10] An ecclesiastical dynasty, the Ó Mealláin family were hereditary keepers of Clog an Eadhachta or the Bell of the Testament, a famous relic now known as St Patrick's Bell. The ornate shrine made for this bell in the early twelfth century was one of the finest treasures in late-medieval Ireland.[11] There were other important

Cavan-Leitrim, p. 58); Cúmhaighe na nGall Ó Catháin, the king of Oireacht Uí Chatháin, who 'died at the height of his good fame' in 1385 was an important noble in the kingdom of Tyrone throughout the middle and later fourteenth century, AC, 1385; he was captured by the English of Coleraine in 1371 and imprisoned for a period afterwards in the great castle at Carrickfergus, AU, 1371; according to legend, he is the man depicted by the ornate late-medieval tomb effigy that survives in the priory church in Dungiven.   9 S. Ó Ceallaigh, *Gleanings from Ulster history* (Ballinascreen, 1994), pp 1–11; J. Develin, *The O'Develins of Tyrone* (Rutland, 1938), pp 15–110; J. O'Donovan, 'The O'Donnellys of Ballydonnelly', *AFM*, vi, pp 2426–30; É. Ó Doibhlín, 'Ceart Uí Néill: a discussion and translation of the document', *Seanchas Ard Mhacha*, 5: 2 (1970), 324–58; the Ó hÁgáin chieftain was known as 'chief of Cinél Fearghusa, and steward of Tullaghoge': AU, 1103; AFM, 1122; K. Simms, *From kings to warlords: the changing political structure of Gaelic Ireland in the later Middle Ages* (Woodbridge, 1987), p. 177.   10 T. Mullin and J. Mullan, *The Ulster clans O'Mullan, O'Kane and O'Mellan* (Belfast, 1966), p. 195; the *'marasgál Uí Néill* – the marshals of Ó Néill' were recruited from the Ó Donnghaile family, while the 'high-stewards ... of Ó Néill' came from the family of Ó Cuinn. Ó Doibhlín was regarded as being among the *'fir-cheithearn* of Ó Néill', 'soldiers with special duties and privileges' (M. Dillon, 'Ceart Uí Néill', *Studia Celtica*, 1 (1966), 10–15).   11 AU, 1353; AFM, 1356, note k; A. Hamlin, 'The early church in Tyrone to the twelfth century' in Dillon and Jefferies (eds), *Tyrone:*

sub-chieftains in Tyrone who recognized the authority of the Ó Néill king. These included Ó Goirmleadhaigh in western Tyrone, MacCathmhaoil, chief of the Clogher valley, and MacCana, chief of extensive lands along the southern shore of Lough Neagh.[12] By the late fourteenth century the Ó hAnluain chieftains, who were kings of Orior, the mountainous district north of the English county of Louth, although they were not of Cinél nEógain descent, were also usually considered as comprising the southern portion of the kingdom of Tyrone.[13]

Like all the Irish kings, Ó Néill of Tyrone had many families who served him on a hereditary basis as soldiers, doctors, lawyers, historians and bardic poets. The lands granted by the kings of Tyrone to their galloglass commander MacDomhnaill Gallóglach, constable of Ulster, were located in eastern Tyrone.[14] The family of bardic poets who served the kings of Tyrone was a very famous one, that of MacCon Midhe.[15] That the kings of Tyrone valued

history and society, p. 117; Gwynn and Hadcock, *Medieval religious houses: Ireland*, p. 34; Mullin and Mullan, *The Ulster clans O'Mullan, O'Kane and O'Mellan*, pp 13, 25, 29, 194–8; Wallace and Ó Floinn (eds), *Treasures of the National Museum of Ireland*, pp 222, 233 and 250; unusually, Ó Mealláin shared custody of St Patrick's Bell with the Ó Maolchalann family.   **12** AU, 1303, 1337, 1338; J. Hogan, 'The Irish law of kingship, with special reference to Ailech and Cenél Eoghain', *PRIA*, 40C (1931–33), 214; AU, 1343, 1355, 1367, 1379, 1432; AFM, 1368; S. Ó Dufaigh, 'The MacCathmhaoils of Clogher', *Clogher Record*, 11: 1 (1957), 25–49; AFM, 1155, note k; 1212, note q.   **13** AU, 1318, 1380; AC, 1391.   **14** The submission of McDonnell, captain of galloglass, 18 May 1542, State papers King Henry VIII, iii, part III continued (London, 1834), p. 383, note 1, states that MacDomhnaill Gallóglach offered to serve the English king 'in Ulster with 120 sparres well harnessed; and … in any other place of this his Realm, I will serve His Majesty with 80 sparres, well harnessed'. (A spar or sparr was made up of 'one *gallóglach*, fully accoutred and accompanied by one or two attendants', G.A. Hayes-McCoy, *Scots mercenary forces in Ireland (1565–1603)*, (Dublin, 1937/reprint, 1996), p. 359); see also K. Nicholls, 'Scottish mercenary kindreds in Ireland, 1250–1600' in Seán Duffy (ed.), *The world of the galloglass: kings, warlords and warriors in Ireland and Scotland, 1200–1600* (Dublin, 2007), pp 97–100.   **15** Although not

Irish learning is evident from the obituaries of many of the Ó Néill nobles and kings recorded in the Irish annals.[16] Both Niall Mór and Niall Óg Ó Néill were great patrons of bardic poets and the intense competition to serve them can be seen in an entry recorded in the Annals of the Four Masters for 1394, which states that 'Tadhg Ó hEachaidhéin, a learned poet, was slain by the family of Cúchonnacht Ó Dálaigh, [in a fight over] the *ollamhship* of Ó Néill'.[17] There were also a number of hereditary coarb and erenagh ecclesiastical dynasties scattered throughout the late-medieval kingdom of Tyrone. Two of the more prominent during the fourteenth century were the Mag Oirc family, coarbs of Termonmaguirk (the sanctuary of Mag Oirc), which lay in the centre of the kingdom, and Ó Mongáin, erenagh of Termonamongan (Tearmonn Uí Mhaoin), in the far west of Tyrone, close to the river Derg.[18]

There was one major ecclesiastical settlement in the late-medieval kingdom of Tyrone, based around the ancient monastery of Armagh. Reputedly founded by St Patrick, by the fourteenth

mentioned in the annals during the fourteenth century, the Four Masters record that Eachmharcach Ruadh MacCon Midhe, 'a learned poet', died in 1420, while they also record that in 1434 Maoiliosa MacCon Midhe 'ollamh and chief poet to Ó Néill' died, AFM, 1420, 1434; the lands of MacCon Midhe known as *'fearann an Reacaire'* ('the Reciter's land') were situated at Loch Í Mhaoldubháin close to Ardstraw, which is believed to be one of the lakes in the Baron's Court demesne, N.J.A. Williams (ed.), *The poems of Giolla Brighde Mac Con Midhe* (Dublin, 1980), p. 2; Dillon, 'Ceart Uí Néill', 8–9. 16 AC, 1392, 1399; AU, 1387, 1403; *Annals of Clonmacnoise*, 1399, p. 322. 17 AFM, 1394; this murder appears to have led to the development of a feud between the two families, ibid., 1408. 18 Gwynn and Hadcock, *Medieval religious houses: Ireland*, p. 407; AFM, 1557, note f; *Inquisitionum in officio rotulorum cancellariae Hiberniae asservatarum, repertorium* (Dublin, 1829), ii, Appendix II, Tyrone, p. 5; B. Smith (ed.), *The register of Nicholas Fleming, Archbishop of Armagh 1404–16* (Dublin, 2003), pp 171, 195–6; each of these families possessed an ancient bell relic, Hamlin, 'The early church in Tyrone to the twelfth century', p. 117. Most authorities state that Mag Oirc was an erenagh

century Armagh was still the seat of the primate of all Ireland, the archbishop of Armagh. Since soon after the Anglo-Norman invasion in the late twelfth century, the archdiocese had famously been divided into two regions *'inter Anglos et Hibernos'*, with the English controlling the southern portion in Co. Louth and Irish clergy retaining control of the northern portion, which lay within the kingdom of Tyrone.[19] From the early fourteenth century an almost unbroken series of English clerics were appointed to the powerful position of archbishop of Armagh. Armagh was built in an imposing location on a hill overlooking the surrounding countryside. By 1394 there was a large cathedral, the very wealthy Augustinian abbey of SS Peter and Paul, a Franciscan monastery as well as two Augustinian nunneries, Temple na Ferta (Temple of the Relics) and Temple Brigid (Templebreed).[20] The Ó Néill family had a *mausoleum regum* at Armagh and the reigning king of Tyrone usually had a house there also.[21] The archbishops, too, had a palace at Drumarg, on the outskirts of the settlement (see figure 15).[22] Armagh must have had quite a large population throughout the fourteenth century, certainly hundreds of people. As a result, this ancient ecclesiastical site provided a much-needed market and educational centre for the entire kingdom of Tyrone.[23]

---

family but the Tyrone *Inquis.*, dating from 1607, clearly states that the family were coarbs.   **19** Gwynn and Hadcock, *Medieval religious houses: Ireland*, pp 59–60. **20** Ibid., pp 29–30, 157 and 242; *Inquis. in officio rotulorum* (Dublin, 1829), ii, Appendix I, Armagh, pp 2–3; Appendix II, Tyrone, pp 1–3, 5–6; Appendix III, Coleraine [Co. Derry], p. 2; C. McCullough and W. Crawford, *Armagh: Irish historic towns atlas, no. 18* (Dublin, 2007), p. 1; Gwynn and Hadcock, *Medieval religious houses: Ireland*, pp 312–13.   **21** F.J. Byrne, *Irish kings and high-kings* (London, 1987), p. 125.   **22** H. Jefferies, 'The visitation of the parishes of Armagh *inter Hibernicos* in 1546' in Dillon and Jefferies (eds), *Tyrone: history and society*, p. 166. **23** *Inquis. in officio rotulorum*, ii, Appendix I, Armagh, p. 2: 'there hath been tyme out of mynde, one markett, weekely, holden in the town or cittie of Armagh, … .

The MacMurchadha kingdom of Irish Leinster was centred on the valleys and forests of the mountain ranges that lie to the south of Dublin. The heartland of Art's kingdom was the double forest of Garryhill (An Gharbhchoill – the Rough Wood) and Laveroc, which covered most of the centre and south of Co. Carlow. Art's main fortress, which was a fortified wooden house, may have been situated in what is today the townland of Garryhill, a small crossroads settlement lying about halfway between the village of Myshall and the small town of Bagenalstown.[24] Art also had a second house in the Laveroc forest. This was a great wooded area that in the fourteenth century ran along the east bank of the Barrow river, through mid and south Co. Carlow. In late-medieval times this forest extended into the Rower area of Co. Kilkenny and also into south Co. Wexford.[25]

Art, as king of the Leinster mountains, was supported by a large number of sub-chieftains in south Leinster.[26] The Ó Nualláin chieftain ruled the territory of Fotharta in north Co. Carlow. Ó Nualláin had the right to inaugurate MacMurchadha as king of Leinster 'on Cnoc an Bhogha', for which the sub-chieftain received MacMurchadha's 'steed and trappings'.[27] Another supporter of

24 In the later fourteenth century, this entire area was one huge forest and the early modern place name Kyllarte, possibly Art's Wood, which appears on sixteenth-century maps of the locality, may refer to Art MacMurchadha's stronghold. 25 Curtis, 'Unpublished letters from Richard II in Ireland, 1394–5', 298–301. 26 Ibid., 301; during the fourteenth century, the MacMurchadha family were often referred to by the Caomhánach (Kavanagh) surname, after Domhnall Caomhánach, King Diarmait's son, who died in 1175. In the late fourteenth century the two surnames were often used together to form one joint surname, MacMurchadha Caomhánach. This practice later died out, leaving just the surname Kavanagh, which is mostly used by members of the family today (ibid.); AFM, 1175, note f: Domhnall was called Caomhánach 'from having been fostered at Cill Chaomhain, now Kilcavan, near Gorey, in the county of Wexford'. 27 Dineen (ed.), *Foras Feasa ar Éirinn*, iii, pp 14–15; Fitzpatrick, *Royal inauguration in Gaelic*

MacMurchadha based in the forests of Co. Carlow was the Ó Riain chieftain.[28] A third of Art's sub-chieftains, Ó Murchadha, descended from an ancient branch of the Uí Cheinnselaig (the Uí Felmeda or Uí Felimy), was situated in south-east Co. Wexford, where he ruled a territory called the Murroes.[29] A large number of branches of the MacMurchadha family possessed lands in north Wexford. These included the Cinnsealach family, descended from Diarmait MacMurchadha's son Énna, and the MacDaibhéid Mór and MacMhadóc families, who were descended from Diarmait's brother Murchadh.[30]

The Ó Broin family, by 1394 based in the forested fastness of Glenmalure in the heart of the Sliabh Ruadh mountain range, were powerful locally.[31] The Ó Broin chieftain was MacMurchadha's most important vassal. The Ó Tuathail family, another of Art MacMurchadha's important sub-chieftains, controlled much of central, north and west Wicklow. The main fastness of the Ó Tuathail chieftains was the glen of Imaal in west Wicklow. There

Ireland, pp 227 and 229; knowledge of the location of Cnoc an Bhogha has been lost for a long time. There is a townland called Knockboy, however, near Rathvilly in north-east Co. Carlow, associated with a later legend of 'King Art Mac Murrough'. Although the legend describes the defeat of one of Art's raids, it intriguingly has a reference to music and 'King Art Mac Murrough's band', which suggests a possible folkloric memory of some sort of celebration at the site, E. O'Toole, 'A miscellany of north Carlow folklore', *Béaloideas*, 1:4 (1928), 318. 28 Orpen, *The song of Dermot and the Earl*, pp 106–7, 146–9, 277; A.K. McHardy (ed.), *The reign of Richard II: from minority to tyranny, 1377–97* (Manchester, 2012), pp 278–9: before the Anglo-Norman invasion of Ireland, Ó Riain had been king of Uí Dróna. By the 1390s, the kingship of Uí Dróna had long passed to MacMurchadha and Ó Riain supported the king of the Leinster mountains in a reduced state as a minor chieftain. 29 AFM, 1381, note m. 30 Orpen (ed.), *The song of Dermot and the Earl*, p. xlii; O'Byrne, *War, politics and the Irish of Leinster*, p. 247; Byrne, *Irish kings and high-kings*, p. 290; nicknamed Murchadh 'na nGaedhal' ('of the Irish'). 31 AC, 1405; ALC, 1405; M. Ronan, 'Killadreenan and Newcastle', *JRSAI*, 63: (1938), 178.

were also some resurgent Irish families in the fourteenth century in that other portion of the ancient kingdom of Leinster reclaimed during the Gaelic revival – the wooded hills of Laois and extensive boglands of Offaly. The Ó Mórdha chieftains of Laois were closely tied to the MacMurchadha kings of the mountains and many of them were recorded as being among Art's adherents. The Ó Conchobhair king of Offaly, however, was more independently powerful.

The monastic settlement of St Mullins, which lay on the southern fringe of the Laveroc forest on the eastern bank of the river Barrow, was an important site in the MacMurchadha kingdom.[32] The monastery contained a number of churches and had a round tower in medieval times. St Mullins was an important pilgrimage site in the fourteenth century.[33] During the fourteenth century the great monastery of Glendalough also survived in the heart of the Wicklow mountains, and at the time was probably a sizeable Irish village. The settlement probably provided for many of the religious and market needs of the Irish population throughout much of the north of Art MacMurchadha's kingdom (see figure 19).

32 Reputedly founded by the early Irish saint Moling Luachra, who was said to have belonged to a minor branch of the Ui Cheinnselaig dynasty. 33 According to the *Annals of Friar John Clyn* (pp 246–7), in the months of September and October 1348, 'bishops and prelates, men of the church and of religion, magnates and others, and commonly all persons of both sexes, gathered from all sides of diverse parts of Ireland, to the pilgrimage and the wading in the water of St Moling in crowds and in multitudes, so that you might see many thousands of men assembling at the same place for many days ... from fear of the plague that then prevailed beyond measure'; Gwynn and Hadcock, *Medieval religious houses: Ireland*, pp 43–4; P. Ó Riain, *A dictionary of Irish saints* (Dublin, 2011), pp 487–90; M. de Paor, *Saint Moling Luachra: a pilgrimage from Sliabh Luachra to Rinn Ros Broic above the stream-pools of the Barrow* (Dublin, 2001).

By 1394 Art MacMurchadha had a good deal of control over the major English town of New Ross which lay on the river Barrow not far south of St Mullins. In fact, New Ross was probably the only substantial English town in Ireland that had fallen under the real control of the Irish. The wars with the MacMurchadha kings of Leinster throughout the fourteenth century had a debilitating effect on the trade of New Ross.[34] The town was no longer the threat it had once been to its great rival, the English city of Waterford. In 1380 New Ross was described as 'situated in the marches near the Irish enemies and rebels, and a great part of the walls and towers have fallen to the ground and the country for four miles on all sides is wasted and destroyed by the Irish, so that no one dares to go to town unless with a great force or by water'.[35] It was still a substantial town and appears to have often hosted Art within its walls, perhaps as its acknowledged local overlord. At Christmas 1393, when the English magnate James Butler, the earl of Ormond, resided in the town with his retinue, probably to prevent MacMurchadha from doing so, the townspeople of New Ross were ordered to supply him with:

> 4,000 good loaves; 2,000 gallons of ale; 40 good bullocks; 20 hogs; two large and good boars; 200 geese; 40 small pigs; a

34 Although a good distance from the open sea, New Ross had once been a thriving port, one of the most successful on the island throughout much of the thirteenth century. It had been founded by William Marshal, the lord of Leinster, around the years 1200–1. A well-known poem in French records the building of defensive walls by the townspeople in 1265. It suggests that in that year the town had a very substantial population, with well over 3,400 able-bodied adult males, divided up among the various trades, as well as hundreds of clergy and sailors. All helped to build the town walls on different assigned days of the week (Crouch, *William Marshal*, p. 109; H. Shields, 'The walling of New Ross: a thirteenth-century poem in French', *Bulletin of the Friends of the Library, Trinity College Dublin*, 12–13 (1975–6), 24–33).   35 89. Nov. 1380, Close Roll 4 Richard II.

quantity of candles; 40 trusses of hay; 100 pair of rabbits; 10 boats of firewood; 5 meases of herring; 100 cod and ling fish; 100 salted salmons; 1,000 whiting; with supplies of all other necessaries and victuals.[36]

CUSTOMS AND CULTURE OF THE LATE-MEDIEVAL IRISH

In the year 1397 Roger Mortimer, the young earl of March and Ulster who had been appointed by Richard II as his lieutenant in Ireland, described the Irish of Tyrone to a Catalan pilgrim as a 'savage, ungoverned people whom no man should trust'.[37] Mortimer was a cousin, once removed, of King Richard, and, besides being one of that monarch's powerful English magnates, held large estates around Trim in English Meath. Mortimer was also heir to the vast de Burgh inheritance in Connacht and the earldom of Ulster. The views of Roger Mortimer towards the Irish inhabitants of large areas of Ireland in the late fourteenth century appear to have been widely held, not only by the ruling elite in England but also by nobles and chroniclers from other areas in late-medieval Western Europe. Jean Creton, the French chronicler who accompanied Richard's final expedition to Ireland in 1399, described the Irish of the Leinster mountains as 'a people who are almost savage'.[38] Viscount Ramon de Perellós, the Catalan pilgrim who visited St Patrick's Purgatory in 1397, was a more sympathetic observer.[39] He was still shocked by the poor manner of dress of the

---

36 71. 11 Nov. 1393, Close Roll 17 Richard II; New Ross was a very strategic site in the fourteenth century, since its bridge, also built by William Marshal, was 'the lowest bridging point on the river on the main land route between Wexford and Waterford', Colfer, 'Anglo-Norman settlement in County Wexford', pp 85–6. 37 Carpenter, 'The pilgrim from Catalonia/Aragon', p. 108. 38 Creton, 'A French metrical history', 34. 39 Carpenter, 'The pilgrim from Catalonia/Aragon', p. 110.

Irish people he encountered, particularly the women in 'the land of the savage Irish where King O'Neill reigned supreme'.[40]

Viscount de Perellós, who visited the court of Niall Óg Ó Néill, the king of Tyrone, around Christmastime in 1397, has left perhaps the best contemporary description of the dress and customs of the late-medieval Irish. De Perellós recorded the style of dress of the nobles of Tyrone who:

> wear tunics without a lining, reaching to the knee. [They wear them] cut very low at the neck, almost in the style of women, and they wear great hoods which hang down to the waist, the point of which is narrow as a finger. They wear neither hose nor shoes, nor do they wear breeches, and they wear their spurs on their bare heels. The king was dressed like that on Christmas Day and so were all the clerks and knights and even the bishops and abbots and the great lords.[41]

This description of the dress of late-medieval Irish nobles is confirmed in two other contemporary descriptions, those of Froissart and Creton. A contemporary illustration of Art MacMurchadha Caomhánach, whom Creton saw at a parley in 1399, depicts the king of Leinster with spurs on his bare feet (see figures 7 and 23).[42] As the modern historian Katharine Simms has pointed out, 'Both these Irish chiefs, who employed hundreds if not thousands of fighting men at a time, could obviously have afforded a pair of shoes, but chose not to wear them, even in the depths of winter'.[43] Simms believes that the contemporary

40 Ibid., pp 109–10. 41 Ibid., p. 110. 42 Froissart, *Chronicles*, p. 414; K. Simms, 'Warfare in the medieval Gaelic lordships', *The Irish Sword*, 12 (1975/6), 105. 43 Simms, 'Late medieval Tír Eoghain', p. 150. 44 Ibid.; K. Simms, 'The barefoot kings: literary image and reality in later medieval Ireland', *Proceedings of*

descriptions dating from the 1390s suggest that 'Irish aristocrats were brought up in a very warlike and Spartan culture' and that this 'cult of Spartan primitivism' may have developed owing to the 'perpetual warfare that accompanied the Gaelic political recovery'.[44]

If this was indeed the case, it appears that late-medieval Irish noblewomen shared the harshness of this Spartan culture with their men. De Perellós writes of the queen of Tyrone, Una, daughter of Domhnall Ó Néill, 'her daughter and her sister were dressed and girded, but the queen was barefoot and her handmaidens, twenty in number, were dressed as I have told you above [wearing an Irish cloak called a mantle], with their shameful parts showing'.[45] Many contemporary descriptions of Irish women right to the end of the sixteenth century echo Viscount de Perellós' depiction of even noblewomen being almost naked under their cloaks.[46] According to one account, it was 'young women and girls [that] have their chests naked to the waist'.[47] Married Irish women wore other garments, for example: 'a shawl that they wrap round themselves and a piece of linen on their heads which is folded several times and knotted at the forehead'.[48] A second source confirms this, adding that married Irish women 'according to ancient custom, wore veils or kerchiefs on their heads ... The

the Harvard Celtic Colloquium, 30 (2010), pp 1–21. **45** Carpenter, 'The pilgrim from Catalonia/Aragon', p. 110; AFM, 1417. **46** Francisco De Cuéllar, 'Letter from one who sailed with the Spanish Armada and tells the story of the enterprise of England' in P. Gallagher and D. Cruickshank (eds), *God's obvious design: Spanish Armada Symposium, Sligo 1988* (London, 1990), p. 239. **47** *Archduke Ferdinand's visit to Kinsale in Ireland, an extract from Le Premier Voyage de Charles-Quint en Espagne, de 1517 à 1518*, Dorothy Convery (ed.), electronic edition, CELT Project, Cork (2012), p. 285 (http://www.ucc.ie/celt/published/T500000-001/index.html, accessed 4 Jan. 2015). **48** De Cuéllar, 'Letter from one who sailed with the Spanish Armada', p. 239.

unmarried women went bare-headed [with their hair filleted up] which they sometimes wore hanging down their backs'.[49] What seems to be common to all accounts of encounters between Irish women and foreign observers, whether in late-medieval or early modern times, is that the Irish women were poorly dressed compared to what Spanish and English visitors were used to.

The frieze cloak or mantle was the most noteworthy item of clothing worn by the late-medieval Irish. It had a:

> fringed or shagged border sowed down the edges of it, [and] was not always made of frieze, or such coarse materials, which was the dress of the lower sort of people; but according to the rank or quality of the wearer was sometimes made of the finest cloth, bordered with a silken or fine woollen fringe, and of scarlet and other various colours. Many rows of this shag or fringe were sowed on the upper part of the mantle, partly to defend the neck the better from the cold, and along the edges run a narrow fringe of the same sort of texture. The women's mantles differed but little from the men's except in length, extending something below the ankles.

Irish men wore their mantles 'almost down to the ankles'.[50] Around 1394 Irish nobles also appear to have generally worn some type of cap or beret. This may have been the:

> sort of bonnet or cap called in Irish Barred ... signifying a covering for the head ... probably [made] the same with the mantle, the better, as that did to defend the head and neck from the cold; and as the mantle was differently ornamented,

---

49 W. Harris (ed.), *The whole works of Sir James Ware concerning Ireland: revised and improved* (Dublin, 1745), i, pp 177–8.   50 Ibid., pp 174–5.

so too the barred varied in that respect according to the quality of the wearer.[51]

The wearing of a distinctive Irish dagger or *scian* appears to have completed what was typical Irish dress in the late fourteenth century. De Perellós preserved a good account of the knives that he saw the Irish in Tyrone carry. The Catalan states that they were 'long, narrow and thin as one's little finger'. The viscount adds that 'they are very sharp' (see figure 8).[52]

When the Irish kings and chieftains encountered Richard II in early 1395, many of their submissions were recorded and these notes often preserve a record of what the Irish nobles were wearing. As a result, it appears that mantle, cap and *scian* may have been typical dress for Irish nobles from all over the island in the late fourteenth century. When Niall Óg Ó Néill, the king of Tyrone in Ulster, submitted to Richard in March 1395, he removed 'his girdle with his dagger and cap'.[53] Toirdhealbhach Ó Conchobhair Donn, a Connacht chieftain, removed 'his mantle, cap, girdle, and dagger' to submit, while Brian Ó Briain the king of Thomond in north Munster removed 'his girdle, sword, and cap'.[54] Tadhg MacCarthaigh Mór, king of Desmond in south-west Munster, removed 'his girdle, dagger, and cap', and the Leinster chieftains Muircheartaigh Ó Conchobhair of Offaly and Gearalt Ó Broin of the Wicklow mountains both removed their 'girdle, sword and cap' before kneeling to submit to the English king.[55]

---

51 Ibid., p. 177.   52 Carpenter, 'The pilgrim from Catalonia/Aragon', p. 110; E. Rynne, 'Three Irish knife-daggers', *JRSAI*, 99: 2 (1969), 137–41.   53 Submission of Niall Óg Ó Néill, 16 Mar. 1395 in Curtis, 'The instruments touching Ireland', p. 159.   54 Submission of Toirdhealbhach Ó Conchobhair Donn, 20 Apr. 1395, ibid., p. 179; submission of Brian Ó Briain, 1 Mar. 1395, ibid., p. 181. 55 Submission of Tadhg MacCarthaigh Mór, 6 Apr. 1395, ibid., p. 192; submission of Gearalt Ó Broin, 12 Feb. 1395, ibid., p. 166; submission of Muircheartaigh Ó

In 1394, most Irish nobles, even the powerful kings, lived in buildings made of wood, wattle and daub. Art MacMurchadha's palace was a fortified wooden building in the middle of the Garryhill forest in the centre of Co. Carlow.[56] Traditionally, the palace of the Ó Néill king of Tyrone had been the rath of Tullaghoge, high on a hill in the east of the modern county. In the fourteenth century Tullaghoge may have been too vulnerable to attack by the rival Ó Néill chieftains of Clann Aodha Buidhe, who were based close by to the east of the river Bann. As a result, as previously stated, the mid fourteenth-century palace of the Ó Néill kings may have been a wooden crannog at a place called Fraochmhagh, which may be Augher, where the O'Neills had an island castle during the sixteenth century (see figure 4).[57]

In the fourteenth century the Irish kings and chieftains did not construct large buildings in stone. Building mostly in wood and wattle may have been a deliberate and shrewd policy that allowed the Irish kings quickly to destroy their main habitations by fire, allowing them to escape with their people and cattle herds into the forests and mountains. In this way, the Irish ensured that English armies did not capture and garrison strategic points. As a result, if an English army wished, for example, to put a garrison into the east of the Tyrone kingdom in the late fourteenth century, they would have had to find and carry all the stone and building materials into Tyrone themselves and then stand guard for as long as it took to build the fortress. This would have been an expensive, dangerous and drawn-out process. One exception to this rule of Irish kings

Conchobhair of Offaly, 12 Feb. 1395, ibid., p. 167.   **56** Curtis, 'Unpublished letters from Richard II in Ireland, 1394–5', 291–3.   **57** Simms, 'Late medieval Tír Eoghain', pp 146–7; J. Andrews, *The queen's last map-maker: Richard Bartlett in Ireland, 1600–3* (Dublin, 2008), pp 107 and 110.

building mostly in wood is the stone castle in western Tyrone, reputed to have been built in the later fourteenth century by the famous nobleman Éinrí Aimhréidh Ó Néill – Henry the Contentious, the brother of Niall Óg Ó Néill, the king of Tyrone.[58] Harry Avery's castle, as the fortress is called to this day, was so deep in western Tyrone that Éinrí Aimhréidh would have had plenty of time to demolish his fortress before an English army could reach it. That the Irish had lost some of their familiarity with building in stone by the late fourteenth century can be seen by the fact that although Harry Avery's castle looks like an English double-towered gatehouse, it is in reality a tower house (see figure 5). It is as if the builder knew what an English castle looked like from the outside but did not really understand its purpose or internal construction.[59] The deliberately temporary nature of most Irish buildings was noticed in Tyrone by Viscount de Perellós in 1397. He recorded that:

> Their dwellings are communal and most of them are set up near the oxen, for that is where they make their homes in the space of a single day and they move on through the pastures, like the swarms of Barbary in the land of the Sultan. Thus in a short space of time their towns can be moved and they travel together always.[60]

58 E. Jope, H. Jope and E. Johnson, 'Harry Avery's castle, Newtownstewart, Co. Tyrone: excavations in 1950', *UJA*, 12:1–2 (1950), 81–92; AFM, 1392, note p; in the early nineteenth century the historian John O'Donovan, while researching for the Ordnance Survey, encountered 'more traditions preserved about this Henry Avrey than about any of the later chieftains of that family, excepting, perhaps Owen Roe and Sir Phelim, who flourished in Cromwell's time'.   59 Jope, Jope and Johnson, 'Harry Avery's castle, Newtownstewart, Co. Tyrone: excavations in 1950', 89–90.   60 Carpenter, 'The pilgrim from Catalonia/Aragon', p. 111.

Cattle farming was practised over all the Irish areas on the island in late-medieval times. The Irish kings and nobles owned huge herds of cattle, often numbering many thousand head.[61] Creton commented on the overwhelming importance of cattle to the economies of the Irish kingdoms when he noticed that 'there was little money in the country, wherefore their usual traffic is only with cattle'.[62] This importance of cattle to many aspects of ordinary life in late-medieval Ireland is seen especially in the diet of the people at that time. Again, a good description is provided by Viscount de Perellós. He states: 'They do not sow corn nor have they any wine. Their only meat is ox-meat. The great lords drink milk and the others meat-broth, and the common people drink water, as I said before. But they have plenty of butter, for oxen and cows provide all their meat'.[63] The Catalan pilgrim continues:

> The king [Niall Óg Ó Néill] received me very well and he sent me an ox and his cook to prepare it. In all his court there was no milk to drink nor bread nor wine, but as a great gift he sent me two cakes as thin as wafers and as pliable as raw dough. They were made of oats and earth and they were black as coal, but very tasty.[64]

The viscount may have exaggerated the lack of the cultivation of cereals by the Irish of Tyrone, which is not surprising given that he visited that kingdom at Christmastime. Many of the characteristics of the diet of the late-medieval Irish that he described are repeated again and again in sixteenth-century descriptions of Ireland written by English observers.[65]

---

61 Curtis, 'Unpublished letters from Richard II in Ireland', 293.   62 Creton, 'A French metrical history', 40.   63 Carpenter, 'The pilgrim from Catalonia/Aragon', pp 110–11.   64 Ibid.   65 For example: 'A note of such oppressions and indirect

With such an abundance of cattle in late-medieval Ireland, blood puddings and similar foodstuffs must also have been an important part of the diet of the population, although de Perellós makes no mention of them. In the early nineteenth century the historian John O'Donovan encountered the custom of the 'bleeding of cattle and using the blood as food' still being carried out in the central mountains of what had once been the late-medieval kingdom of Tyrone. According to O'Donovan the practice began 'from the beginning of May until the 20th of August', with the cattle 'improved not injured by being thus bled'. After being allowed to settle and congeal, the blood was salted and then almost boiled, 'but if the water should be boiling at the time ... it will not do'. It was then 'mixed with butter, and variously prepared according to taste'. The resulting food was 'considered a great luxury by the mountaineers'.[66] The lack of references to native alcoholic drinks is a surprising omission by the Catalan pilgrim. Certainly, mead – in Irish *miodh* and *mil-fíon* (honey wine) – would have been brewed by the Irish in the late fourteenth century. From the early fifteenth century Irish whiskey (*uisce beatha – aqua vitae*), which had a reputation for being 'excellent', became popular, while ale, called *leann* by the Irish, is also often mentioned in late-medieval sources.[67] The Irish did drink imported wine in late-medieval times, but the quality was often poor and wine could be very scarce at times.[68] Fish was also eaten by the medieval Irish, although, again de Perellós never mentions the practice.

---

courses as hath been held in Tír Chonaill and other places', 21 Dec. 1594, TNA SP63/177/170–3. **66** Herity (ed.), *Ordnance Survey letters: Londonderry, Fermanagh, Armagh-Monaghan, Louth and Cavan-Leitrim*, pp 72–3. **67** Harris (ed.), *The whole works of Sir James Ware*, i, p. 183; K. Simms, 'Guesting and feasting in Gaelic Ireland', *JRSAI*, 108 (1978), 86–8. **68** Simms, 'Guesting and feasting in Gaelic Ireland', 86–8; AC, 1310.

Horses, too, were important to the late-medieval Irish. Native Irish horses were smaller than the norm in Western Europe and were called *hobbies* in the fourteenth century. Despite their small stature, Irish horses were 'held in great esteem for their easy amble'.[69] The early modern author Philip O'Sullivan Beare stated that 'The biggest of them is assigned to fighting as it stands out in strength, courage and ferocity'.[70] The sure-footedness of the native Irish horse was important to the Irish warrior of the late fourteenth century, who often used the cover provided by forest, mountain and bog to attack the more heavily armed and horsed English knights who opposed them on the battlefield. Creton recorded in 1399 that Art MacMurchadha Caomhánach galloped down from a mountain to meet the English on a horse 'so fine and good, that it had cost him, they said, four hundred cows'.[71] Creton adds 'I never, in all my life, saw hare, deer, sheep or any other animal, I declare to you for a certainty, run with such speed, as it did'.[72] Creton demonstrated that he was a good observer when he noticed that the king of the Leinster mountains 'had a horse without housing or saddle'.[73] De Perellós noticed this too, when he recorded that the household cavalry of Niall Óg Ó Néill 'ride without a saddle on a cushion'.[74] The Irish never adopted the stirrup, preferring to sit on cushions and use spurs on their bare feet to help control the horse. According to Viscount de Perellós, Niall Óg Ó Néill in 1397 'had then three thousand horses or more'.[75]

---

69 Harris (ed.), *The whole works of Sir James Ware*, i, p. 166.   70 O'Sullivan (ed.), *The natural history of Ireland*, pp 72–5.   71 Creton, 'A French metrical history', 40.   72 Ibid.   73 Ibid.   74 Carpenter, 'The pilgrim from Catalonia/Aragon', p. 110.   75 Ibid.; Mhág Craith (ed.), *Dán na mBráthar Mionúr*, i, p. 2; ii, p. 1.

The courts of the Irish kings by the 1390s appear to have been quite Spartan. De Perellós describes the 'great court' held on Christmas Day 1397 by the king of Tyrone, Niall Óg Ó Néill:

> his table was of rushes spread out on the ground while nearby they placed delicate grass for him to wipe his mouth. They used to carry meat to him on poles, in the same way as they carry *semals* [tubs], in this country, and as you can imagine, the squires bearing this were badly dressed.[76]

Yet Ó Néill had a dignified air about him in the Catalan's account. According to the viscount, 'There was a great number of poor people following him and I saw the king giving them great alms [in the form] of ox-meat.'[77] Niall Óg also spoke to de Perellós 'at length, asking me about the Christian kings, especially the kings of France, Aragon and Castile, and about their customs and the way they lived'. De Perellós adds: 'It appeared to me from his words that they consider their own customs to be better than ours and more advantageous than any others in the whole world.'[78]

The same high regard that the Irish nobility had for their customs is evident in Froissart's chronicle. Froissart received an account from the English squire Henry Cristall of how he successfully prepared a group of Irish kings that may have included Niall Óg Ó Néill, the king of Tyrone, when they were staying together in early 1395 for a ceremony in which they were to be knighted by Richard II. Cristall stated that his 'mission' was 'based on the King's [Richard's] expressed wish that in behaviour, bearing and dress they should conform to the English pattern'. Although they eventually complied, at first the Irish kings, when urged to

76 Carpenter, 'The pilgrim from Catalonia/Aragon', p. 110.   77 Ibid.   78 Ibid., p. 111.

make their men sit apart from them at table, 'looked at each other and refused to eat, saying it was a breach of the excellent custom in which they had been brought up'. Over the first few days, Cristall observed how the Irish kings 'get their minstrels and their principal servants to sit with them and eat off their plates and drink from their goblets. They told me that such was the custom of the country. Except for their beds, they had everything in common.'[79] Cristall got himself into some trouble with the Irish kings when:

> Once I asked them about their faith, and what they believed in, but they were not at all pleased by the question and I had to stop. They said that they believed in God and the Trinity, just the same as us, with no difference whatever. I asked them which pope they inclined to. They replied: 'To the one in Rome, with no compromise.'[80]

Throughout the late-medieval period the Irish staunchly opposed any attempt by the English to portray them as anything other than good Christians.

Cristall also gave Froissart a shrewd assessment of the general characteristics of the late-medieval Irish:

> who are very dour people, proud and uncouth, slow-thinking and hard to get to know or make friends with. They have no respect for pleasant manners or for any gentleman, for, although their country is ruled by kings, of whom there are a large number, they will have nothing to do with courtly behaviour, but cling to the rough ways in which they have been brought up.[81]

79 Froissart, *Chronicles*, pp 413–14.   80 Ibid., pp 414–15.   81 Ibid., pp 410–11.

As a result, it is perhaps no surprise that Cristall added for Froissart that:

> It must be said that they were thoroughly stared at by the English and others who were present, and not without reason, for they were foreign and different in appearance from the English and other nationalities, and people are naturally curious to see some new things.[82]

In return, the late-medieval Irish referred to the English of Ireland as the gall – the foreigners. Englishmen from the kingdom of England were called Saxons.[83]

Froissart (1395), de Perellós (1397) and Creton (1399) have all left valuable contemporary accounts of the late-medieval Irish at war. This is appropriate given that warfare was probably the main occupation of the Irish kings and nobility throughout the fourteenth century. This period was a time of great military innovation in Gaelic Ireland. The once highly traditional Irish warriors adopted metal armour, archery, fighting on horseback and the employment of battalions of heavily armed mercenaries recruited from Gaelic Scotland.

By the 1390s most Irish nobles served as horsemen (*marcach*) in the armies of their kings. The Irish horseman wore a coat of mail with padded undergarments and a conical metal helmet, and was armed with sword and *scian*. The main weapon of the fourteenth-century Irish horseman was the spear, which the warrior carried overarm, not couched like a lance in the manner of English knights. Some spears used by the Irish horseman, such as the *ga*, were thrown, while others, such as the *craoiseac*, were 'retained in

---

82 Ibid., p. 416.   83 'The description of Ireland', p. 67.

the hand' by the mounted warrior.[84] The Irish horseman of the late fourteenth century used a native cushion instead of a saddle and stirrups, which meant he could not couch a lance. As a result, he could not charge English knights on a level battlefield and expect to emerge victorious. The overarm use of spears may have suited the style of warfare in Ireland at this time.[85] Much of the fighting between the Irish and English armies took place in mountainous, forested and bogland regions, where Irish horsemen could dart in and out of cover, firing spears and then retreating to safety. This was to prove very effective throughout the century.

Viscount de Perellós has left a very good description of Niall Óg Ó Néill's household cavalry. He states that:

> there are several kings on that island ... But he [Ó Néill] is the greatest king and he has forty horsemen. They ride without a saddle on a cushion and each one wears a cloak according to his rank. They are armed with coats of mail and round iron helmets like the Moors and Saracens. Some of them are like the Bernese. They have swords and very long knives and long lances, like those of that ancient country which were two fathoms in length. Their swords are like those of the Saracens, the kind we call Genoese. The pommel and the hilt are different; the pommel is almost [as big] as a man's hand.[86]

This description of Irish horsemen corresponds closely with Creton's picture, dating from 1399, of Art MacMurchadha when the French chronicler saw the king of the Leinster mountains fully

---

84 P. Harbison, 'Native Irish arms and armour in medieval Gaelic literature, 1170–1600', *The Irish Sword*, 12:49 (1976), 272–3.   85 Ibid., *The Irish Sword*, 12:48 (1976), 173–99; ibid., 12:49 (1976), 270–84.   86 Carpenter, 'The pilgrim from Catalonia/Aragon', p. 110.

armed and mounted. The accompanying illustration of the Irish king could almost be drawn from the Catalan viscount's description of the Tyrone horsemen, and is the first contemporary depiction of an Irishman wearing metal armour (see figure 23).[87] English horsemen wore more metal armour than their Irish opponents, although owing to the difficult nature of the terrain in much of Ireland, even the English of Ireland may not have worn as much heavy armour as soldiers from the English kingdom did in late-medieval times.

From surviving records, it appears that Art MacMurchadha and both Niall Mór and his son, Niall Óg Ó Néill, all fought throughout their active years as horsemen. It may be that their people at that time expected Irish kings to be skilled and accomplished warriors. Cristall, who lived among the Leinster Irish for seven years, provided an account of how the young sons of Irish kings were trained as warriors. He informed Froissart that 'in Ireland a king knights his son at the age of seven; and that if the father is dead, his nearest blood-relative does it'.[88] The young boy then learnt 'to joust with light lances, such as he can easily hold, against a shield set up in a meadow on a post. The more lances he breaks, the greater the honour for him.'[89]

The next most important type of Irish soldier after the horseman during the fourteenth century was the galloglass (*gallóglaigh* – foreign warriors).[90] These soldiers originated in Gaelic Scotland and seem to have been recruited from families dispossessed by the Bruces in the wars for Scottish independence,

---

87 Harbison, 'Native Irish arms and armour in medieval Gaelic literature', 187–8.
88 Froissart, *Chronicles*, p. 415.   89 Ibid.   90 Simms, *From kings to warlords*, p. 175.

fought throughout the late 1200s and early 1300s. They first took service with Irish kings in west Ulster and north Connacht. By the fifteenth century, galloglass families had begun to spread to serve the Irish and English lords of south Connacht and Munster. They were called 'foreign warriors' not because they came from Gaelic Scotland but because most of them had some Norse ancestry.[91] By the 1390s one of the greatest of all the galloglass families, the Clann Alasdair branch of the Hebridean MacDomhnaill dynasty, had monopolized galloglass service to Ó Néill, king of Tyrone. Ó Néill granted them much land and the title 'constable of Ulster' in return for the provision of hundreds of heavily armed warriors. Compared to Irish foot soldiers, galloglass battalions were very well armed. Their main weapon was the battleaxe, but most were also armed with a sword or *scian*. They were protected by a coat of mail with padded undergarments, and a conical metal helmet, just like the Irish horsemen. Some galloglasses in every battalion were archers and this may explain the soldiers armed 'with bows which are not long – only half the size of English bows, but their range is just as good' that Viscount de Perellós encountered in Tyrone in 1397.[92]

Niall Óg Ó Néill sent his galloglass constable to welcome Viscount de Perellós into Tyrone, to ensure that the Catalan pilgrim reached his court safely. The viscount states that 'I met King O'Neill's constable with a hundred men on horseback, armed also in their manner, and I conversed with this constable'.[93] This man was probably Eoin Maol MacDomhnaill, who submitted to Richard II at Drogheda in March 1395. At the time MacDomhnaill was indistinguishable from the other Irish nobles

91 Hayes-McCoy, *Scots mercenary forces in Ireland*, p. 18.   92 Carpenter, 'The pilgrim from Catalonia/Aragon', pp 109–10.   93 Ibid.

since he spoke Irish and dressed in exactly the same manner as the rest of the chieftains.[94] MacDomhnaill claimed that the great Scots Gaelic overlord 'MacDonald, Lord of the Isles' was his 'kinsman' but had 'expelled me from my country ... whereupon I came to O'Neill's country'.[95] The MacDomhnaill battalion in the service of the king of Tyrone was an elite unit, and both Niall Mór and Niall Óg Ó Néill knew that they would get a good fight out of their galloglass constable and his battleaxe men and archers whenever they went into battle against their English or Irish enemies.[96] In the 1390s the galloglass families had not yet reached the province of Leinster. Art MacMurchadha hired Irish mercenaries from Munster when he needed additional soldiers.

The most numerous Irish foot soldiers in late-medieval times were the lightly armed and usually unarmoured kerne (*ceatharnaigh*). Each armed with a sword or *scian*, a small shield called a 'target' and a handful of darts (small spears), kerne were not much use in pitched battles against well-armed English soldiers. Their forte was guerrilla warfare: for example, running in and out of forests to attack English columns, or setting fire to houses and seizing livestock on raids. If a force of kerne, even a very large one, was caught in the open by an English force, the result was inevitably a massacre of the Irish light infantry by their heavily armed opponents. Nevertheless, a skilful Irish commander could prevent this from happening simply by sticking to favourable terrain, where most of the serious fighting took place in Ireland

---

94 Curtis, 'The instruments touching Ireland', pp 149–51.   95 Ibid., pp 175–6; Nicholls, 'Scottish mercenary kindreds in Ireland, 1250–1600', pp 97–100.   96 For example, see the actions of MacDomhnaill Gallóglach in support of Ó Néill and his son Éinrí in battle against Ó Domhnaill and MacSuibhne Fanad at the Rash (Mountjoy forest, Co. Tyrone) in 1435, AFM, 1435; T.W. Moody, F.X. Martin and F.J. Byrne (eds), *NHI*, viii: *A chronology of Irish history to 1976* (Oxford, 1982), p. 161.

throughout the fourteenth century. Creton appears to have recorded attacks by mixed forces of kerne and horsemen on columns of Richard II's troops during the king's second expedition into the Leinster mountains in 1399:

> Thus we passed straight through the woods, for the Irish were much afraid of our arrows. There they raised such a shouting and noise that, in my opinion, they might easily have been heard at the distance of a long league. They did not all escape, owing to the archers, who were often up with them. Very frequently they assailed the vanguard, and threw their darts with such force that they pierced haubergeon [small mail shirts] and plates [plate armour], through and through.[97]

Irish warriors proved themselves to be skilled and dangerous opponents throughout the fourteenth century. Large English armies found no one to fight and small armies were defeated. On an individual level the best Irish warriors appear to have been highly skilled. Cristall gave Froissart a detailed description of the perils of warfare for the English in Irish parts of the island. He states that 'Ireland is one of the most difficult countries in the world to fight against and subdue, for it is a strange, wild place consisting of tall forests, great stretches of water, bogs and uninhabitable regions.' Cristall continues:

> It is hard to find a way of making war on the Irish effectively for, unless they choose, there is no one there to fight and there are no towns to be found. The Irish hide in the woods and forests, where they live in holes dug under trees, or in bushes

97 Creton, 'A French metrical history', 33–4; Bradbury, *The Routledge companion to medieval warfare*, pp 256 and 258.

and thickets, like wild animals. When they learn that you have entered their territory to make war on them, they come together in various places by different paths, so that it is impossible to reach them. But they, if they see they have advantage, can attack the enemy as it suits them, for they know the country backwards and are skilled fighters.[98]

A major difference between warfare in Ireland and the wars the late-medieval English were more used to, was the tendency of the Irish to kill their prisoners. In continental Europe the capture and ransoming of knights was a big feature of late-medieval warfare.[99] The Irish did not exactly slit throats, as Cristall apparently recounted to Froissart, and 'remove the heart, which they take away. Some who know their ways, say that they eat it with great relish.'[100] The beheading of an enemy was a ritualistic part of ancient Irish warfare, however, that continued right to the end of the sixteenth century.

Warfare in Ireland throughout the fourteenth century was usually small-scale and involved cattle raiding and the harrying of enemy territory. Much of the fighting took place at the rear of Irish armies, as the warriors either defended their own retreating people and herds of cattle, or protected from pursuers the spoils taken in a raid.[101] However, the two expeditions of Richard II to Ireland in 1394–5 and 1399, and possibly also some of the earlier campaigns conducted by Art MacMurchadha or Niall Mór and Niall Óg Ó

---

98 Froissart, *Chronicles*, p. 410. 99 J. Gillingham, 'Killing and mutilating political enemies in the British Isles from the late twelfth to the early fourteenth century: a comparative study' in B. Smith (ed.), *Britain and Ireland, 900–1300: insular responses to medieval European change* (Cambridge, 1999), pp 114–34. 100 Froissart, *Chronicles*, p. 410. 101 Simms, 'Warfare in the medieval Gaelic lordships', 98–108.

Néill, involved much greater numbers on both sides and more intense fighting than cattle raiding. Art MacMurchadha in the Leinster mountains and Niall Mór and Niall Óg Ó Néill in Gaelic Ulster probably put armies of around 2,000 warriors into the field regularly against their Irish and English opponents. Although the Irish nobility of the fourteenth century was almost bred for warfare, and both the terrain and the tactics they adopted favoured them during these years, it was still important for Irish armies to be well led and for the Irish kings to know the limits of their capabilities. In Art MacMurchadha, Niall Mór and Niall Óg Ó Néill, the late-fourteenth-century Irish found leaders who had these essential skills.

CHAPTER 3

Richard's first expedition to Ireland, 1394–5

Cing Risderd, king of England, came to Ireland this year and Art MacMurchadha, king of Leinster, was greatly weakened by the king and the rest of the English.[1]

There was great activity in the kingdom of England in preparation for Richard's expedition to Ireland during the summer of 1394. In July the sheriff of every county in the kingdom issued a proclamation:

> that all yeomen and archers of the crown of whatsoever condition, being at the king's wages and fees ... draw with speed to the king's presence, so as to be there on 3 August next at latest, ready every man ... arrayed to sail with the king to Ireland in his army for repression of the malice of certain Irish the king's enemies who have long been in rebellion against him.[2]

1 AC, 1398 (recte: 1394); 'Cing' is the Old English form of 'king'. This entry in the Annals of Connacht is recorded in relation to Richard's second expedition, but appears misplaced and is more relevant to his first. 2 1 July 1394, Calendar of

At the same time Richard gathered a large fleet to transport his army to Ireland.[3] The king ordered John de Bellemonte, the constable of Dover castle and the warden of the Cinque Ports, 'to summon the barons of singular the said ports and of the members thereof to be at Bristol on the feast of the Exaltation of Holy Cross next with ships and seamen in array, ready at their pain and peril to sail with his fleet'.[4] Richard wanted the Cinque Ports to supply him with: '57 ships, and in every ship twenty men and a master armed and arrayed to do his service' at their own cost for fifteen days. If in service longer, the king agreed to pay 'the master taking 6d a day, the constable 6d and every other man 3d'.[5] Other ships such as *La Typhayne* and *Le Michel* from the island of Guernsey were 'by Henry Rither esquire arrested and detained by command of the king to sail on his service to Ireland'.[6] While waiting for Richard to gather his army and fleet together, Rither allowed both ships to continue to trade in the English Channel.[7] In September, when preparations for the expedition to Ireland were almost complete, more orders were issued to the sheriffs of the western counties of England to arrange food supplies for the king's army once it was on the island. The sheriffs of the western counties were:

> to cause proclamation to be made, that all who have wine, any kind of corn or malt, flesh, fish or other victuals whatsoever for sale shall take the same or cause them to be taken to Ireland from time to time for sustenance of the king and his army, and that on coming thither prompt payment shall be made them for the same.[8]

Close Rolls, 18 Richard II, pp 301–2. 3 2 Aug. 1394, Calendar of Close Rolls, 18 Richard II, p. 308. 4 Ibid., p. 307. 5 Ibid. 6 3 July 1394, Calendar of Close Rolls, 18 Richard II, p. 297. 7 Ibid. 8 28 Sept. 1394, Calendar of Close Rolls, 18 Richard II, p. 364.

Taken together, all the preparations suggest that Richard II's first expedition to Ireland in 1394 was very well organized indeed.

Richard may have assembled a fleet of well over two hundred ships to take his army to Ireland.[9] A surviving wardrobe account records that the English king had more than 5,000 men-at-arms and archers with him in Ireland in October 1394.[10] This large figure does not include the 1,000 to 2,000 Cheshire archers who formed Richard's personal bodyguard, or the approximately 2,000 local English soldiers who joined the king's army once he had landed.[11] As a result, Richard II may have commanded a field army of between 8,000 and 10,000 men in Ireland in October 1394, an immense number comparable to any English army that campaigned in France during the second half of the fourteenth century.[12] Richard also took many of his most important supporters among the English nobility to campaign with him in Ireland, including blood relations. Among these were his cousin (once removed) Roger Mortimer, the young earl of March and Ulster; Thomas Mowbray, the earl of Nottingham, the marshal of England and a distant relative of the king; another cousin of the king, Edward of Aumerle, the earl of Rutland, who was the admiral of the king's fleet; John Holland, the earl of Huntingdon and the king's half-brother; Lord Thomas Holland, the king's nephew, who was the son of the king's other half-brother, Thomas Holland, the earl of Kent; Thomas of Woodstock, the duke of Gloucester, who was Richard's uncle; Sir Thomas Percy, a brother of the earl of Northumberland and the king's steward of the household; as well

9 Allmand, *The Hundred Years War*, pp 82–90; Lydon's estimate of 500 ships appears to be far too high; J.F. Lydon, 'Richard II's expeditions to Ireland', *JRSAI*, 93 (1963), 139–40; C. Allmand describes an English fleet of 146 ships assembled in 1347 as 'impressive', *The Hundred Years War*, p. 89. 10 Lydon, 'Richard II's expeditions to Ireland', 142. 11 Ibid. 12 Ibid., 142–3.

as many other supporters, such as Sir John Beaumont, Sir Thomas Despenser and Sir William Scrope.[13]

The royal fleet sailed from the port of Milford Haven in south Wales and made landfall at Waterford on 2 October 1394. In a letter written soon afterwards, Richard commented on the smooth nature of his sailing to Ireland. The king wrote:

> we had the finest and most favourable crossing, with full health of body, without being troubled or upset by the weather or rough sea in any way, that ever God allowed – a thousand thanks to Him – in such fashion that we were only a day and a night at sea in our crossing; and so we arrived at our city of W.[aterford] in I.[reland] where we were by our citizens there received very honourably and with great joy.[14]

Considering the fact that a reigning English monarch had not visited the island since 1210, the Irish annals are very terse in their recording of this important event – if they took notice of Richard's arrival at all. Most merely record that 'the king of the Saxons (namely, Richard II) came to Ireland this Harvest and the earl of March came with him'.[15] The Annals of Clonmacnoise even record that 'The earle of March arrived in Ireland of a purpose to get his rents of the Inhabitants of the kingdome,' and do not mention Richard at all.[16] The Annals of Saints' Island are fuller. They state that 'the king of England came to Ireland with an immense force, including English and Welsh, and such a fleet

---

13 Curtis, 'Unpublished letters from Richard II in Ireland, 1394–5', 301; Lydon, 'Richard II's expeditions to Ireland', 138 and 141; Saul, *Richard II*, pp 243–7; A.W. Boardman, *Hotspur: Henry Percy, medieval rebel* (Stroud, 2003), pp 24–5, 27–8, 48.   14 Curtis, 'Unpublished letters from Richard II in Ireland, 1394–5', 289–90; CIHM, 1394.   15 AU, 1394.   16 *Annals of Clonmacnoise*, 1394, p. 316.

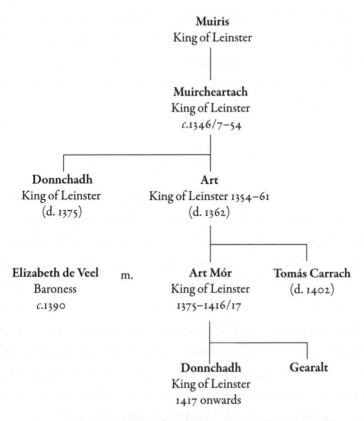

Muiris
King of Leinster

|

Muircheartach
King of Leinster
*c.*1346/7–54

Donnchadh
King of Leinster
(d. 1375)

Art
King of Leinster 1354–61
(d. 1362)

Elizabeth de Veel   m.   **Art Mór**   **Tomás Carrach**
Baroness   King of Leinster   (d. 1402)
*c.*1390   1375–1416/17

Donnchadh   **Gearalt**
King of Leinster
1417 onwards

4. The MacMurchadha Caomhánach kings of Leinster.

did not come to Ireland since the Norse fleets came. They landed at Waterford.'[17]

Richard spent quite a few days at Waterford, organizing his army after it had disembarked from the fleet. The English king also spent some of this time arranging for a number of his ships to blockade the south Leinster coastline.[18] He states in a letter that he found 'victuals in great plenty and very cheap', and that the English lords from the surrounding territories 'come in to offer us

17 ASI, 1394.   18 Lydon, 'Richard II's expeditions to Ireland', 145.

their services'.[19] The Annals of Saints' Island record the king's first objective – an attack on Art MacMurchadha in the Leinster mountains. These annals continue: 'and from there MacMurchadha [was] attacked, and the Gaels of Leinster were overthrown'.[20]

ART MACMURCHADHA CAOMHÁNACH

Art was an able king of the Leinster mountains. He could put armies of thousands of Irish warriors into the field and threatened the English settlements of south Wexford, north Carlow, Kildare and the vale of Dublin itself. MacMurchadha was born, according to a later set of Irish annals, sometime in 1356–7.[21] Warfare between the English and the Irish in the mountains of south Leinster had been almost continuous throughout much of the fourteenth century. Many if not most of Art MacMurchadha's predecessors as kings of the Irish of the Leinster mountains had died violent deaths at the hands of their English enemies.[22] Art's grandfather Muircheartach MacMurchadha, who was king of the Leinster mountains from c. 1346/7, was executed in 1354 by the English ('MacMurchadha was drawn by the foreigners', pulled apart between horses). The annals state that his death led to 'great war ... between foreigners and Gaels'.[23] Art's father, who was also called Art MacMurchadha, succeeded Muircheartach as king of the Leinster mountains. He was taken prisoner in 1361 by Edward

---

19 Curtis, 'Unpublished letters from Richard II in Ireland', 290; many of the English from Co. Kilkenny 'were in the K.[ing]'s service by order of the steward of the royal household in the K.[ing]'s expedition at le Garwell', 40. 19 Dec. 1394, Close Roll 18 Richard II. 20 ASI, 1394. 21 AFM, 1416 and 1417. 22 Frame, 'Two kings in Leinster: the crown and the MicMhurchadha in the fourtennth century', p. 166. 23 AC, 1354; AFM, 1354; *Annals of Friar John Clyn*, 1347, pp 244–5.

III's son Lionel, duke of Clarence, the lieutenant of Ireland and died in his custody, probably in 1362.[24] Art succeeded to the kingdom of Irish Leinster in 1375, following the violent deaths of two intervening MacMurchadha kings at the hands of the English.[25]

It is in 1375 that Art first appears in historical records, when his uncle Donnchadh MacMurchadha, king of Irish Leinster, 'was treacherously slain by the foreigners' in the English town of Carlow.[26] In May 1376, Richard Wade of Carlow admitted that it was he who had ordered the killing of Donnchadh MacMurchadha, but 'on the advice and with the assistance of Arturus McMurgh [Art MacMurchadha], now captain of the said nation'. Wade added that Art immediately turned on him and burnt down his house in Carlow, costing Wade goods and armour that he states were worth £100.[27] Wider war with the English broke out soon afterwards and lasted into early 1378 before Art succeeded in securing the king's peace.[28] This war appears to have been launched in a successful effort to ensure continued payment of Art's annual black rent of 80 marks, which had been paid since King Edward III's reign to his predecessors.[29] The English of Leinster had underestimated Art by attempting to buy him off with a single payment of 20 marks.[30]

MacMurchadha, from the beginning, appears to have had the support of substantial numbers of Irish mercenaries from the north

24 AC, 1361; AFM, 1361; O'Byrne, *War, politics and the Irish of Leinster*, p. 247; D. Beresford, 'Lionel ('of Antwerp')', *DIB*, v, pp 511–12.   25 AFM, 1368, 1369, 1375; AC, 1369, 1375; *Annals of Friar John Clyn*, 1375 ('written in a new hand'), pp 252–5.   26 *Annals of Friar John Clyn*, 1375, note l.   27 24. 15 May 1376, Close Roll 50 Edward III.   28 38. 26 June 1377[8?], Close Roll 1 Richard II; 49. 28 Mar. 1378, ibid.   29 38. 26 June 1377[8?], ibid.; 7. 19 Oct. 1379, Close Rolls 3 Richard II.   30 31. [8 Feb. 1377], Close Roll 51 Edward III.

Munster region. In 1377–8 they were commanded by nobles from the Ó Cearbhaill and Ó Briain of Ara families.[31] As a result, MacMurchadha was able to put a very large force of warriors into the field. The English claimed that in March 1378, when MacMurchadha again attacked Carlow, he did so with '2,000 horse and foot'.[32] On this occasion the town was burnt down but the castle (see figure 9) succeeded in holding out.[33] Art's exploits are recorded in the Irish annals for the years 1380 and 1381, as he consolidated his hold over his kingdom.[34] The records indicate a period of activity in the north and east Wexford areas. In 1386 he won a victory over the English of Co. Kilkenny.[35] For much of the 1380s, however, Art was at peace with the English as long as his black rent of 80 marks was paid every year. Occasionally there were incidents when the local English raided MacMurchadha's followers, but restitution was usually quickly offered and accepted.[36]

In 1385 Sir Philip Courtenay (the king's lieutenant) withheld Art's black rent, and this led to the outbreak of war, as MacMurchadha sought to maintain his right to tribute from the English.[37] The fighting did not last long and in November 1386 a new king's lieutenant, Robert de Vere, the earl of Oxford and marquis of Ireland, one of Richard II's great favourites, 'admitted' Art:

> chieftain of his lineage ... to the peace of the king and the marquis ... whereupon it was agreed that he might have 80 marks per annum from the exchequer of the marquis of Ireland, by name of a fee, for as long as he conducts himself

31 17. 24 Mar. 1378, Close Roll 1 Richard II; 104. [no date], ibid.   32 36. 14 Mar. 1378, ibid.   33 49. 28 Mar. 1378, ibid.   34 AFM, 1381; two entries for the same year record the same process.   35 AU, 1386; AFM, 1386.   36 24. 21 Nov. 1384, Close Roll 8 Richard II.   37 1. 13 July 1385, Patent Roll 9 Richard II.

well and faithfully towards the king and the marquis, and their faithful subjects.[38]

This peace held and even survived an incident in 1389 when the English of Carlow killed some of Art's followers. They knew they had done wrong and collected 10 marks 'assessed among themselves and granted to Arthurus McMurgh [Art MacMurchadha] ... in part satisfaction of damages that the said commons lately inflicted on Arthurus in killing his men'.[39]

A bardic poem composed for Art by the poet Eoghan MacCraith records some of the most notable characteristics of MacMurchadha's style of kingship. Two stanzas record Art's strong overlordship of his Irish vassals, and possibly over some of his English neighbours as well:

> *Ní hionann béas is báidh leam*
> *d'Art agus d'uaislibh Éireann*
> *Fiú leis gach neach teacht 'n-a theagh*
> *'s a mbí tearc teach i n-a dtéid-sean.*

> Art's ways are – I rejoice –
> not those of the other nobles of Erin;
> All are glad to give him homage,
> few receive his.

> *Umhluighthear dhó i mbonnaibh bean*
> *'s i gclochaibh aolta Éireann*
> *Do ní a mbí san fhionn-mhuir d'Art*
> *'s a mbí san fhiodhbhuidh umhlacht.*

---

38 48. [1 Nov. 1386], Patent Roll 10 Richard II.   39 177. 4 Aug. 1389, Close Roll

Homage is paid him on hilltops,
and in Erin's white castles;
All things in the bright sea
and in the forest submit to him.[40]

Other stanzas refer to Art's martial prowess:

Sleagh bhaoghlach 'n-a bhais tana
fraoch Catha ar Mhac Murchadha
Go n-athraigh Art gné an ghall-gha
Gan é i n-alt a agallmha.

His dread lance in graceful hand,
Battle fury seizes Art MacMurchadha;
He cannot be spoken to
till he has changed the direction of the foes' lances.[41]

Art was a cultured patron of the church and Irish learned families. In 1399 the annals record that 'MacEochaidh Eolach [the knowledgeable], *ollamh* of the house of Caomhánach in poetry and general protector of the men of Ireland' died, while for 1404/5 they state that 'Ulliam Ó Deoráin, law-*ollamh* to the house of Caomhánach, died'.[42] The Annals of Ulster refer to this brehon as 'the best *ollamh* of Leinster in jurisprudence'.[43] The high regard that the ruling MacMurchadha family had for Irish learned men can be seen by the fact that the annals also record in 1402 that Art's brother Tomás Carrach MacMurchadha 'was drowned when going

12 Richard II.   40 McKenna, 'To Art MacMurchadha Caomhánach', 98–101. 41 Ibid., pp 100–1. This bardic poem needs a more up-to-date translation; R. Frame, 'Art MacMurchadha Caomhánach', *ODNB*, xxxv, pp 917–18.   42 AC, 1399, 1404.   43 AU, 1405.

past Ceann Eich to pay poets'.[44] In 1402 Art himself commissioned the restoration of the *cumdach* or book shrine of the Book of Mulling, a small gospel book written *c.*750–800 AD, and associated with St Moling Luachra. In the fourteenth century the book shrine was kept at the monastery of St Mullins and Art had it decorated with silver and rock crystals. Under a large central oval rock crystal, Art had inscribed a record of his generosity that begins 'King Arthur, lord of Leinster' (see figure 10).[45] The bardic poem by Eoghan MacCraith may refer to this restoration of the *cumdach* of the Book of Molling when the poet states of Art:

> *Do mhéaduigh neimheadh gach naoimh*
> *Sochair do chlannaibh Chathaoir*
> *Glór laoidheadh agus leabhar*
> *Glór aoidheadh dá n-uaisleaghadh.*

> He has enriched saints' shrines,
> a blessing for Cathaoir's families;
> Words of songs and books
> and guests glorify them.[46]

Art's family also preserved the famous 'vessell or cup to drinke out of called the Corne-cam-more', better known today as the Kavanagh Charter Horn. Described as 'the only piece of Irish regalia to have survived the middle ages', the horn itself is of elephant ivory, with a decorated brass mounting commissioned in the fifteenth century (see figure 11).[47]

---

44 ASI, 1402; Ceann Eich ('hill of the horse'), now Kineagh near Kilcullen, Co. Kildare, a ford on the river Liffey, AFM, 526, note f. 45 Ó Riain, *A dictionary of Irish saints*, p. 489; R. Foster (ed.), *The Oxford illustrated history of Ireland* (Oxford, 1989), p. 92; O'Neill, *The Irish hand*, p. 66. 46 McKenna, 'To Art MacMurchadha Caomhánach', 99. 47 Byrne, *Irish kings and high-kings*, p. 153; Wallace and Ó

MacCraith's poem makes particular reference to the presence of large amounts of gold at MacMurchadha's court. Much of it appears to have come from the English in the form of tribute or compensation for injury done to MacMurchadha's property or followers. MacCraith states:

> *Ór uatha i ndíol gach dána*
> *ór chuca 'n-agcíos-chána*
> *laoich ó tholaigh mhóir Mhogha*
> *monaigh óir a n-almsodha.*

> Gold for poems is given
> by the heroes of Mogh's hill;
> They get gold in tribute;
> Their alms are gold coins.
> [...]

> *Ní dleaghar ionmhas eile*
> *mar éiric 'n-a n-oirbhire*
> *Einiochlann d'ór ó gach fhior*
> *do shlógh geimhiol-throm Ghaoidheal.*

> In gold they must receive
> honour price as *éiric* [compensation] for injury
> from all in the troop
> of heavy-chained Gael.[48]

Floinn (eds), *Treasures of the National Museum of Ireland*, pp 260, 267 and 279; H. McDowell, *Irish family treasures* (Dublin, 1985). 48 McKenna, 'To Art MacMurchadha Caomhánach', 99–100.

Although his relations with the surrounding English were mainly peaceful, this was seriously upset around the year 1390 when Art married the English heiress baroness Elizabeth de Veel.[49] De Veel was the heiress to the barony of Norragh in the fertile plains of south Kildare. Her father, Sir Robert de Veel, baron of Norragh, died sometime around 1378. The historian Edmund Curtis calls her marriage to Art 'a love-match', and there may be something to this. Elizabeth was a widow twice over. Her first husband had been Sir John Staunton, lord of Otymy, in the far north of Co. Kildare. Elizabeth and Sir John had two daughters, Margaret and Anastasia.[50] Her second husband was Leonard Freyne of Cloyne in Co. Kilkenny. Elizabeth appears to have had a son James with Freyne.[51] When it was discovered, this unlikely marriage between an Irish king and an English heiress must have made the English nobility of Leinster wonder just where the limits of Art's ambitions lay.[52] According to the Statute of Kilkenny, an Irishman had no right to inherit English land.[53] Perhaps Art and Elizabeth should have sought an exemption before marrying. From what we know of Art's character and personality, he may well have

---

49 The family was often called 'Calf' locally. The family coat of arms 'contained three calves'. **50** E. Curtis and E. St John Brooks, 'The barons of Norragh, Co. Kildare, 1171–1660', *JRSAI*, 5:1 (1935), 84, 88–9; W. Fitzgerald, 'Norraghmore and the barons of Norragh', *Journal of the Kildare Archaeological Society*, 7 (1913), 242–53. **51** Curtis and St John Brookes, 'The barons of Norragh, Co. Kildare', 99. **52** Frame, 'Art MacMurchadha Caomhánach', p. 918; O'Byrne, *War, politics and the Irish of Leinster*, pp 104, 109–11; Cosgrove, *Late medieval Ireland*, p. 14. **53** Hardiman (ed.), *A statute of the fortieth year of King Edward III., enacted in a parliament held in Kilkenny, AD 1367, before Lionel, duke of Clarence, lord lieutenant of Ireland*, p. 9–11: http://www.ucc.ie/celt/published/F300001-001/index.html, accessed 5 Jan. 2015. The relevant piece states: 'Also, it is ordained and established, that no alliance by marriage, gossip-red, fostering of children, concubine-age or by amour, nor in any other manner, be henceforth made between the English and Irish of one part, or of the other part.'

wondered why he should have to. The decision of the English administration to then deny MacMurchadha his rights by marriage to the barony of Norragh struck at his already demonstrated most sensitive point. This was Art's perception of his legitimate rights, in defence of which he had gone to war or threatened to go to war on a number of previous occasions. With Art's marriage to Elizabeth de Veel, the stage was set for a major confrontation with the English administration in Ireland, and, in turn, with Richard II himself.

THE 1394–5 EXPEDITION CONTINUES

Richard and his army left Waterford on Monday 19 October and marched via Jerpoint in south Kilkenny. By Saturday they had reached the borders of the great wood of Garryhill in the centre of Co. Carlow, 'the chief fortress that our enemy MacMurrough has'.[54] The Annals of Saints' Island was well informed when it recorded that Richard's army, 'laid siege to Garbhchoill'.[55] Richard encamped on the edge of the forest awaiting the arrival of his uncle, Thomas of Woodstock, the duke of Gloucester. He joined the English king on a Saturday night. Richard and his army stayed in camp on Sunday as it was a day of rest.[56]

The late-medieval English usually made excellent soldiers. The force that Richard brought to Ireland in 1394 had the typical composition of a fourteenth-century English army. This was a core of a substantial number of men-at-arms, supported by a larger force of elite mounted archers. Mounted archers were paid twice the wages of foot archers. They could keep up with the men-at-arms

---

54 Curtis, 'Unpublished letters from Richard II in Ireland', 290–1.   55 ASI, 1394.
56 Curtis, 'Unpublished letters from Richard II in Ireland', 290.

because they were on horseback, and dismounted to fight.[57] The English probably did not relish fighting the Irish in late-medieval times. The favoured English tactics used in the wars in France were a *chevauchée*, a march by the entire army through the French countryside, plundering and burning along the way, sometimes followed by a pitched battle in which the English knights dismounted and fought from semi-fortified defensive positions. This was where the massed ranks of the skilled English archers could be used to best effect.[58] These tactics did not suit the mountains and forests of Ireland. There was also very little plunder to be had by the English soldiers from the Irish, apart from immense herds of cattle.

Despite the very large forces deployed against him, Art MacMurchadha decided to fight. Given the favourable terrain of the mountains and forests of south-east Leinster, the Irish chieftains may have felt that their chances of holding out were good. While Richard and his army were still organizing at Waterford, 'An army was led by Art MacMurchadha, king of Leinster, against the foreigners' to plunder the town of New Ross. The annals record that MacMurchadha burned the town 'with its houses and castles, and carried away from it gold, silver, and hostages'.[59] This was probably an attempt to deny Richard a local urban base from which to attack him.

Art's main plan was to defend the Garryhill forest. In the sixteenth century Irish armies were highly skilled at plashing the branches of trees together to hinder the progress of English armies and in building earthen defences within the forests. This appears

57 Allmand, *The Hundred Years War*, pp 58–67.   58 Saul, *Richard II*, pp 6–9, 33–4; Bradbury, *The Routledge companion to medieval warfare*, pp 31, 200 and 205; W. Cafferro, *John Hawkwood: an English mercenary in fourteenth-century Italy* (Baltimore, 2006).   59 AFM, 1394.

to be what MacMurchadha's men did in October 1394.[60] Richard noted 'all the fortress[es] and defences of the forest', where Art 'stood on his defence'.[61] Art made a grave error in staying within the Garryhill forest to fight Richard. The English monarch records that 'On Monday very early we thought to encamp in the said wood of Garryhill, which is, as we said before, the chief fortress that our enemy MacMurrough has, and which he thought, as was reported to us, to hold by force against us on our entry upon the lands which the said MacMurrough claims to be his'. The English king's account continues: 'we were at last lodged in the said strong wood of Garryhill, our said enemy dislodged, and his principal house burned in our presence; and there that day and the night following were fought several skirmishes'.[62] Art was on the run after only one day's fighting.

On Tuesday Richard was in pursuit of MacMurchadha in the Laveroc forest to the south. Art was dependent on the immense size of the woods for protection 'and could not move any resistance against us [Richard's army]'.[63] Indeed Richard and his commanders demonstrated a good grasp of the tactics required to defeat the Irish of Leinster. The English army broke up into a number of large detachments, referred to as 'wards', and Richard 'set certain garrisons very cunningly, as it seemed ... round about the Irish enemies'.[64] The king's cousin Edward, earl of Rutland, who was accompanied by Sir John Beaumont 'with certain men-at-arms and archers', formed one ward. Thomas Mowbray (see figure 12), earl of Nottingham, the earl marshal, again with a force of men-at-arms

---

60 Sir Henry Docwra to Sir Robert Cecil, 12 Feb. 1601, TNA SP 63/208PT1/121–4; P. Walsh (ed.), *Beatha Aodha Ruaidh Uí Dhomhnaill* (London, 1948), i, pp 218–19.   61 Curtis, 'Unpublished letters from Richard II in Ireland', 291.   62 Ibid., 291.   63 Ibid.   64 Ibid., 292; Lydon, 'Richard II's expeditions to Ireland', 145.

and archers, formed another. The king's nephew, Lord Thomas Holland, supported by Sir Thomas Percy 'well supported with men-at-arms and archers' formed a third main detachment.[65] The exact dispositions of the English forces are not recorded except that the earl marshal was 'very near the woods of Garryhill and Laveroc'.[66] Here the marshal 'had several fine encounters with them [the Irish], in one of which he slew many of the people of the said MacMurrough, and burned around nine villages, and preyed of his cattle up to the number of 8,000'.[67]

The earl marshal was now in close pursuit of MacMurchadha. In fact, Mowbray:

> broke in upon him, and, if he had not been foreseen, he would have found the said MacMurrough and his wife in their beds. But they, being told of the affray, escaped with great difficulty and at such short warning that they were nearly taken.[68]

Art MacMurchadha was too able a king to be captured asleep in his bed, but his escape appears to have been a narrow one. Although Art and his wife Elizabeth got away, the earl marshal 'found a coffer belonging to the said MacMurrough's wife, in which were certain articles of feminine use, but of no great value'.[69] The English also captured Art's seal, which bore the inscription 'Sigillum Arthurii MacMurgh Dei Gracia Regis Lagenie' or 'Seal of Art MacMurchadha, by the grace of God, king of Leinster'.[70] Thwarted by MacMurchadha's successful escape, a 'sorely vexed'

---

65 Curtis, 'Unpublished letters from Richard II in Ireland', 292–3.   66 Ibid., 292.
67 Ibid., 293.   68 Ibid., 292.   69 Ibid., 293.   70 Ibid.; Saul, *Richard II*, pp 282–3; Cosgrove, *Late medieval Ireland*, p. 20.

earl marshal 'had his [Art's] house burned ... as also some fourteen villages round about the said wood, and had four hundred cattle driven away with him'.[71] The earl marshal then proceeded into the Duffry forest east of the Blackstairs mountains, 'a strong country, which was all bog ... wherein no Englishman has commonly entered before this time, and there slew certain persons, and among others one of their greater captains and evildoers of the country ... and had him beheaded and sent his head to the king'.[72]

The earl of Rutland's detachment also enjoyed success in Fotharta against the Ó Nualláin chieftain. Rutland's men killed over a hundred Irish warriors and:

> with great hardihood and in the face of the enemy, he entered a strong country, ... and the earl, along with his men, with great travail, made a great bridge out of certain trees, cords, and boughs across the river ... in order to vex the enemy. And there he slew a great number, and prey-d and drove away with him more than 6,000 cattle, and he sent 360 of them to the king.[73]

By Wednesday the lands of Ó Nualláin were on fire and 'great burnings were made in the aforesaid lands'.[74] Janico Dartas, in command of yet another detachment of English soldiers, captured an additional herd of cattle.[75]

The English appear to have deliberately chosen the best time of year to attack MacMurchadha. This was when the leaves had fallen from the branches of the deciduous trees in the forests of the Leinster mountains. Richard's initial delay at Waterford may have been partly to allow time for the last leaves to fall from the oak

71 Curtis, 'Unpublished letters from Richard II in Ireland', 293.   72 Ibid.
73 Ibid., 292.   74 Ibid., 291.   75 Ibid., 292; E. Curtis, 'Janico Dartas, Richard II's "Gascon squire": his career in Ireland, 1394–1426', *JRSAI*, 63:2 (1933), 182–6.

trees in the woods of Leinster.[76] As a result, Art's soldiers were vulnerable to the skilled archers in Richard's detachments. These archers, who were on horseback, had the potential to inflict severe casualties on MacMurchadha's warriors.[77]

The depiction of the warfare recorded in Richard's letters – of a vastly superior English army that had its Irish opponents on the run – will be familiar to anyone who has studied the campaigns of destruction against the Irish carried out by English armies during the latter stages of the Nine Years War. With the burning of villages and the capture of livestock, Art's people faced starvation during the ensuing months. They also faced outright massacre if cornered by English forces. MacMurchadha was an intelligent king, however, and never let it come to that. Knowing that the game was up, he decided to submit to Richard. His war in defence of his mountain kingdom had lasted less than a week. Both sides suffered casualties during the fighting, although exact numbers are not recorded.

According to Richard's account, the Ó Nualláin chieftain and his son submitted first, appearing before the English king 'bareheaded, disarmed, their girdles undone, holding their swords by the points, with the pommels erect, and put themselves unreservedly at our mercy, without any conditions'. Richard adds that on 'the same day and in like manner there came humbly to obey us and to surrender and submit themselves the said MacMurrough and three other captains, kneeling and acting in the above-said manner'.[78] The Annals of Saints' Island confirm the king's account and add detail by recording that Ó Broin, Ó Nualláin and Ó Mórdha, along with MacMurchadha, submitted

76 Lydon, 'Richard II's expeditions to Ireland', 145.　77 Ibid.　78 Curtis, 'Unpublished letters from Richard II in Ireland', 291.

to the king.[79] Richard had MacMurchadha and his chieftains swear on the famous Irish relic, St Patrick's crozier or staff, that they would become loyal subjects.[80] Richard then decided to take the minor chieftains with him to Dublin as hostages, to ensure Art's future loyalty, but released the Irish king of Leinster. The Annals of Saints' Island state that 'MacMurchadha went home safely, having promised to return'.[81] It may seem strange that the English king released his most formidable opponent in Ireland, and it probably was a major error. He appears to have underestimated Art, perhaps influenced by how quickly the resistance of the Irish in the Leinster mountains collapsed in October 1394. Richard may also have released MacMurchadha in an effort to impress the Irish kings elsewhere on the island with his good intentions, and in this respect his gamble may have paid off. There may also have been an element of calculated risk to Art's submission to the English king. Art must have had the fate of many of his predecessors on his mind as he travelled to submit to Richard. As a result, it took some personal courage on his part to do so.

MacMurchadha's submission led to the end of most serious fighting in Leinster. Nobles from the Ó Díomasaigh family, kings of Clanmalier in the midlands, continued to fight with the English, but this may have been an independent local quarrel, begun before Richard's arrival in Ireland. Nevertheless, when Tomaltach Ó Díomasaigh, 'an excellent king's son, was killed by the foreigners', his body was decapitated 'and his head was brought to Dublin to the King'.[82] Roger Mortimer, the earl of March, was active in the north Leinster/south Ulster region. A number of references in the

---

79 ASI, 1394; AFM, 1394.   80 See AFM, 1537, note g, for a good description of the Staff of Jesus, destroyed in Dublin in 1537.   81 Curtis, 'Unpublished letters from Richard II in Ireland', 291; ASI, 1394.   82 ASI, 1394; AFM, 1394.

annals dating from this year record raids by Mortimer's forces on the 'Muinntear Mhaoil Mhórdha' and 'Clann an Chaoich', two branches of the Ó Raghilligh family, who were the kings of East Breifne, and on the MacMathghamhna family of Oriel.[83] The earl of March also summoned the Ó Fearghail chieftain, king of Annaly, to submit to him at his castle at Trim. The annals record that Ó Fearghail 'returned with honour on that occasion'.[84] There was also some fighting in north Munster when Toirdhealbhach Ó Briain, the son of the famous Murchadh na Raithnighe, 'waged war with the people of the king in Munster and Leinster, and burned and plundered the county of Limerick'.[85] He was not the paramount Irish king in his locality however. A violent incident occurred in Dublin when the bardic poet Cam Cluana Ó Dubhagáin, 'ollamh of history, eloquence, and poetry', who may have foolishly travelled to the town to spy on the English king, was 'put to death by stuttering foreigners while in captivity'.[86] The Annals of the Four Masters record that the bardic poet 'was slain at Dublin by the people of the king of England'.[87]

Richard's military victory over the Leinster Irish in late October and early November 1394, in the end, was rapid and relatively easy. Careful preparation and choice of tactics by the English royal army contrasted with some major errors made by Art MacMurchadha. This may have led the English king to seriously underestimate the military capabilities of the Irish kings, a view that may have been confirmed by the massive rush of Irish kings and chieftains to submit to the English monarch in late 1394 and early 1395. Although this did not impact the remainder of Richard's first expedition to Ireland, it would seriously impact his second, and in the end it even undid his rule over England.

83 ASI, 1394.　84 Ibid.　85 AFM, 1394.　86 ASI, 1394.　87 AFM, 1394.

The well-informed historian who compiled the Annals of Saints' Island was aware that Richard called a parliament to meet at Dublin on 1 December 1394.[88] Very little record of the business transacted at this parliament has survived, bar one ordinance:

> that no liege of the K.[ing], of whatever estate or condition he may be, shall give, sell, send, bring or lend to any Irishman not residing among the K.[ing]'s English lieges, any grain, malt, bread, wine, ale, salt, iron, horses, armour, or other victuals whatever under a certain penalty determined in that ordinance.[89]

Much other urgent business must have been discussed with the king at the Dublin parliament at this time. Somebody informed the king that the great Munster lord Gerald Fitzgerald, the earl of Desmond, had taken possession of the manor of Dungarvan in Co. Waterford that had once been part of the royal demesne.[90] In mid-January 1395 Richard sent the earl an 'order, on his faith and allegiance, to be before the K.[ing] in person on Monday ... wherever the K.[ing] may then be in Ire[land], to declare [his] right and estate if he claims to have any'.[91] The recent destruction visited on New Ross by Art MacMurchadha, which Richard may have seen, may also have been discussed in the Irish parliament. A surviving record of a patent dating from January 1395 states that Richard 'has considered the great losses, damages and destructions which the K.[ing's] beloved lieges, the sovereign and commons of the town of New Ross, have long sustained from the K.[ing's] Irish rebels dwelling around that town'.[92] Richard noted that 'the walls

88 ASI, 1394. 89 41. 19 Dec. 1394, Close Roll 18 Richard II. 90 3. 18 [Jan. 1395], Close Roll 18 Richard II. 91 Ibid. 92 71. 26 Jan. 1395, Patent Roll 18 Richard II.

of that town have fallen down and the town is so greatly impoverished that the residents cannot repair them without aid, as is said'. As a result, the patent states that the townspeople 'may have the k.[ing's] custom within that town called le cocket for the next ten years ... in aid of improving, fortifying and repairing the walls of that town'.[93]

Although not recorded in a close roll until November 1395, long after the English monarch had returned to England, the decision to move the Irish exchequer from Carlow back to its old location in Dublin may also have been discussed at the December parliament.[94] Carlow town, with its important castle, was situated in an exposed location and was vulnerable to attack by the Irish. The Irish exchequer had been brought to the town in 1366 by King Edward III's son Lionel, duke of Clarence, for this very reason, in order to bolster Carlow's defences through greater English activity.[95] The measure did not succeed, however, and the town continued to be very vulnerable. Fears were even expressed for the security of the exchequer records, which colonial officials believed would eventually be burned by the Irish.[96] As a result:

> for the greater comfort of the people, the K.[ing] ordained with the advice of his council that the Ex.[chequer] and [common] bench of the K.[ing], which have long been held at the town of Carlow until now, shall henceforth be held at Dublin.[97]

Another important plan that may also have been discussed at the December parliament was the directive agreed to by Art

93 Ibid.   94 54. 6 Nov. 1395, Close Roll 18 Richard II.   95 105. 8 Feb. 1378, Close Roll 1 Richard II.   96 33. 10 July 1393, Close Roll 17 Richard II.   97 54. 6 Nov. 1395, Close Roll 18 Richard II.

MacMurchadha on 7 January 1395 at a meeting with Thomas Mowbray, the earl marshal, near Tullow. MacMurchadha promised that having delivered:

> to our Lord the king ... full possession of all lands, tenements, castles, fortresses, woods, and pastures, with all their appurtenances, which have been of late occupied by the said Art or his allies, men, or adherents within the land of Leinster ... that by the first Sunday of Lent next, he will leave the whole country of Leinster to the true obedience, use, and disposition of the king, his heirs, and successors, ... saving and excepting always to him all his moveable goods ... and that all the armed men, warriors, or fighting men of the following, household, or nation of the said Art shall quit the whole lands of Leinster aforesaid and shall go with him and shall have fitting wages from the king, for the time being, to go and conquer other parts occupied by rebels of the said Lord King, and that Art and all his men aforesaid shall have all lands which they may thus acquire and hold them of the said Lord King.[98]

Art also discussed with the earl marshal other areas of contention between himself and the English, such as the grant 'of 80 m.[arks] p.a. to be received as his ancestors received it from the K.[ing]'s progenitors, together with his wife Elizabeth's inheritance of the barony of Norragh', which were awarded to him by patent on 24 January 1395.[99]

The exact nature of Richard's demand that Art leave his kingdom in the Leinster mountains with all his fighting men is

98 Curtis, 'Instruments touching Ireland', pp 169–70. 99 24 Jan. 1395, Patent Roll 18 Richard II.

unclear. Some modern historians believe that the English king wanted the Irish of Leinster to leave eastern Ireland and conquer new lands for themselves in other areas of the island. Others state that Richard wanted Art and his sub-chieftains to surrender any illegally conquered lands in Leinster and that he offered compensation by employing them as soldiers in the royal army, to be subsequently granted lands conquered from Irish enemies elsewhere on the island.[100] Whichever was the case, Art must have been taken by surprise and felt that he had no option but to agree following his defeat by the royal army in October 1394.

Around Christmastime in 1394 the English monarch may have had difficulty keeping all his men in Ireland for the festive season. Richard issued orders to the authorities in Dublin and Drogheda 'to cause it to be proclaimed publicly that no one of whatever condition may cross to foreign parts without special licence ... and no mariner or master of a vessel is to take any such person to those parts'.[101] Throughout his seven months in Ireland Richard attempted to keep up to date with the government of England, which was of course his main kingdom. In December two of his knights, Richard Abberbury the younger and Nicholas Ribenuzo or Ryvenys, were sent on an important embassy to Rupert, Count Palatine of the Rhine in Germany. Having completed their mission, the two knights travelled west to Ireland to report to the king.[102] Richard sent many letters to the chancellor of England, the archbishop of York, detailing the early success of his campaign in Leinster.[103]

100 Curtis, 'Unpublished letters from Richard II in Ireland', 277; Johnston, 'Richard II and the submissions of Gaelic Ireland', 15–16; Cosgrove, *Late medieval Ireland*, pp 26–7.   101 38. 6 Nov. 1394, Close Roll 18 Richard II.   102 230. Historical Notes, in E. Perroy (ed.), *The diplomatic correspondence of Richard II* (London, 1933), xlviii, p. 253; J. W. Zophy (ed.), *The Holy Roman Empire: a dictionary handbook* (Westport, 1980), pp 395–7.   103 Richard II to the

On 16 February 1395 Art MacMurchadha had another meeting with Thomas Mowbray near Carlow. By now Richard had left it to the earl marshal 'to distribute lands and habitations to captains and leaders of fighting men quitting and leaving the land of Leinster, even as it shall seem best to the said earl'.[104] At the February meeting, MacMurchadha submitted again to the English king and reaffirmed his agreement to leave Leinster with his warriors. On this occasion and over the ensuing days most of MacMurchadha's sub-chieftains again submitted to Richard. All the sub-chieftains agreed to pay the English king substantial fines if they reneged on their submissions. Art bound himself to pay 20,000 marks sterling to the papacy, an enormous sum of money.[105] One wonders whether many of the Leinster sub-chieftains realized the full implications of what they had agreed to. Art MacMurchadha, however, was an intelligent king, and may have been horrified by Richard's plan. In any event, on 28 February, when Lent began in 1395, none of the Leinster Irish moved. It is unclear whether this owed more to the large numbers of Irish kings and chieftains who submitted to the English king, thus removing the need for any royal campaigns in recalcitrant Irish regions, or to stubbornness and a refusal to leave their territory.

Early February 1395 was also the time when Richard sent his famous letter to his uncle Edmund of Langley, duke of York and the 'custos of England', in which in Anglo-Norman French the English king described the three different types of people he

archbishop of York, chancellor of England (Oct. 1394?) in Curtis, 'Unpublished letters from Richard II in Ireland', 289–90; Richard II to the archbishop of York, chancellor of England (Oct./early Nov. 1395?], ibid., 290–2.   104 Curtis, 'Instruments touching Ireland', pp 165–6; 80. 12 Feb. 1395, Patent Roll 18 Richard II.   105 Curtis, 'Instruments touching Ireland', pp 167–9.

encountered in Ireland: 'Pource ensement qen nre terre Dirland sont trios maners des gentz J cestas-savoir Irrois savages noz enemis Irroix rebelx t Engleis obeissantzi' ('There are three manner of people in our land of Ireland, Irish savages our enemies, Irish rebels and obedient English').[106] There has been much debate among modern historians as to who exactly Richard was referring to. In Richard's own writings, Irish savages 'our enemies' often became Irish rebels once they negotiated with him, or if it was established that they or their ancestors had ever submitted to him before or to one of his predecessors. The obedient English were the loyal English of Ireland.[107] Whatever the exact definitions, the letter does capture the complex situation that Richard encountered in Ireland with competing ethnic groups and a fluid concept of loyalty to the English king.

106 H. Nicolas (ed.), *Proceedings and ordinances of the privy council of England*, vol. 1, 10 Richard II to 11 Henry IV (London, 1834), p. 52.   107 Johnson, 'Richard II and the submissions of Gaelic Ireland', 6–7.

CHAPTER 4

Richard and the Ó Néill kings of Tyrone

Hurry and claim all
the land of Ulster, Elystan's fame;
there's a domain full of false balk,[1]
demand it as yours on the edge of Dundalk.
After capturing Great Niall [Gred Nïal – Niall Mór Ó Néill],
my lord,
misshapen dog, blockhead of Ulster,
you will cut down, bell tower of praise,
the people of Ulster with every other stroke.[2]

> – A poem by the Welsh bard Iolo Goch (*c.*1398),
> offering posthumous (possibly) advice for
> Roger Mortimer, earl of March and Ulster

While Richard was in Dublin the Ó Néill kings of Tyrone opened
a line of communication with him through the elderly, semi-retired

---

1 Land that is arable but not properly ploughed.   2 K. Simms, 'The Ulster revolt
of 1404: an anti-Lancastrian dimension' in B. Smith (ed.), *Ireland and the English
world in the late Middle Ages* (Basingstoke, 2009), p. 148; G.A. Williams, 'Cywydd
Iolo Gach I Rosier Mortimer: Cefndir a Chyd-Destun', *Llên Cymru*, Cyfrol 22

Niall Mór Ó Néill, probably in December 1394. Niall Mór's son, Niall Óg Ó Néill, was the active king of this kingdom and the most powerful Irish leader on the island. The Ó Néill family were one of the most distinguished of the Irish royal dynasties, with a heritage stretching back many centuries.

AODH REAMHAR Ó NÉILL

The story of Niall Mór and Niall Óg Ó Néill really begins with the career of Niall Mór's father Aodh Reamhar (Hugh the Fat) Ó Néill.[3] Aodh Reamhar was a successful Irish king. When he died in 1364 he was acknowledged as 'the best king of the Half of Conn [the northern half of Ireland] that came in the late time to the kingship of the fifth of Ulster'.[4] Other annals call him 'the very best king of his time'.[5] In 1345, the year he became king of Tyrone, Aodh Reamhar acted like a pre-invasion high-king when he put 'a fleet on Lough Neagh'.[6] Towards the end of his reign, in 1358, Ó Néill led a great raid on his western neighbour, the Ó Domhnaill kingdom of Tír Chonaill.[7] This raid may indicate that Aodh Reamhar had almost subjugated that kingdom, and if Fermanagh and Oriel are added, Ó Néill by this year must have been the real overlord of what are now the six western counties of the province of Ulster – Derry, Tyrone, Armagh, Monaghan, Fermanagh and Donegal.

(1999), 57–79; Johnston, 'Iolo Goch and the English: Welsh poetry and politics in the fourteenth century', 87–9; D. Johnston (ed.), *Iolo Goch: poems* (Llandysul, 1993), pp 88–9.   3 Epithets in this family were always to the point and often unflattering.   4 AU, 1361; AFM, 1364.   5 AC, 1364.   6 AFM, 1345.   7 AU, 1355, the Annals of Ulster appear to be out by three years in their record for this period; despite these successes, Aodh Reamhar did not have it all his own way in Gaelic Ulster. The warriors landed in Co. Antrim by his Lough Neagh fleet in 1345

Aodh Reamhar, as king of Tyrone, appears to have made use of the ancient mythological Ulster Cycle of legends to form a basis of propaganda for his kingship. These tales, with their stories of Conchobhar mac Neasa, the king of Ulster, Cú Chulainn the heroic warrior who defended the borders of the province against invaders, and the *Táin*, the story of a great cattle raid, proved to be powerful propaganda in the hands of the Ó Néill kings. Aodh Reamhar made skilful use of them. At some stage during his reign, this Ó Néill king commissioned a finely made seal, which contains on it a depiction of the Red Hand of Ulster surrounded by dragons or monsters and the Latin inscription 's. odonis oneill regis hybernicorum ultonie' ('The seal of Aodh Ó Néill, king of the Irish of Ulster') (see figure 13).[8] This emblem may have been taken from the Ulaid people, the Irish who still lived in east Ulster in the English earldom.[9] These people were regarded as the descendants of Conchobhar mac Neasa and the ancient people of Ulster. Their power had been broken by the English, however, and it was the Ó Néill family, who were of Uí Néill not Ulaid descent, who adopted the powerful mythology of the ancient Ulster Cycle. If the statements about the Spartan nature of the dress and culture of the natives of Tyrone in the 1390s are correct, as well as the success of their warriors on the battlefield, they may provide evidence that the entire population of the kingdom of Tyrone, both men and women, bought into the propaganda of the Ó Néill kings.[10]

were repulsed by the Clann Aodha Buidhe, and in 1354 Aodh Reamhar was again heavily defeated by the Clann Aodha Buidhe allied to the English townsmen of Dundalk: AFM, 1345; AU, 1354; K. Nicholls, AFM, 'Appendix: additional marginalia from TCD MS 1301 (H.2.11), 1354'; AC, 1354.   8 W. Reeves, 'The seal of Hugh O'Neill', *UJA*, 1 (1853), 255–8; Simms, 'Late medieval Tír Eoghain', p. 146.   9 K. Simms, 'Propaganda use of the *Táin* in the later Middle Ages', *Celtica*, 15 (1983), 146; Reeves, 'The seal of Hugh O'Neill', 255–8.   10 Ó hÓgáin, *Myth*,

Just before his death, Aodh Reamhar Ó Néill may have performed one more good service for his kingdom – the provision of sage advice to his son and successor Niall Mór. Four stanzas at the end of a bardic poem written by a Franciscan poet for Niall Mór record Aodh Reamhar's words of advice:

Dob hí a comhairle dá chloinn
ria ndol d'Aodh mhór, mhac Domhnaill,
báidh um chongnamh re chéile
dáibh gér orlamh aimhréidhe.

The advice of great Aodh, son of Domhnaill, before death, to his family was this: to set their minds of cooperating with one another even though they were disposed to quarrel.

'Ní do isleochadh ibh fein
-mian bhur n-easgcarad eiséin –
na deanaidh' ar Aodh Eamhna,
'féagaidh fur gaol geineamhna'.

Said Aodh of Eamhain: 'Do not do anything that might weaken yourselves – that is what your enemies desire. Be mindful of your blood relationship'.

Beannacht Aodha, [a]their Néill
ar Niall do fhagaibh a[i]nnséin
's gan labhra d'fhairbríogh ná d'fhioll
do dhamhna airdrí[o]gh [n]Éirionn.

legend and romance, pp 111–14, 131–9, 413–17; Simms, 'Propaganda use of the *Táin* in the later Middle Ages', 142–9; T. Kinsella (trans.), *The Táin*, (Dublin, 1969).

Niall's father, Aodh, then left him his blessing: and not a word was spoken by the heir of the high-kings of Ireland about force or violence.

Teagasg Aodha dá oighre-
ní théid céim don chomhairle;
fuaighfidh le a ghníomh gach gartmhagh;
tuairfidh brí[o]gh na beandachtan.

[Niall] departs not by [even] a [single] step from the advice of Aodh to his heir. He will unite together every plain and field, by his exploits. He will merit the efficacy of the blessing.[11]

If factual, these were wise words and allowed Aodh's sons and heirs to achieve great things when they eventually did take his death-bed advice.

NIALL MÓR Ó NÉILL

Despite Aodh Reamhar's wise words, his son Niall Mór Ó Néill inherited a civil war with his brother Domhnall along with the kingdom of Tyrone. Both brothers had the support of substantial numbers of MacDomhnaill galloglasses. Niall Mór hired MacDomhnaill reinforcements from the Clann Alasdair in the Hebrides Islands off Scotland.[12] Domhnall Ó Néill had the support of closely related members of the Clann Alasdair already serving as galloglasses in Tyrone.[13] Domhnall Ó Néill soon acknowledged his brother's growing power, especially after the

11 Mhág Craith (ed.), *Dán na mBráthar Mionúr*, i, pp 8–9; ii, p. 4. 12 AFM, 1366. 13 Ibid., 1366.

defeat of his MacDomhnaill galloglasses by those of his brother at the battle of Ath an Imuricc, fought on a river somewhere in Tyrone in 1366.[14] In 1370 the annals record that 'A firm and sincere peace was made by the Cinél nEógain with each other. Domhnall gave hostages to Niall, that he would not contest the lordship with him; and Niall then gave Domhnall a share of territory and lands.'[15] The Annals of Ulster add that 'hostage and kingship were ceded by Domhnall to Niall'.[16]

This peace between the brothers was the making of the late-medieval kingdom of Tyrone. It led to a great expansion in the power of the Ó Néill king all over the province of Ulster. It also may have encouraged other close family members to treat the authority of the ruling Ó Néill king with more respect.[17] For example, another of Niall Mór's sons who became a powerful figure in west Tyrone was known as Éinrí Aimhréidh – Henry the Contentious. The Annals of Connacht state that this was *'per antiphrasim'*, because he was not in any way contentious and he should perhaps have been called Henry the Peaceful. Although the exact nature of this noble's personality is disputed in the annals, he does seem to have been a loyal supporter of the kingship of his father Niall Mór and brother Niall Óg Ó Néill. Whether the brothers eventually saw the wisdom of the advice given by their dying father Aodh Reamhar is uncertain.

Niall Mór must have been able to recognize the advantages of the peace, for he treated his brother with the requisite amount of respect for the remainder of their lives. Niall arranged for his eldest son, Niall Óg, already perhaps his recognized heir, to marry Domhnall's daughter Una, who thus became the future queen of

14 AC, 1366; AU, 1363; AFM, 1366; Nicholls, 'Scottish mercenary kindreds in Ireland, 1250–1600', p. 98.   15 AFM, 1370.   16 AU, 1367.   17 AC, 1392.

Tyrone.[18] Domhnall, too, possibly recognized the advantages that would accrue to his entire family and indeed to the wider kingdom of Tyrone once he made peace with his brother. This agreement between the two brothers was quite important in the context of late-medieval Gaelic Ireland. Most Irish dynasts were never able to come to such agreements and often destroyed their kingdoms in bitter civil wars. The destruction of the Ó Conchobhair kingdom of Connacht in the thirteenth century is an excellent example. In this instance an astonishing expansion of Ó Néill power was felt immediately in the surrounding lordships.[19]

In 1374 Niall Mór led an expedition east of the Bann and Lough Neagh to attack the English in the earldom of Ulster. The annals say that 'Defeat was inflicted by Niall Ó Néill, namely, by the king of the fifth of Ulster, on the foreigners, wherein fell the Knight [Roche] and Bogsa of the Rock and the Sandal and the de Burgh and William of Baile-Dalat, head of the splendid hospitality of Ireland.'[20] This battle may have taken place somewhere in the northern portion of the earldom of Ulster, as some of the English casualties in the battle have been tentatively identified as Bocksa of Carrickfergus, Sandal of Mount Sandal (a hill on the east bank of the Bann close to Coleraine), and William of possibly Ballynadolly (a place name in south Co. Antrim).[21] The battle, which may have

---

18 Simms, 'Late medieval Tyrone', p. 147.   19 AFM, 1370; AU, 1367; AC, 1370.
20 AFM, 1374; AU, 1369; a John de Burgh may have been granted lands near Coleraine in the early fourteenth century, McNeill, *Anglo-Norman Ulster*, p. 68; Bogsa of Carrickfergus may have been descended from the Scottish de Bosco family, supporters of Edward and Robert Bruce. See Duffy, 'The Bruce invasion of Ireland: a revised itinerary and chronology', p. 17.   21 AFM, 1374, notes d and e; McNeill, *Anglo-Norman Ulster*, p. 82; the Sandal family had extensive lands surrounding Coleraine, see: R. Frame, 'A register of lost deeds relating to the earldom of Ulster, c.1230–1376' in Seán Duffy (ed.), *Princes, prelates and poets in medieval Ireland: essays in honour of Katharine Simms* (Dublin, 2013), pp 96–100.

been quite fateful given the number of English casualties involved, was unusual because it was rare for an Irish army to defeat an apparently large English one in the heart of a major English area. There may have been a number of contributing factors to this. An English population possibly in distress was one, and substantial numbers of MacDomhnaill galloglasses and Irish horsemen being available after the ending of the Ó Néill civil war must have been another. Niall Mór Ó Néill followed up his victory over the English of Co. Antrim with an even greater victory (probably later the same year, 1374) over the English of the southern portion of the earldom of Ulster in Co. Down. The annals record that:

> A great hosting by Niall Ó Néill to Dun da Lethglas [Downpatrick] and great defeat was inflicted on the foreigners by him, wherein fell Sir James de la Hyde, deputy of the king of the Saxons, and the de Burgh of Caimlinn and many other others were slain therein.[22]

Caimlinn has been identified with the place name Camlin, the site of one of John de Courcey's early fortifications in south Co. Antrim.[23] A branch of the de Burgh family was settled there throughout the 1300s.[24]

---

22 AU, 1370; AFM, 1375; AC, 1375 (again, the Annals of Ulster are out by five years here). The annals record that this second battle at Downpatrick took place in 1375 although an earlier date towards the end of 1374 may be more correct. 23 AFM, 1375, note s. 24 John de Burgh of Camlin is recorded commanding the defence of Antrim castle during the 1350s. He was also seneschal of Ulster from 1363–6. A Richard de Burgh, 'S[eignur] de Camalyn', surrendered his rights to the earl of Ulster in 1302, Frame, 'A register of lost deeds relating to the earldom of Ulster', pp 90, 99; McNeill, *Anglo-Norman Ulster*, p. 64; Flanders, *De Courcy – Anglo-Normans in Ireland, England and France*, p. 175; Simms, 'The Ulster revolt of 1404: an anti-Lancastrian dimension', p. 144.

Richard II and his queen, Anne of Bohemia, from the illuminated 'R' of the Shrewsbury Charter (1389) (courtesy of Shrewsbury Museum Service).

2. Interior of the left wing of the Wilton Diptych: Richard II presented by John the Baptist, Edward the Confessor, and Edmund, king and martyr; interior of the right wing of the Wilton Diptych: the Virgin and Child with eleven angels (*Wilton Diptych, c.*1395–9) (© National Gallery, London).

3. Rock and castle of Dunamase (courtesy of National Library of Ireland).

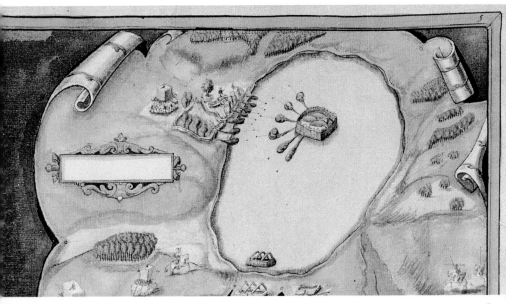

The rath of Tullaghoge and a crannog in Tyrone (1602) (courtesy of National Library of Ireland)

5. Harry Avery's castle, Newtown-Stewart, Co. Tyrone (photograph by Frank McGettigan).

6. The O'Kane tomb, Dungiven priory, Co. Derry (photograph by Frank McGettigan).

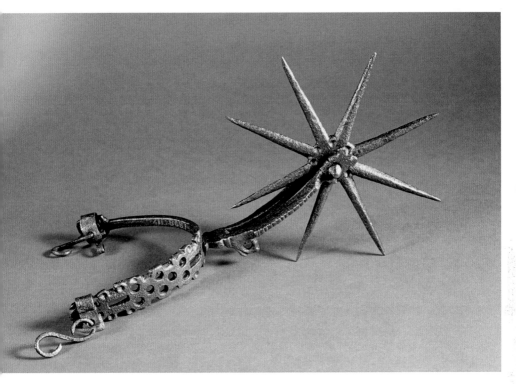

7. Late-medieval Irish spur (courtesy of National Museum of Ireland).

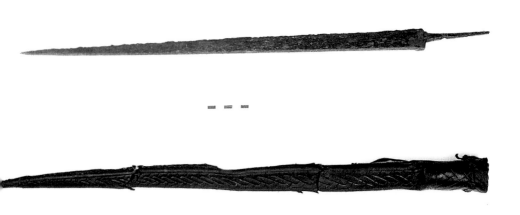

8. Late-medieval Irish dagger with scabbard (courtesy of National Museum of Ireland).

9. The castle of Carlow (courtesy of National Library of Ireland).

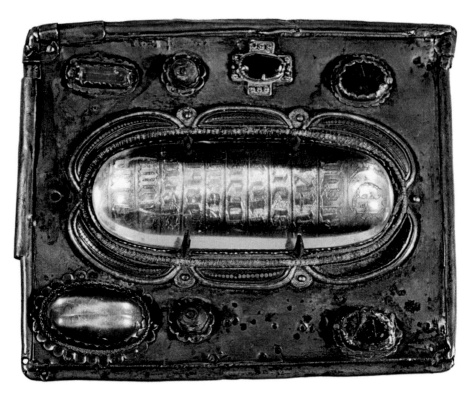

10. Shrine of the Book of Mulling (courtesy of National Museum of Ireland).

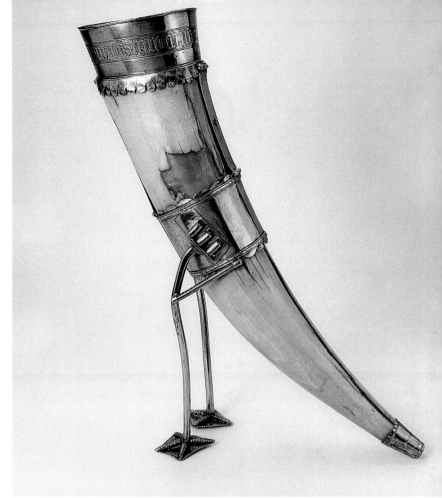

11. (*above*) The Kavanagh Charter Horn (courtesy of National Museum of Ireland).

12. Thomas Mowbray, earl of Nottingham and marshal of England, with Richard II (detail from fo. 85r of Cotton MS Nero D VI, © The British Library Board).

14. Carrickfergus castle (courtesy of National Library of Ireland).

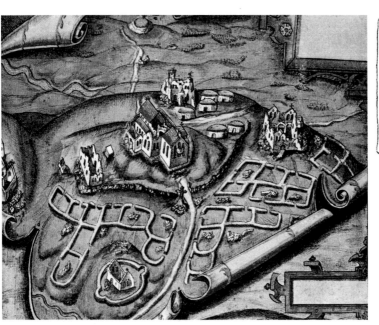

13. Seal of Aodh Reamhar Ó Néill.

15. The ecclesiastical settlement of Armagh, as it lay destroyed in 1602. The hill of Eamhain Mhacha can be seen in the background (courtesy of National Library of Ireland).

16. Trim castle, Co. East Meath (courtesy of National Library of Ireland).

17. Teach Midchuarda: plan of the banqueting hall at Tara – in 1387, Niall Óg Ó Néill built a house at Eamhain Mhacha in which to entertain the learned men of Ireland (detail from columns 243 and 244 of the Yellow Book of Lecan, TCD MS 1318, a late-fourteenth-century/early fifteenth-century composite manuscript, courtesy of the Board of Trinity College Dublin).

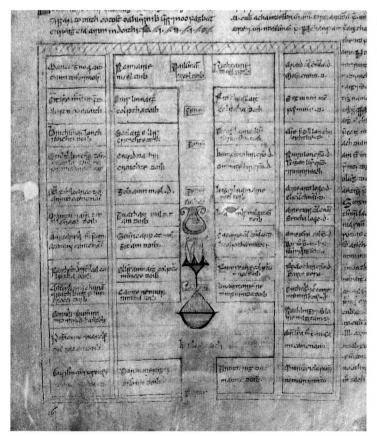

18. Tower of
Mary Magdal
Drogheda, Co
Louth (courte
of National
Library of
Ireland).

19. The Seve
Churches,
Glendalough,
Co. Wicklow
(courtesy of
National Libr
of Ireland).

20. A duel with daggers (detail from fo. 82r of Cotton MS Nero D VI, © The British Library Board). On 16 September 1398, Richard II famously called off the trial by battle being held before him, between Henry Bolingbroke, duke of Hereford, and Thomas Mowbray, duke of Norfolk.

21. Richard II knighting Henry of Monmouth, the future King Henry V (detail from fo. 5 of Harley MS 1319, © The British Library Board). 22. Relief ships arriving on the Leinster coastline (detail from fo. 7v of Harley MS 1319, © The British Library Board).

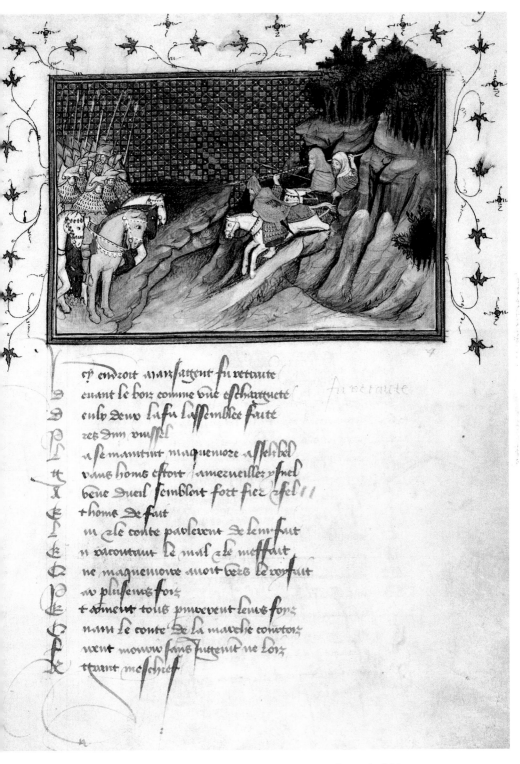

cy endroit maxfargent fu retrait
enant le bois comme une eschanguete
eulp deux lafu laffemblee fuite
zes din vuiffel
a se manitut maquemore affeilbel
vaus home effoit / amezueilles yfuel
bene dueil semblort fort fiez efel
thome de faut
m ele conte pavlerent de lenxfaut
n vacontaut le mal ele meffaut
ne maquemore auoit bers le rorfut
m plufeurs fors
t commeut tous pmuevent leurs fors
nam le conte de la marche conutois
nent mouu sauns fuireut ne loix
ttaunt meschief

23. Art MacMurchadha parleys with Sir Thomas Despenser, the earl of Gloucester
(detail from fo. 9 of Harley MS 1319, © The British Library Board).

n ttales fu la ormes nonuelle
e lemprise du duc qui fu couelle
nomes ie croy on ne puisla deteslle
n nul prus
au on nous dist qul auoit sa compus
auile teive la plus gtant pr cptis
illes chasteaulx office desnus
t en son nom
aux par tout aut institueon
ous ceulx quloy onumt aynacon
usont mondw sans lem sp pon
omme seycyn

Q uant le conte oy scelle doulem
tenesu pas merueilles sl ot peur
av des nobles la purie etveiruem
eurs leteiux.

25. Richard II's fleet returns to Britain (detail from fo. 18 of Harley MS 1319, © The British Library Board).

24. (*opposite*) Jean Creton and John Montagu, the earl of Salisbury, arrive at Conway in Wales (detail from fo. 14v of Harley MS 1319, © The British Library Board).

ifint an rop febone atore queux

on droit Seigneur ne bone bueille depfleu

in le papit eft efmeu pom la mieux

on bone Sanex

ffin que menluo fotez affenuez

ore Dift leroy se fouffe bien alez

me tout se ttens qui en mande mez

L meft Smie

ne ce neft pas ce que manez promiz

ouf me Seiftez quon bone auoit trainiz

ouf soiefme par Sieu se parasiz

eft tresmal fatt.

26. Richard II is captured by Henry Percy, the earl of Northumberland
(detail from fo. 44 of Harley MS 1319, © The British Library Board).

These were great victories by Niall Mór Ó Néill and for the Irish warriors of the kingdom of Tyrone. A decade later Niall Mór Ó Néill rounded off his conquest of Ulster when in 1384 his warriors burnt down the English town of Carrickfergus (see figure 14).[25] This may have been the occasion when John Rynaux, the chamberlain and treasurer of the liberty of Ulster, was killed and the records of the earldom, 'tallies and ... writs ... were burnt in the town of Carrickfergus by rebels'.[26] It does not appear to have been Niall Mór's objective to destroy completely all the English areas within the earldom of Ulster. Although the colony in much of south Co. Antrim seems to have been substantially destroyed during these years, English lords remained in control of Lecale and the Ards farther to the south-east and the Coleraine region known as *Twescard* (the north) for the remainder of the fourteenth century. What does appear to have happened is that the lords of these English districts agreed to recognize Niall Mór Ó Néill as high-king of the fifth of Ulster and to pay him any tributes or levies of troops demanded. As such, Niall Mór, after his great victories of 1374, was the provincial king of Ulster, with little exaggeration. This was an astounding achievement, especially considering the odds stacked against him.[27]

---

25 AFM, 1384; AU, 1384.   26 2. 19 July 1398, Close Roll 22 Richard II; Frame, 'Deeds relating to the earldom of Ulster', pp 85–106.   27 Although these two great victories by Niall Mór Ó Néill over the English of Ulster are not recorded by the English chroniclers, there is English evidence that they did indeed take place. A set of annals from St Mary's Abbey in Dublin records 'Lord James de la Hyde, a distinguished knight', who it states was killed by MacAonghusa, king of Iveagh. These annals state that Sir James was acting as 'legate [*missus*] by means of the earl of March and Ulster' rather than having the title of deputy to King Edward III, although he may still have been on the king's business, 'Annales Monasterii Beate Marie Virginis, Juxta Dublin – Annals AD 1370–76' in Gilbert (ed.), *Chartularies of St Mary's Abbey, Dublin*, ii, p. 283; in the close rolls of King Edward III for December 1374 we find James de la Hyde's widow Joan who had been 'left six

The provincial high-kingship of Ulster was the limit of realistic Ó Néill ambition and Niall Mór knew it. The bardic poets composed stanzas of poetry stating that Niall would become high-king of the island like the pre-invasion high-kings of old and reconquer Ireland from the foreigners. A famous bardic poem beginning *'Bean ar n-aithéirghe Éire'* ('Ireland is a woman who has recovered from terrible disasters') was composed for Niall Mór by the Franciscan bardic poet Tadhg Camchosach Ó Dálaigh.[28] However, Niall Mór seems to have realized that this was not in any way feasible and indeed could lead the kingdom of Tyrone and the Ó Néill family to disaster. As a result, although the king of Tyrone's warriors threatened Carlingford and Dundalk throughout the 1380s and seemed about to overrun the Cooley peninsula, the summit of Niall Mór's ambition – the high-kingship of the fifth of Ulster – had largely been realized in 1374.[29]

In 1374 Niall Mór Ó Néill may have attempted to celebrate his two major victories over the English of the earldom of Ulster by building a new *longphort* or fortress on the hill of Eamhain Mhacha near the ecclesiastical settlement of Armagh ('Hewynnae near Armagh') (see figure 15).[30] Eamhain Mhacha was an ancient place, the site of the mythological palace of Conchobhar mac Neasa, the legendary king of Ulster from the Ulster Cycle of

orphans' after her husband 'James was killed in the K.[ing's] service', petitioning for the return of stock and crops seized by overzealous royal officials 'because of some debts that he owed the K.[ing]'. The Irish council ordered the return of the goods to Joan: 146. 11 Dec. 1374, Close Rolls Edward III 48; Simms, 'The Ulster revolt of 1404: an anti-Lancastrian dimension', p. 144.   **28** Mhág Craith (ed.), *Dán na mBráthar Mionúr*, i, pp 1–9; ii, pp 1–4.   **29** 41. 23 Nov. 1384, Patent Roll 8 Richard II; 255. 18 Aug. 1388, Patent Roll 12 Richard II.   **30** Simms, 'Propaganda use of the *Táin* in the later Middle Ages', 142; letter to Masters Odo (Mcdinim), dean, and Maurice (O'Corry), 6 Aug. 1374, in Lalor, 'A calendar of the register of Archbishop Sweteman', 221–2; Smith (ed.), *Register of Milo Sweteman*, pp 11–12.

tales.[31] To build such a fortress would have been quite a statement by Niall Mór Ó Néill. It would have symbolically confirmed that he was high-king of the fifth of Ulster, a new Conchobhar mac Neasa to rule the province. In the end Niall Mór never did build a fortress at Eamhain Mhacha. Perhaps the pre-Christian ethos of the Ulster Cycle put him off taking the final step. More important perhaps, was the exposed location of Eamhain Mhacha, south of the river Blackwater. Any fortress built there by Niall Mór would potentially have offered a target for invading English armies to attack or even garrison.

Despite his threats and boasting, Niall Mór, by his actions, demonstrated that he wished to improve relations between the king of Tyrone and the English archbishop of Armagh, Milo Sweteman. Although in 1374 Archbishop Sweteman complained to the king's Irish council that Ó Néill 'has been publicly threatening, and threatens daily, that he wishes to make his manor and *longphort* at Hewynnae near Armagh', and that 'like a pope or an emperor' ('si esset papa vel imperator') he planned to seize all the archbishop's lands within the kingdom of Tyrone 'and leave the archbishop and his clerks nothing at Armagh except the cathedral church', some of the wilder accusations made against Ó Néill in 1374 may be exaggerated hearsay.[32] In 1375 Niall Mór's sons Éinrí Aimhréidh and Cú-Uladh Ruadh let their soldiers rampage through the archbishop's lands, raping the women of his tenantry and creating such a bad situation that the inhabitants of Armagh and the archbishop's tenants in the surrounding area threatened to

31 Ó hÓgáin, *Myth, legend and romance*, p. 413.   32 Letter to Masters Odo (Mcdinim), dean, and Maurice (O'Corry), 6 Aug. 1374, in Lalor, 'A calendar of the register of Archbishop Sweteman', 221–2; Smith (ed.), *Register of Milo Sweteman*, pp 11–12; the accusations were made 'under the seal of confession by persons who would not otherwise have dared to make them'.

surrender their lands and depart from the region 'on account of their iniquities'.[33] When the archbishop protested to the king of Tyrone, Niall Mór immediately put a stop to his sons' depredations. As a result, it is unclear how much store can be put in the veracity of some of the more grandiose allegations.

Niall Mór Ó Néill gained some valuable experience of top-level negotiations with a major English lord in 1380 when Edmund Mortimer, the earl of March and Ulster, appeared in Ireland determined to recover his vast inheritance. The Mortimers were one of the greatest English noble families.[34] Mortimer, the young third earl of March, in 1368 had married Philippa, the only surviving heir to her parents, Lionel, duke of Clarence, the son of King Edward III, and Elizabeth de Burgh, the heiress of the Brown earl of Ulster.[35] In 1379 Richard II appointed Mortimer lieutenant of Ireland. The earl was potentially heir to an immense inheritance encompassing both the provinces of Connacht and Ulster, as well as extensive territories in Meath and the Irish midlands also. Although Niall Mór was a powerful native king and could have ignored the arrival of the earl of March and Ulster in Ireland, Ó Néill appears to have realized the value of peaceful negotiations. According to the Irish annals, Niall Mór was the most prominent of the many Irish nobles from all over Ireland who 'came into his house' to pay court to the earl. Niall Mór's meeting with Mortimer appears to have gone tolerably well and he returned to Tyrone. Another prominent Ulster chieftain, Art MacAonghusa, the king of Iveagh, was not so fortunate. Although probably a vassal of Ó Néill, Art MacAonghusa was an independently powerful chieftain.

33 Letter, 18 July 1375, in Lalor, 'A calendar of the register of Archbishop Sweteman', 258.   34 D. Beresford, 'Edmund Mortimer', *DIB*, vi, p. 707; Davies, *The revolt of Owain Glyn Dŵr*, p. 37.   35 D. Beresford, 'Lionel ('of Antwerp')', *DIB*,

In fact, just before he met with the earl of March, he inflicted a severe defeat on some of the English, killing their local ally Ó hAnluain, king of Orier in the process.[36] The annals record that MacAonghusa 'was taken prisoner in treachery in the house of the Mortimer. And the Gaels of Ireland took fear of the latter from that out, so that they and also the foreigners of Ireland avoided him.'[37] Mortimer's sojourn in Ireland had gotten off to a disastrous start. The unfortunate Art MacAonghusa died of plague in the dungeon of Trim castle in 1383, never having been released (see figure 16).[38]

The high-handed actions of the earl of March and Ulster towards Art MacAonghusa must have made Niall Mór fear for his personal safety at any future meeting. The arrest destroyed any trust that existed between the mature Irish king of Tyrone and the young English earl. Possibly having had further communication rebuffed, Mortimer led a punitive expedition into Ulster to attack the kingdom of Tyrone. He first visited Coleraine, perhaps to survey the destruction caused by Ó Néill in parts of his earldom. While he was in Coleraine the earl made repairs to 'the bridge of Culrath [Coleraine] and the towers at each end thereof'.[39] This must have been an imposing structure to span a river as big as the Bann. The earl of March also began repairs to 'the great tower and other buildings within the castle of Carrickfergus', and to the castles of Drumtarcy near Coleraine on the west bank of the river Bann and Greencastle in south Co. Down, 'which were wasted by the Irish'.[40]

v, pp 511–12.   36 AFM, 1380; AU, 1380.   37 AU, 1380; AFM, 1380.   38 AFM, 1383.   39 223. 14 Mar. 1382, Patent Roll 5 Richard II.   40 G. Orpen, 'The earldom of Ulster', *JRSAI*, 45:2 (1915), 124–6.

The earl may have marched overland from Coleraine to Derry. He then proceeded on a destructive foray through the kingdom of Tyrone, burning the churches of Urney and Donaghmore in the Derg valley before marching through central Tyrone where churches were also burnt at Errigal-Keeroge and Clogher. This raid may have been modelled on a *chevauchée*, a favoured English tactic of the wars in France.[41] In the midst of all this activity and perhaps on the brink of a recovery of at least some power in east Ulster, Mortimer died very unexpectedly in 1381.[42] Ó Néill had gained some valuable experience in negotiating with an English high-nobleman, experience that would stand him in good stead when Richard II came to the island in 1394–5.

NIALL ÓG Ó NÉILL

In 1387 Niall Mór Ó Néill may have decided to go into semi-retirement and appoint his son Niall Óg to be the active king in his place. Niall Óg was probably given almost full control of the government of the kingdom and its large Irish army at this time. Possibly to mark this important event the annals record that 'A house was built in Eamhain Mhacha by Niall Óg Ó Néill to recompense the [learned] companies of Ireland therein [see figure 17].'[43] This building of what may have been a substantial wooden complex on the hill of Eamhain Mhacha (no trace of any stone building was found during archaeological excavations) and the extension of invitations to the learned men of Ireland to attend the celebrations record an important ceremony held by Niall Óg Ó Néill. It was not quite Niall Mór's building of a *longphort* at the

41 AFM, 1380, notes s, t, u and v.   42 AU, 1381; AFM, 1381; Cosgrove, *Late medieval Ireland*, p. 10.   43 AU, 1387; AFM, 1387.

site, but the event must have been an impressive celebration and possibly marked the beginning of Niall Óg's reign as high-king of Ulster.[44]

Disaster nearly struck Niall Óg quite soon into his kingship. In 1389, he was captured by the English.[45] Niall Mór's conquest of the earldom of Ulster during the 1370s and 1380s may have caused Niall Óg to underestimate the military abilities of the English, who were still formidable opponents. During the first year of his reign, Niall Óg appears to have had his mind set on a conquest of the Cooley peninsula, the final portion of the earldom of Ulster that lay outside the control of the Ó Néill kings. Certainly by 1388 the English freeholders and clergy of the peninsula were complaining to the Irish council of 'the losses, wastes, damages and dangers they had sustained by the war raised and carried on by Nelanus Oneel [Niall Óg Ó Néill] and his accomplices, the K.[ing's] Irish enemies'.[46] The Cooley peninsula was just north of the English town of Dundalk and was within easy reach of the major area of English settlement in Co. Meath. The peninsula could also be assisted from the great English city of Dublin. As a result, Niall Óg perhaps should have approached military activity in the area with more caution. In the difficult mountainous and wooded heartlands of Gaelic Ulster, Ó Néill was a powerful and dangerous opponent. Many of the Ó Néill kings, however, seemed to have to learn personally that there was a definite limit to their ambitions. Once the king of Tyrone began to campaign in low-lying English areas with urban centres and depth to their defences, the advantage swung dangerously in favour of his enemies.

44 Simms, 'Propaganda use of the *Táin* in the later Middle Ages', 143–4. 45 AFM, 1389; AU, 1389; AC, 1389. 46 255. 18 Aug. 1388, Patent Roll 12 Richard II; the English defences on the Cooley peninsula were well organized and

Niall Óg's capture by the English captain Edmund Loundres could have spelt the end of his kingship. His father, Niall Mór, however, emerged from semi-retirement to organize Niall Óg's release. A deal was negotiated whereby Niall Óg was set free, and three prominent hostages from the ruling Ó Néill family were surrendered to the English in his place. These hostages included Niall Óg's son Brian, 'his first born'.[47] The release agreement was comprehensive and Niall Mór Ó Néill and his sons:

> swore to become the K.[ing's] lieges; that they would not interfere concerning the 'bonaght' of Ulster; and that the K.[ing] (and Roger Mortimer, earl of March and Ulster, when he came of age) should have all lordships, rents, exactions, and answering of the Irish of Ulster, as fully as they used to have them of old, reserving to Oneele and his successors such things as they used to have of ancient custom.[48]

commanded by a capable soldier, Edmund Loundres, 28. 28 June 1389, Patent Roll 13 Richard II; Loundres was granted £40 in Jan. 1390 'for his service in taking Nelanus Oneil [Niall Óg Ó Néill] of Ulster', 40. 12 Jan. 1390, Patent Roll 13 Richard II.   47 222. [12 Mar. 1390], Patent Roll 13 Richard II; some of the hostages surrendered by Niall Mór and Niall Óg appear to have been very young children. In 1394, John Clifford, the deputy constable of Dublin castle, was paid £11 12s. 'for the wages and expenses of Bernadus Oneel [Brian Ó Néill], recently a hostage of Oneel being in his custody in that castle, and for the carriage of Bernadus at Trim, Drogheda, Ardee and Dundalk, and others of his company; and also for the wages of Shan McBrien [identity uncertain] and Catholicus s.[on] of Catholicus Oneel [Cú-Uladh son of Cú-Uladh Ruadh Ó Néill] and John s.[on] of Shan McBrien [identity uncertain]; and also for the transport of four hostages of Oneel and their nurses from Dundalk to Dublin castle, with various expenses for their safe conduct.' The reference to 'their nurses' may mean that Niall Mór and Niall Óg, concerned for the welfare of their young hostages, who were sons, grandsons, and possibly also nephews and grand-nephews, sent female servants to look after them. There are few records of other late-medieval Irish kings doing anything similar, 19. [No exact date, 1394?], Close Roll 17 Richard II.   48 240. 20 Feb. 1390, Patent Roll 13 Richard II; D. Beresford, 'Sir John Stanley', *DIB*, ix, p. 10.

The terms agreed to by Niall Mór and his sons, if implemented in full, could have seen a substantial diminishing of the power of Ó Néill as high-king of Ulster and perhaps the return of the Ó Néill family to little more than kings of Tyrone. Certainly the Ó Néill conquests and any effective overlordship of areas within the earldom of Ulster were potentially lost.[49] As it turned out, the Ó Néill ruling family did little to implement the agreement and even resumed war with the English before their hostages were released. The 1390 indenture was, however, another important precursor to Niall Óg's negotiations with Richard II and Roger Mortimer in 1395.

Niall Óg was as able a king as his father Niall Mór and appears to have been a good horseman and warrior.[50] By 1392 he was again at war with the English when he led 'A great hosting ... with the nobles of the Fifth around him, against the foreigners of Sraidbhaile [Dundalk] and sway over the foreigners was obtained by him on that expedition'. This was the occasion on which Niall Óg met Geoffrey (Seifin) White, keeper of the peace for Co. Louth, in single combat, and killed the Englishman.[51] Ó Néill may have killed a second English knight, '*an Dúdálach*', on the same occasion.[52]

THE 1394–5 EXPEDITION CONTINUES

When the semi-retired Niall Mór Ó Néill opened communication with Richard in 1395, he gave himself the title 'Princeps Hibernicorum Ultonie' or 'Prince of the Irish of Ulster'. Niall Mór

49 AU, 1391. 50 McKenna (ed.), *Aithdioghluim Dána*, i, p. 56; ii, pp 33–4.
51 Simms, 'The Ulster revolt of 1404: an anti-Lancastrian dimension', p. 147.
52 This might refer to 'the Dowdall' – the Dowdalls were a prominent Dundalk

wrote to Richard, 'When I heard of your joyful coming to your land of Ireland I greatly rejoiced and do now rejoice', and asked for justice for some recent English attacks on the kingdom of Tyrone. Niall Mór especially requested that Richard 'be shield and helmet of justice to me between my lord the earl of Ulster and me in case he be provoked by stern advice to exact more from me than by right he should'.[53] From the start of negotiations the Ó Néill family correctly identified the greatest threat to their dominant position in Ulster: the potential claims inherited by Roger Mortimer over the province.

The English king's reply must have been favourable, and on 6 January 1395, from a place called Maydown just south of the Blackwater river, opposite Benburb, Niall Óg Ó Néill sent a letter to the English king appointing his 'beloved and right worshipful father' as 'my deputy, proxy, agent, and special envoy' to meet and negotiate with Richard.[54] Memories in Ulster of the treacherous treatment of Art MacAonghusa, the king of Iveagh, in 1380 were still very raw.[55] As a result, Niall Óg may have felt it wise not to put himself in danger by meeting the English king too early before he could determine whether Richard was trustworthy and that the negotiations were going well. Niall Mór was authorized to treat with the English king and also with Roger Mortimer 'and conclude

family. T. Ó Donnchadha, (ed.), *Leabhar Cloinne Aodha Buidhe* (Dublin, 1931), pp 33–4; *Leabhar Cloinne Aodha Buidhe* clearly states that it was Niall Óg Ó Néill who commanded this expedition and who personally slew '*Seiffin Dufait*'; B. Smith, 'The murder of John Dowdall, sheriff of Louth, 1402' in Duffy (ed.), *Princes, prelates and poets in medieval Ireland*, p. 194.   53 Niall Mór Ó Néill to King Richard II [Dec. 1394?], in Curtis, 'Letters sent to the king when in Ireland', pp 211–12.   54 Letter of proxy written by Niall Óg Ó Néill, 6 Jan. 1395, in Curtis, 'Instruments touching Ireland', pp 173–5; Curtis, *Richard II in Ireland, 1394–5*, p. 34. 55 Muircheartach MacAonghusa to King Richard II [*c*.Jan./Feb. 1395], in Curtis, 'Letters sent to the king when in Ireland', pp 176–9.

in my name with them ... to make and enter into a certain composition for obtaining and having peace to me and my nation, my subjects, and country'.[56] Niall Mór was also allowed to discuss the return of any lands taken unjustly over the years by the kings of Tyrone from the English, as well as the bonnacht of Ulster, the valuable military levy on Gaelic Ulster once owed to the earls of Ulster that had long been appropriated by Ó Néill.[57]

The by now quite elderly Niall Mór Ó Néill travelled south to negotiate with Richard and Mortimer soon afterwards. The talks took place within a special room inside the enclosure of the Dominican priory of St Mary Magdalene in Drogheda (see figure 18).[58] Niall Mór spoke Irish throughout the negotiations and interpreters were used to translate the speeches of both sides. Niall Mór appears to have been a confident negotiator and he was not overawed by being in the presence of the English king. This is evident from the record of 'some dissension [that] had arisen between the earl [Roger Mortimer] and Niall [Mór] Ó Néill in presence of the king concerning the immediate homage and tenure of certain Irishmen of Ulster' that survives from the negotiations.[59]

The main points of dispute were between the Ó Néill kings and Mortimer, who claimed to be their immediate overlord. The Mortimer claim to overlordship also concerned the bonnacht of Ulster and 'all other services which Niall senior and junior and their ancestors rendered or ought to have rendered to the ancestors of the said Earl'.[60] It had long been the ambition of the Ó Néill

---

56 Letter of proxy written by Niall Óg Ó Néill, 6 Jan. 1395, in Curtis, 'Instruments touching Ireland', pp 173–5. 57 Ibid., p. 174. 58 Notarial Instrument XXIX, 19 Jan. 1395, in Curtis, 'Instruments touching Ireland', p. 190; Gwynn and Hadcock, *Medieval religious houses: Ireland*, p. 224. 59 Deed, 20 Jan. 1395, in Curtis, 'Letters sent to the king when in Ireland', pp 223–4. 60 Ibid., p. 223; K. Simms, '"The king's friend"': Ó Néill, the crown and the earldom of Ulster' in J.F.

family to hold Tyrone directly from the kings of England, with no intervening overlord. Niall Óg, on another occasion, demonstrated this when he asked Richard to make a firm decision on 'the liberties and lordships which the king's Majesty is to confirm to us, and which our ancestors had from the king's ancestors'.[61]

Whatever the difficulties were that had caused the argument between Niall Mór and Roger Mortimer, they must have been straightened out, however temporarily, and around 19/20 January 1395, Niall Mór 'did liege homage to our lord Richard the Second, king of England and France, duke of Aquitaine, and lord of Ireland, for himself, his sons, his nation, and his subjects in Irish, publicly rendered into Latin by interpreters'.[62] Niall Mór then made a second 'concord with Lord Roger Mortimer, earl of March and Ulster, in presence of the said Lord King ... having touched the holy Gospels [and] took corporal oath with mature and perfect deliberation on the missal and cross of the Archbishop of Armagh'.[63]

When Niall Mór returned to Tyrone, he carried letters from Richard to Niall Óg. In a subsequent reply to the English king, Niall Óg stated that 'I received your Majesty's letters stating that part cause of your coming to Ireland was that you would do justice to every man'.[64] Niall Óg, who referred to himself as 'the king's liegeman and subject, Governor of the Irish of Ulster', complained that some of the English on the border of Oriel had ignored the English king's peace 'granted by you to my father' and committed

Lydon (ed.), *England and Ireland in the later Middle Ages* (Dublin, 1981), pp 214–24.   61 Niall Óg Ó Néill to the Archbishop of Armagh, 26 Feb. 1395, in Curtis, 'Letters sent to the king when in Ireland', p. 222.   62 Notarial Instrument XXIX, 19 Jan. 1395, in Curtis, 'Instruments touching Ireland', pp 190–1.   63 Ibid., pp 191–2.   64 Niall Óg Ó Néill to Richard II (late Jan./early Feb. 1395?), in Curtis, 'Letters sent to the king when in Ireland', p. 210.

'thefts, robberies, reivings, and other endless injuries, in contempt of your Majesty's peace'.[65] The essence of Richard's letters to Niall Óg may be preserved in a statement the English king made in February 1395 that was written into the Irish patent rolls:

> The K.[ing] believes it to be pious and pleasing to God that, having now come to the land of Ire.[land] for the sake of justice and the good government of his people and subjects there, under divine trust, he should restore grace to his subjects at his first coming, and especially to those who humbly seek his grace. Therefore he wishes, out of reverence towards God, as becomes his clemency, to temper justice with mildness, so that those of the K.[ing]'s subjects who have behaved badly may the more quickly take an opportunity of bearing themselves better in future.[66]

Even though his father's negotiations with Richard had gone well, if Niall Óg did not complete the negotiation process, hostilities between the English and the warriors of Tyrone may have been the result. In February 1395 Niall Óg called an important provincial gathering and 'made come to us all the great men among the Irish of Ulster, to consult and deliberate with them about my going to the king's court'.[67] Ó Néill later wrote to the archbishop of Armagh that envoys from Ó Briain, king of Thomond, Ó Conchobhair, king of the Irish of Connacht, and MacCarthaigh, king of Irish Desmond, also attended. These envoys apparently advised Niall Óg 'strongly not to go to the king', advice that Ó Néill shrewdly decided to ignore.[68] It would have

---

65 Ibid., pp 210–11.   66 83. 20 Feb. 1395, Patent Roll 18 Richard II.   67 Niall Óg Ó Néill to the Archbishop of Armagh, 26 Feb. 1395, in Curtis, 'Letters sent to the king when in Ireland', pp 221–3.   68 Ibid., p. 222.

been greatly to the advantage of the Irish of Connacht and Munster for Richard to become embroiled in a major dispute with Ó Neill in the north of the island. The more intelligent Irish kings must have realized that Richard's time in Ireland was limited and that he must return with his large forces to England sooner rather than later. Niall Óg and his advisors, too, were intelligent men and realized that any conflict with the English king would only benefit the southern Irish kings and not the Ó Néill family and the kingdom of Tyrone. Niall Óg decided to travel south to meet personally with the English monarch.

Niall Óg was still concerned for his personal safety. On 11 March 1395, he wrote a letter to Richard from Armagh stating that he would 'come on Monday next to meet my lord the primate of Armagh in the marches of Dundalk, and on the Tuesday then next following I will, please God, see your gracious face'. Niall Óg asked that the English king 'will deign to send a safe-conduct under your great seal and trustworthy escorts together with the said Lord Primate to meet me at the day and place fixed'.[69]

On 16 March, in the king's rooms in the Dominican priory in Drogheda, in the presence of Richard, Niall Óg Ó Néill took an oath in Irish, translated into English by his secretary, Master Tomás Ó Luchráin, that:

> I, Niall junior, captain of my nation swear to be faithful liegeman of my Lord Richard, King of England and France and Lord of Ireland, my sovereign lord, and of his heirs and successors, being kings of England, from this day henceforth. So help me these God's holy Gospels.[70]

---

69 Niall Óg Ó Néill to Richard II, 11 Mar. 1395, in Curtis, 'Letters sent to the king when in Ireland', p. 208.   70 Notarial Instrument VIII, 16 Mar. 1395, in Curtis,

Niall Óg also agreed that 'if he should violate the said oath, he would pay to the Papal Camera 20,000 marks of English money', again an enormous sum.[71] Although Niall Óg Ó Néill returned safely to Tyrone, Roger Mortimer was dissatisfied with the outcome of the negotiations at Drogheda. This would soon become violently evident to both Richard and Ó Néill.

It was in March 1395 – on Lady Day, 25 March, to be precise – that Froissart set the story of the knighting of four Irish kings (Niall Óg Ó Néill, Art MacMurchadha Caomhánach, Brian Ó Briain and probably Toirdhealbhach Ó Conchobhair Donn) by Richard 'in the cathedral church of Dublin'.[72] It is very unlikely, however, that the ceremony as recounted by Froissart took place in the manner recorded in the chronicle. Cristall's story, as preserved by Froissart, is probably an amalgam of a number of separate knighting ceremonies, involving Niall Óg Ó Néill possibly alongside Brian Ó Briain, the later individual knighting of Toirdhealbhach Ó Conchobhair Donn, but probably no ceremony involving Art MacMurchadha. There is enough circumstantial evidence from other contemporary sources, however, to save Froissart's famous account from being dismissed as a complete fabrication.[73]

Niall Óg Ó Néill appears to have been knighted by Richard in Drogheda, 'knight by your creation – *de vestra creacione miles*', probably on 16 March 1395 when he paid liege homage to Richard. Niall Óg went back to Tyrone after that and was at Lisloney, near Armagh, on the day before the date of Froissart's

'Instruments touching Ireland', p. 159; Niall Óg Ó Néill to Richard II (after 16 Mar. 1395), in Curtis, 'Letters sent to the king when in Ireland', p. 215. 71 Notarial Instrument VIII, 16 Mar. 1395, in Curtis, 'Instruments touching Ireland', p. 160. 72 Froissart, *Chronicles*, p. 416. 73 Johnston, 'Richard II and the submissions of Gaelic Ireland', 1–2; Cosgrove, *Late medieval Ireland*, pp 24–5.

ceremony.[74] Niall Óg Ó Néill's later interaction with de Perellós over Christmas 1397 suggests that the king of Tyrone had indeed been subjected to Cristall's training in how to become an Englishman. This training must have occurred immediately before 16 March, and the Irishman appears to have resented it.[75]

Intriguingly, the Annals of the Four Masters record that 'Niall Óg, the son of Niall, son of Aodh Ó Néill, and Ó Briain, i.e. Brian, the son of Mathghamhain, went into the king of England's house', which suggests that these two Irish kings may possibly have met the English king together.[76] Brian Ó Briain, the king of Thomond, submitted to Richard in Dublin on 1 March 1395.[77] Further circumstantial evidence from English records, however, suggests that he was knighted by Richard along with Ó Néill. Robes for both were paid for at the same time.[78] Nevertheless, if they were both knighted together it must have been in a ceremony that probably took place in Drogheda on 16 March, rather than in Dublin on 25 March.

Although the Annals of the Four Masters record for 1395 that [Art] 'MacMurchadha had gone into the king's house', they add that 'he did not afterwards keep faith with him'.[79] Other contemporary sources suggest that Art MacMurchadha remained aloof from Richard after his release, following his first submission in late October or early November 1394.[80] Indeed, the English monarch may never have had Art within his personal grasp again.

---

74 Curtis, 'Instruments touching Ireland', pp 159–60; ibid., 'Letters sent to the king when in Ireland', pp 213–14.   75 Carpenter, 'The pilgrim from Catalonia/Aragon', p. 111; Curtis, *Richard II in Ireland, 1394–5*, pp 41–3.   76 AFM, 1395. 77 Curtis, 'Instruments touching Ireland', pp 163–4, 181–2.   78 Johnston, 'Richard II and the submissions of Gaelic Ireland', 2; K.R. Mem. Roll 22 R.II, E 159/175, Michaelmas term, *brevia directa baronibus*, m. 31, National Archives, Kew, London.   79 AFM, 1395.   80 Curtis, 'Unpublished letters from Richard II

Toirdhealbhach Ó Conchobhair Donn was knighted by Richard, but this ceremony took place on board a ship in Waterford harbour on 1 May.[81]

The English king regarded his agreements with Niall Mór and Niall Óg Ó Néill as the highlights of his expedition to Ireland in 1394–5. Richard wrote to the archbishop of York in January 1395 to inform him of the success of his meeting with Niall Mór in Drogheda:

> know that on the 20th day of this present month of January there came into our presence in D.[rogheda], our council being around us, The Great O'Neill the father, having sufficient proxy and authority on the part of The Great O'Neill his son, and with all humility kneeling, did liege homage, subjection, and fealty to us, and swore both in his name and in the name of and for his son to be to us loyal and obedient liegeman, and to make up as far as in them lies for all that in which they have offended against us or any of our lieges for all past time.[82]

One of the king's cousins, Edward of Aumerle, the earl of Rutland, presented Richard with a valuable gift of a 'silver cup decorated with a golden beech tree ... at Drogheda' at this time, perhaps in celebration of the accord made with Niall Óg Ó Néill. The cup cost £20 10s.[83] The Ó Néill dynasty was possibly known to some of the ruling elite in late-medieval England. As a result, the fact that Richard had managed to come to an agreement with the two

in Ireland', 291. 81 Curtis, 'Instruments touching Ireland', pp 186–7. 82 Richard II to the archbishop of York, chancellor of England, Jan. 1395, in Curtis, 'Unpublished letters from Richard II in Ireland', 294. 83 J. Stratford, *Richard II and the English royal treasure* (Woodbridge, 2012), pp 25, 83, 87, 192, 309.

Ó Néill kings may have impressed noble opinion in his English kingdom.

On 16 March 1395, again in the Dominican priory in Drogheda, Eoin Maol MacDomhnaill, the constable of Ulster, and Muircheartach MacAonghusa, the king of Iveagh, also submitted to Richard.[84] MacDomhnaill made a fulsome declaration promising to serve Richard whenever and wherever required.[85] MacAonghusa had previously complained to Richard that even after the king's peace had been declared, his lands were being raided by Niall Óg Ó Néill's men, by Ó Néill's brother Cú-Uladh Ruadh, by Ó hAnluain king of Orior and by the men of Edmund Savage.[86] Seán MacMathghamhna, the king of Oriel, submitted to Richard in Drogheda on 10 March 1395, while Adam MacGiolla Mhuire and the galloglass constable MacCába did so on 19 March 1395 in Dundalk.[87] The king of Tyrone's most important sub-chieftain, Maghnus Ó Catháin, the king of Oireacht-Uí-Chatháin, was also in communication with Richard via Archbishop John Colton of Armagh. Ó Catháin was determined that the English king be made aware 'that before that Ó Néill senior returned in peace from the king's land, the men of Edmund Savage preyed my people in five hundred cows'.[88] Ó Catháin added, for the archbishop's information, that 'Ó Néill as he asserts made peace both for himself and his vassals and so it was against the king's

---

84 Notarial Instrument 1, 16 Mar. 1395, in Curtis, 'Instruments touching Ireland', pp 149–51; Notarial Instrument IX, 16 Mar. 1395, ibid., p. 160; Notarial Instrument X, 16 Mar. 1395, ibid., p. 161; Notarial Instrument II, 16 Mar. 1395, ibid., pp 151–2; Nicholls, 'Scottish mercenary kindreds in Ireland and Scotland, 1250–1600', pp 98–9. 85 Notarial Instrument 1, 16 Mar. 1395, in Curtis, 'Instruments touching Ireland', p. 150. 86 Muircheartach MacAonghusa to Richard II (Feb. 1395?), in Curtis, 'Instruments touching Ireland', pp 176–9. 87 Notarial Instrument XXI, 19 Mar. 1395, in Curtis, 'Instruments touching Ireland', pp 184–5. 88 Maghnus Ó Catháin to the Archbishop of Armagh (early

peace that my men were preyed, whereby I humbly beseech your Paternity to see how far you can get assistance for me in the king's court to recover from Johnock MacQuillan, Edmund's man, for the said cows'.[89]

Brian Ó Briain, the king of Thomond, sent letters to Richard in late January 1395 in which he referred to himself as prince of Thomond.[90] Ó Briain must have been using an impressive seal because the notary who took a copy of the letter for the English king made special mention of the wax seal 'containing three leopards'.[91] As I have already mentioned above, Ó Briain travelled to Dublin where he submitted to Richard II on 1 March in the Augustinian abbey of St Thomas the Martyr.[92] In early February Thomas Mowbray had been given a commission by Richard to 'receive in the K.[ing]'s place and name the liege homages of all manner of the K.[ing]'s Irishmen of Thomond, of whatever estate', with James Butler, the earl of Ormond, and Gerald Fitzgerald, the earl of Desmond, to assist him.[93] It must have been the earl marshal who brought Brian Ó Briain back to Richard in Dublin. The king of Thomond, too, agreed to 'bound himself in 20,000 marks of English money', to keep his oath of homage to Richard II, and it was Butler, 'one skilled in the Irish speech', who acted as interpreter on this occasion.[94] Richard also received letters at this time from Tadhg MacCarthaigh, prince of the Irish of Desmond, and from Muircheartach Ó Ceallaigh, the Irish archbishop of Tuam, who assured the English king:

Feb. 1395?), in Curtis, 'Letters sent to the king when in Ireland', pp 220–1. **89** Ibid. **90** Notarial Instrument XIV, 4 Feb. 1395, in Curtis, 'Instruments touching Ireland', pp 163–4. **91** Ibid., p. 164. **92** Notarial Instrument XVIII, 1 Mar. 1395, in Curtis, 'Instruments touching Ireland', pp 181–2; Gwynn and Hadcock, *Medieval religious houses: Ireland*, pp 172–3. **93** 81. 12 Feb. 1395, Patent Roll 18 Richard II. **94** Notarial Instrument XVIII, 1 Mar. 1395, in Curtis,

that since the time when I last left you I have laboured for the good of your realm in Connacht according to my powers and with all remedies known to me, and have sought to bring your lieges and subjects into true obedience and submission.[95]

By the end of March, Richard and the bulk of his army were on the move again, back south through the English areas of Co. Kildare and north Co. Carlow. His destination was Kilkenny, situated in the midst of the large area of English settlement in south-west Leinster and east Munster. On 28 March Richard was at Great Connell (near Newbridge), in mid Co. Kildare, and on the 29 March he was at Castledermot in the south of the county. By the 30th he had reached Carlow.[96] Richard was at Leighlin Bridge on 1 April 1395, and soon after, reached Kilkenny. Once there he took up residence again with the Dominicans 'in the church of the Friars Preacher outside the walls in the suburbs of Kilkenny' – the Holy Trinity priory in Irishtown.[97] His mind had already turned towards his return to England. On 1 April, Sir John Beaumont had been ordered to commandeer 'a certain ship called *La Trinite* of Dublin, which is presently in Eng.[land], as soon as it arrives at the port of Dublin, for the passage of great horses'.[98]

'Instruments touching Ireland', p. 181. **95** Notarial Instrument VII, 8 Mar. 1395, in Curtis, 'Instruments touching Ireland', pp 158–9; Muircheartach Ó Ceallaigh, archbishop of Tuam, to Richard II, 11 Mar. 1395, in Curtis, 'Letters sent to the king when in Ireland', pp 208–9; Curtis, *Richard II in Ireland, 1394–5*, p. 39; A. MacShamnráin, 'Muircheartach (Mauricius, Maurice) Ó Ceallaigh', *DIB*, vii, pp 174–5. **96** Notarial Instrument XXXI, 28 Mar. 1395, in Curtis, 'Instruments touching Ireland', p. 193; Notarial Instrument XXIV, 29 Mar. 1395; ibid., pp 187–8; Notarial Instrument XXVIII, 30 Mar. 1395, ibid., p. 189. **97** Notarial Instrument V, 1 Apr. 1395, in Curtis, 'Instruments touching Ireland', p. 155; Notarial Instrument XXVII, 16 Apr. 1395, ibid., p. 189; Gwynn and Hadcock, *Medieval religious houses: Ireland*, p. 226. **98** 10. 1 Apr. 1395, Close Roll 18 Richard II.

This ship was reserved for Richard's personal use and was directed to wait for him at Waterford.

While in Kilkenny Richard took the submissions of many of the remaining prominent southern and western Irish kings. The major Irish figures from Desmond were brought to the English king by his cousin, Edward of Aumerle, the earl of Rutland.[99] When Tadhg MacCarthaigh Mór submitted to Richard, the southern king also 'bound himself in 20,000 marks' as surety for his future loyalty.[100] On 25 April the warlike chieftain Toirdhealbhach Ó Briain submitted.[101] Richard was in Waterford when he took the submission of the king of the Irish of Connacht, Toirdhealbhach Ó Conchobhair Donn.[102] Ó Conchobhair Donn submitted on behalf of his sub-kings and sub-chieftains, who were from the MacDonnchadha, Ó Dubhda, Ó hEaghra, Ó Gadhra, MacDiarmada, Ó Ceallaigh, Ó Madáin, Ó Maoilriain, Ó hÁinle, Ó Beirn, Ó Flannagáin and Ó Ruairc families.[103] Two Irish bishops – Patrick of Kilfenora and Gregory of Kilmacduagh – who were also present at the ceremony, confirmed that Toirdhealbhach Ó Conchobhair Donn had the authority to represent these families.[104]

In April 1395 Ó Conchobhair Donn wrote what was probably the most colourful letter that Richard received from an Irishman.

99 Edward, earl of Rutland and Cork, to Richard II, 5 Mar. 1395, in Curtis, 'Letters sent to the king when in Ireland', pp 204–5.   100 Notarial Instrument XXX, 6 Apr. 1395, in Curtis, 'Instruments touching Ireland', pp 192–3.   101 Notarial Instrument XXXIII, 25 Apr. 1395, ibid., pp 195–6.   102 Notarial Instrument, 20 Apr. 1395, in Curtis, 'Instruments touching Ireland', p. 179.   103 Ibid., pp 180–1.   104 Ibid., p. 180; the two bishops also declared that Brian Ó Briain, 'Prince of Thomond', who does not appear to have been present on this occasion, 'had power to do liege homage' for his sub-chieftains, listing the MacConmara, MacMathghamhna, Ó Conchobhair of Corcomroe, Ó Lochlainn, Ó Deághaidh and Ó hAichir families. The bishops' statement may have referred retrospectively

Toirdhealbhach had a bitter rivalry with a neighbouring Ó Conchobhair petty king, Toirdhealbhach Ó Conchobhair Ruadh, and was determined not to allow his opponent to gain any advantage over him with the English king. Ó Conchobhair Donn wrote to Richard on 3 April to:

> Let your Majesty know that all the chief Irish of Connacht, a few only excepted, have been up to this, and now are, subject, with the permission of your royal Majesty, to me, as true and lawful heir of my predecessors; to whom formerly your predecessors gave lands and lordships.[105]

Ó Conchobhair Donn continued:

> another of my race, Toirdhealbhach Ruadh by name, wishful with the aid of some Irishmen who have since been expelled by me to appropriate to himself my lordship and that of my ancestors (though he is a bastard and son of a bastard), has aspired to the name and title by which I am called in Irish fashion, that is to say Ó Conchobhair; a man of little power, he possesses some pieces of land with my permission near to my lordship. Please give no credence to his messengers until my coming to you.[106]

Although the aspersions that Toirdhealbhach Ó Conchobhair Donn cast on Toirdhealbhach Ó Conchobhair Ruadh's ancestry and legitimacy were apparently unfounded (Ó Conchobhair Ruadh was actually senior to Ó Conchobhair Donn in the family hierarchy), his letter seems to have had a substantial impact on

to the earlier submission of Ó Briain to Richard in Dublin on 1 Mar. 1395. 105 Notarial Instrument XXXIV, 21 Apr. 1395, in Curtis, 'Instruments touching Ireland', pp 196–7.   106 Ibid., p. 197.

Richard, whose notary recorded the letter as being from 'Theotricus O'Conor, Lord of Connacht, a famous Irishman'.[107] Ó Conchobhair Ruadh may have written a more subdued letter to Richard on 15 April 1395 in which he complained of 'a certain rival of my blood [who] prevents me from coming to your lordship's feet'.[108] Ó Conchobhair Ruadh too requested of the English king 'Therefore I beseech your lordship not to listen to any adversary of mine to my prejudice until my coming to your presence.'[109]

Towards the end of his time in Ireland Richard began to grant vast estates among the Leinster mountains to his favourites and senior noblemen. By then it may have already been evident that there was a large element of unreality to these proceedings. Thomas Mowbray, heir to the lordship of Carlow, was awarded Carlow castle, while the able soldier Janico Dartas was granted a wide section of the southern marches of the vale of Dublin, to be taken from rebellious branches of the Harold and Archbold families.[110] Sir John Beaumont was granted a great estate in north Wexford that stretched

> from the bank of the water of the Slane [the river Slaney] on the south side and from la Blakewatyr of Arklow [now called the Avoca river] on the north side, and from the high sea on the east side and from the bounds of Co.s Carlow and Kildare on the west side ... except the lands ... that belong to the earl of Ormond if he should have any within those boundaries.[111]

107 Ibid., p. 196; Curtis, *Richard II in Ireland, 1394–5*, p. 46.　108 Toirdhealbhach Ó Conchobhair of Connacht to Richard II, 15 Apr. 1395, in Curtis, 'Letters sent to the king when in Ireland', p. 203.　109 Ibid.　110 5. 26 Sept. 1396, Close Roll 20 Richard II; 52. 12 Dec. 1395, Close Roll 18 Richard II.　111 53. 28 Apr. 1395, Patent Roll 18 Richard II.

Dartas wrote with black humour to the bishop of Salisbury in England that:

> our lord the king has granted me a parcel of land in the country of the Irish rebels, which if it were in the parts of London would be worth by the year fifty thousand marks, but by my faith, I have so much trouble holding on to it that I would not like to lead such a life for long for even a quarter of the land.[112]

There were signs that Richard's endeavours in Ireland were in difficulty even before he left the island and returned to England. As already mentioned, following his release after his first submission, Art MacMurchadha remained elusive, despite submitting again on numerous occasions to Richard's senior noblemen. Once Richard's 'wards' were removed from south Leinster after the end of the fighting in the mountains, MacMurchadha had room to manoeuvre again.[113] Art's last submission to Richard occurred on 14 April 1395, when Art met Thomas Mowbray near O'Brennan's cross in north Co. Kilkenny.[114] It is obvious that Art realised that Richard's expedition to Ireland had entered its final phase. Even Art's location in April 1395, in the Irish midlands, with their forested hills, bogs and numerous potential escape routes into Connacht, Munster or Ulster, suggests that he anticipated trouble and did not intend to become trapped by English forces, as had occurred the previous October. Richard made a big effort to cut passes through MacMurchadha's Garryhill and Laveroc forests in early April 1395,

---

112 Janico Dartas to the bishop of Salisbury (after Apr. 1395?), in Curtis, 'Unpublished letters from Richard II in Ireland', 296–7. 113 Lydon, 'Richard II's expeditions to Ireland', 146. 114 Notarial Instrument XXII, 14 Apr. 1395, in

when he ordered the sheriffs of Cos. Dublin, Kildare, Carlow and Waterford, 'and the seneschals and sheriffs of the Cross-lands of the liberties of Kilkenny and Wexford', to assemble 'four men, strong in body, from each carucate of cultivated land ... each with his axe and victuals for eight days', to be 'at the bridge of Leighlin on Tuesday ... there to do what shall be enjoined on behalf of the K.[ing]'.[115]

Richard's agreement with Niall Óg Ó Néill, the king of Tyrone, was also beginning to unravel before he left Ireland. This was because of the opposition of Roger Mortimer, along with many of the local English, to the deal the English king had struck with the ruling family of Tyrone. The first difficulty arose in Dundalk, which was situated on the border with this Irish kingdom. Niall Óg wrote to Richard to complain 'that toll is charged upon my men, *viz.* one penny on every horse in spite of your Majesty's prohibition'.[116] Niall Óg Ó Néill's subsequent letters to the English king record that he felt a major explosion of violence was now imminent between himself and Mortimer. On 14 April 1395 Niall Óg wrote with alarm to Richard that 'I understand from the tidings of some, both English and Irish, that your Lordship intends to take his way to England, and that immediately after your departure the earl of March plans to attack me with his followers'.[117] When Niall Óg wrote a second time to Richard, he again warned that 'it is openly foretold that after your departure my lord the earl of Ulster will wage bitter war against me, and if I make no resistance he will crush me without pity, so it is

Curtis, 'Instruments touching Ireland', pp 185–6.   **115** 65. 4 Apr. 1395, Close Roll 18 Richard II; 66. 4 Apr. 1395, ibid.; 67. 4 Apr. 1395, ibid.   **116** Niall Óg Ó Néill to Richard II (after Mar. 1395?), in Curtis, 'Letters sent to the king when in Ireland', pp 212–13.   **117** Niall Óg Ó Néill to Richard II, 14 Apr. 1395, ibid., p. 205.

believed'.[118] The king of Tyrone clearly recognized the dilemma he was in and he spelt it out for the English monarch, stating:

> Now of the two evils that may befall me I know not without your wise counsel which to choose, for, on the one hand, if I do not resist, in obedience to your Majesty, he will make war on me *à outrance*, and all my supporters will proclaim me dastard [coward]; on the other hand, if I resist him my rivals will say that I have become rebel and traitor to your Majesty, which, God be witness, I never intend to be.[119]

This is an able analysis but Richard does not appear to have responded. By now the English king was being advised to return to England as soon as possible, and he appears to have gone into denial in regard to many of the unresolved Irish problems.

On 1 May 1395 Richard was on board the ship *La Trinite* of Dublin, which was berthed in Waterford harbour, preparing for his return to England. Before he did so he knighted Toirdhealbhach Ó Conchobhair Donn, along with two prominent English nobles from Connacht, William de Burgh and Walter Bermingham, in an elaborate ceremony performed onboard the ship. Much of the detail of the ceremony was recorded. When Ó Conchobhair and the two Englishmen were received by the English king in his cabin they, 'lying prone there did obeisance'. Richard 'desiring that they should not leave him without some gift or honour, created them and belted them knights, and as token of that Order, admitted them to the kiss of peace and granted each of them a sword to be honourably used'. Two bishops were present, the Dominican friar, Robert Rede, bishop of Lismore, and Richard Mitford, bishop of

118 Niall Óg Ó Néill to Richard II (date unknown – Apr. 1395?), ibid., pp 214–16.
119 Ibid., p. 215.

Chichester, as well as Lord Henry Percy and Sir William Arundel. Percy and Arundel 'placed gilded spurs upon' the heels of the three noblemen 'as token of that order'.[120]

Richard set sail for England on 15 May 1395 and landed soon afterwards at Bristol. He had been in his Irish lordship for a little over seven months. He may have cut short his Irish sojourn because of English considerations, particularly because of fears of an upsurge in activity by the Lollards, adherents of a heretical sect in his English kingdom.[121] Regardless of whether this was the real reason, the return of the English king to his home kingdom was inevitable. Some of the Irish annalists regarded Richard's first visit to Ireland as a success. The compiler of the Annals of Saints' Island recorded for 1395 that 'King Richard, i.e. the king of England, went across again [to England] with power and honour from all Irishmen, as he deserved, for there were few men in his time as estimable as he.'[122] This set of annals also noted approvingly that 'The nobles of the Gaels of Ireland submitted, and they all returned safely,' which demonstrates that Richard's honourable treatment of the Irish kings and nobles was recognized and appreciated by the Irish population of the island.[123] The Chronicle of Adam Usk, a contemporary Welsh source written by a supporter of Roger Mortimer, was less congratulatory. Adam Usk wrote of the English king: 'he accomplished little there, however, for although the Irish pretended at the time to submit to his will, as soon as he departed news arrived that they had rebelled.'[124] The Annals of the Four Masters record for 1395 that:

120 Notarial Instrument XXIII, 1 May 1395, in Curtis, 'Instruments touching Ireland', pp 186–7. 121 Curtis, *Richard II in Ireland, 1394–5*, pp 48–9; Hardy (ed.), '156. The year 1395 according to the St Albans Chronicle', *The reign of Richard II*, pp 301–2. 122 ASI, 1395. 123 Ibid. 124 *Chronicle of Adam Usk*, 1395, pp 18–19; *Knighton's Chronicle* is more positive, reporting of Richard's first

The king of the Saxons departed from Ireland in May, after a great number of the foreigners and Gaels of Ireland had gone into his house; and Mortimer was left by the king in Ireland as his representative.[125]

At first glance, Richard II's expedition to Ireland from October 1394 to May 1395 was a great success. Eighty Irish kings and chieftains and gaelicized English lords submitted to the English king while he was on the island.[126] These submissions were from every part of Ireland except the very far north-west and some isolated territories on the Atlantic seaboard. They included every major Irish king in every province, except for Ó Domhnaill, king of Tír Chonaill, Mag Uidhir, king of Fermanagh and Ó Flaithbheartaigh, king of Iar-Chonnacht.[127] Although these submissions compare very favourably to what King Henry II achieved when he visited Ireland in 1171–2, Richard's land grants to English nobles and soldiers were a failure. Henry's grants in the twelfth century transformed many parts of Ireland forever.

Richard's expedition in 1394–5 diminished the power of Art MacMurchadha, the king of the Irish of Leinster, but MacMurchadha was able to thwart the English king's plans to remove him and his warriors to other parts of Ireland. Art was still in south Leinster in May 1395 when Richard sailed back to England. MacMurchadha was also in control of most of his sub-kings and was able to recover his full authority in the Leinster mountains in the years after 1395. Despite being forced to endure months of intense negotiations in Drogheda, the Ó Néill kings of

expedition: 'In AD 1395, about the month of May, King Richard returned from Ireland to England, having subdued the land,' in G.H. Martin (ed.), *Knighton's Chronicle, 1337–96* (Oxford, 1995), 1395, pp 550–1. **125** AFM, 1395. **126** Curtis, *Richard II in Ireland, 1394–5,* p. v. **127** Ibid., pp 48–9.

Tyrone, Niall Mór and Niall Óg, managed to see off Richard II's first expedition to Ireland without any major attack on their own kingdom. The shrewd decision by Niall Óg Ó Néill not to take the advice of the southern Irish in February 1395, when they wanted him to offer resistance to the English king, was crucially important. By negotiating with Richard, Niall Óg Ó Néill saved the kingdom of Tyrone from invasion by a large and capable English army. The warriors of Tyrone could certainly have fought Richard's army from the mountainous and forested interior of their kingdom, but large-scale destruction and loss of life would have occurred in fertile inhabited areas.

The greatest success of Richard's expedition to Ireland in 1394–5 was probably the fact that the English king personally saw and became more aware of the serious plight that many vulnerable English areas were in, in regard to attacks by their Irish neighbours. This growing awareness is evident in the number of small towns – for example, Kinsale, Callan, Galway, Drogheda and Youghal – that were granted permission by Richard in the years after the 1394–5 expedition to retain royal taxes for a set period. These previously had been sent to the central exchequer, but Richard ordered that they be retained by the townsmen to build new walls or repair old, run-down defences.[128]

THE AFTERMATH TO THE FIRST EXPEDITION, 1395–8

Even before Richard left Ireland, Art MacMurchadha was rebuilding his power within the Wicklow mountains. The Ó

128 2. 1 May 1395 [Kinsale], Patent Roll 18 Richard II; 4. 18 Nov. 1395 [Galway], Patent Roll 19 Richard II; 7. 20 Jan. 1396 [Callan], ibid.; 6. 12 Feb. 1397 [Youghal], Patent Roll 20 Richard II; 9. 28 Feb. 1399 [Drogheda], Patent Roll 22 Richard II.

Tuathail chieftain, Feidhlim Ó Tuathail, wrote to the English king while he was still on the island, to complain that 'the Irishmen of Hy Kinsella came against me your subject and preyed me in thirty head of mares out of my stud and carried them off, also they took my son and hold him hostage'.[129] If Ó Tuathail's son was handed over to Art by the raiders then the allegiance of this sub-king may have been won back by MacMurchadha for his kingdom in the Leinster mountains. The Annals of the Four Masters record that soon after the English king returned to England 'The foreigners of Leinster attempted to make MacMurchadha (Art) prisoner, by treachery ... but this was of no avail to them, for he escaped from them by the strength of his arm, and by his valour, so that they were not able to do him any injury'.[130] Although small 'wards' or garrisons were reset about south Leinster, Art must have been successful in reimposing his authority over the Irish of the region.[131] In 1396 Feidhlim Ó Tuathail, the very chieftain MacMurchadha had had to raid the previous year, won a major victory over 'the foreigners of Leinster and the Saxons ... in which the foreigners were dreadfully slaughtered; and six score heads were carried for exhibition before Ó Tuathail, besides a great many prisoners, and spoils of arms, horses, and armour'.[132]

---

129 Feidhlim Ó Tuathail to Richard II (1395?), in Curtis, 'Letters sent to the king when in Ireland', pp 206–7. 130 AFM, 1395. T. D'arcy McGee, *A memoir of the life and conquests of Art MacMurrogh, king of Leinster* (Dublin, 1847), pp 41–3. 131 D. Johnston, 'The interim years: Richard II and Ireland, 1395–99' in Lydon (ed.), *England and Ireland in the later Middle Ages*, pp 176–7; Dr Johnston wrote that Richard's 1394–5 settlement endured for years after his departure from Ireland. My analysis suggests that it was in difficulty in many areas even before he left the island. 132 AFM, 1396; the Annals of Saints' Island state that 'Numerous Welshmen were killed by Ó Tuathail', ASI, 1395; the battle that Henry Marleburrough records for 1398, in which 'on Ascension day, the Tothills slue forty English men. Among them were accounted as principall Iohn Fitzwilliams, Thomas Talbot, and Thomas Comyn', may refer to the same engagement, CIHM, 1398.

There was also much violence in Gaelic Ulster after Richard II left Ireland. Domhnall Bog (the Soft) Ó Néill, one of the many sons of Éinrí Aimhréidh, captured his uncle Niall Óg's eldest son and heir Brian Ó Néill in late 1395.[133] Not content with an attack on the heir apparent, Domhnall Bog continued what must have been a deliberately personal assault on the king of Tyrone, by attacking 'the town of Ó Néill' (probably Dungannon), where he captured Niall Óg's wife Una, the queen of Tyrone. Domhnall Bog handed the royal captives over to the English, which raises the question of whether he was acting on behalf of the earl of March. By 1396 Roger Mortimer was at war with many of the Irish kings of north Leinster and south Ulster. The annals record that in that year he attacked the Clann Sheoáin, a branch of the Ó Fearghail family of Annaly.[134] He also attacked the Ó Raighilligh kingdom of East Breifne, where he cut passes through two forests and killed the noble Mathghamhain Ó Raighilligh.[135]

As noted earlier, even before Richard left the island, Niall Óg Ó Néill had been in dispute with the young earl of March. The main area of contention was Mortimer's claim to be the

---

133 AFM, 1395; Éinrí Aimhréidh Ó Néill died in 1392. The annals give him the title of *ríoghdhamhna*, which was a prestigious one, meaning one eligible for kingship, AU, 1392; AFM, 1392; Simms, *From kings to warlords*, p. 177; the Annals of Clonmacnoise refer to him as 'tanist and next successor of the principality of Ulster, after his brother Neale Oge O'Neale's death (if he had lived)', 1392, p. 315; the Annals of Connacht gave him an impressive obituary, recording that 'Éinrí the Quarrelsome *per antiphrasim*, son of Niall Mór Ó Néill, eligible prince of Ireland *de jure* and undoubtedly destined to be king of Ulster if he had lived, the man who of all the descendants of Niall son of Eochu Muigmedoin was the most generous of rewards and presents, and at another time the most marvellously and extravagantly bountiful, died a good death at the feast of St Brendan,' AC, 1392; the Annals of Saints' Island were less generous, recording that 'Éinrí Aimhréidh Ó Néill, renowned for hospitality and valour, an unjust, wicked, and sinful man, died this year,' ASI, 1392. **134** ASI, 1396. **135** Ibid.

intervening lord between Ó Néill and Richard II. Niall Óg also feared for the safety of his son Feidhlimidh, who was held as a hostage by Mortimer in Trim castle.[136] Niall Óg, possibly owing to his own experience of imprisonment, appeared genuinely to care for the welfare of young family members surrendered as hostages to the English. As a result, he wrote to Richard, urging him 'to entrust the other boy hostages to worthy men, as it was agreed, otherwise all of them will die, since those in whose charge they are care little or nothing for their lives, even as they cared nothing for the lives of the dying who are and have been tortured with divers, dire, and dread torments'.[137] In early 1396 Mortimer 'made a treacherous raid on Ó Néill' before launching a larger assault on Tyrone, accompanied by 'the earl of Ormond, the earl of Kildare, the foreigners of Ireland, and a host of Gaels'.[138] The annals record that 'They went to Armagh [see figure 15], plundered the city, remained a fortnight there, and finally burned it together with the great church of Patrick ... and may God restore it! They turned and took sway over Ulaid after that.'[139] This great raid must have been very destructive for the ecclesiastical settlement of Armagh. As the annals state, Mortimer gained some authority east of the Bann and Lough Neagh, the Ulaid mentioned in the text. In 1396 Niall Óg succeeded in ransoming his son Brian from Domhnall Bog Ó Néill.[140]

Niall Óg's father, the semi-retired Niall Mór Ó Néill, died in 1397. According to the Annals of Ulster the deceased Niall Mór had been 'high-king of Ulster and contender for the kingship of Ireland'.[141] During his long and successful career Ó Néill had

---

136 Niall Óg Ó Néill, captain of his nation, to Richard II, [after Mar. 1395?], in Curtis, 'Letters sent to the king when in Ireland', p. 213.   137 Ibid., pp 213–14.   138 ASI, 1396.   139 Ibid.   140 AFM, 1396.   141 AU, 1397.

demonstrated that he was both a talented warrior and capable negotiator. Shrewd, highly ambitious and ruthless when the circumstances demanded, he could also think strategically and appreciated the value of a hard-won compromise. Loyalty and personal bravery were also evident in his personality. Indeed, he and Art MacMurchadha were probably the two most able Irish kings of the fourteenth century.

By 1398 Niall Óg Ó Néill had the measure of his opponents in west Ulster. He invaded the kingdom of Tír Chonaill, plundered the great Cistercian abbey at Assaroe, and put to flight Toirdhealbhach an Fhiona ('of the Wine') Ó Domhnaill, the king of the territory.[142] Soon afterwards, the annals record that 'the foreigners and Gaels of the fifth of Ulster (Ó Domhnaill only excepted) went into the house of Ó Néill and gave him hostages and other pledges of submission'.[143] Niall Óg Ó Néill was as powerful as he ever had been.

Elsewhere in Ireland during these years Toirdhealbhach Ó Briain was back on the warpath. In 1398 he sacked Mullingar in alliance with '[the people of] south Leinster'.[144] The annals at this time record much fighting between the English and the Irish of Leinster. In 1397 they record: 'an attack by the earl [of March] on the Leinstermen, and he took sway over this side of Leinster'.[145] In 1398 they note another attack on the Leinster Irish by the English of Dublin.[146] That was the same year the ancient monastery of Glendalough was finally destroyed for good in an English raid. The Annals of Connacht state that 'Glendalough was burned by Englishmen and Irish foreigners again this summer', and the monastery was sacked and subsequently abandoned. The

---

142 AFM, 1398; AC, 1398; Gwynn and Hadcock, *Medieval religious houses: Ireland*, p. 127.   143 AFM, 1398.   144 ASI, 1398.   145 Ibid., 1397.   146 Ibid., 1398.

manuscript known as the Drummond Missal may have been taken as plunder from Glendalough at this time.[147]

Relations between the Irish and the English broke down long before those between Richard II personally and the Irish kings. In November 1395 the English king wrote to Niall Óg Ó Neill, inviting the king of Tyrone to visit England and meet him at Westminster.[148] The violence in Tyrone in late 1395 as well as Roger Mortimer's attacks on Ó Néill in 1396, however, prevented this. The news that Mortimer openly attacked Niall Óg Ó Néill in late 1396, in what appears to have been a major raid, must have been very disheartening for Richard. In 1397 Roger Mortimer's uncle, Sir Thomas Mortimer, fell foul of the king in some palace intrigue and fled to Ireland in fear for his life.[149] The Welsh chronicler Adam Usk recounts that when the earl of March later attended parliament in England in 1398, 'He bore himself carefully and with discretion'. Usk adds that:

> the king, and others who took his side, envying the earl's good character, set traps for him, searching out excuses to proceed against him; but he feigned indifference towards the misfortunes of the people, pretending when he was with the king that he approved of what he did, whereas in fact he strongly disapproved of it. Nevertheless the king remained suspicious and hostile towards him, planning to put him to death ... and continually seeking a chance to destroy him.[150]

---

147 AC, 1398; AFM, 1398; *Annals of Clonmacnoise*, 1398, p. 321; S.C. Casey, 'Glendalough: liturgy and music' in C. Doherty, L. Doran and M. Kelly (eds), *Glendalough: City of God* (Dublin, 2011), p. 243.   148 Johnston, 'The interim years: Richard II and Ireland, 1395–99', p. 180; letter from Richard II concerning, among other matters 'macmourgh & le grand Onel', British Library, Cotton MS Titus B XI, one of the documents numbered 7.   149 *Chronicle of Adam Usk*, 1397, pp 26–33, 40–1; ASI, 1397.   150 *Chronicle of Adam Usk*, 1398, pp 39–41.

Mortimer returned to Ireland still Richard's lieutenant for the island. The English king planned to replace him with his nephew Thomas Holland, who by 1398 had been given the title duke of Surrey. Holland was appointed on 26 July 1398.

Events in Ireland, however, had outpaced those at the English court. On 20 July 1398, Roger Mortimer had given battle to Feidhlim Ó Tuathail, the king of Imaal, and to the Ó Broin chieftain, at Kells, a prominent hill now called Kellistown, close to Carlow.[151] The Ó Nualláin and MacDaibhéid Mór chieftains, as well as 'Mortagh McLoaghlen capitaneum turbariorum McMurchardi – Muircheartach MacLochlainn, captain of the kerne of MacMurchadha', may also have fought alongside Ó Broin and Ó Tuathail in this battle.[152] According to Adam Usk, Mortimer 'through an excess of military ardour which led him rashly to advance in front of his own troops, he fell amidst the ranks of his enemies and was killed, to the great distress of the English kingdom'.[153] The Irish annals add that many local English were also killed, in what was a major victory for the Irish of the Wicklow mountains and their allies.[154] The statement by the later Annales Breves Hiberniae that Mortimer's mother 'gave two chalices, one to Myshall, the other to Garryhill, to have him alive or dead to convey into England', is corrupt in that Mortimer's mother Philippa had died in 1378. Perhaps Mortimer's

---

151 O'Toole, 'The parish of Ballon, County Carlow', 261–74; there has been a lot of confusion among modern historians as to the location of this battle. Edward O'Toole's 1933 article, however, makes a very strong case for it to have taken place in north Co. Carlow. In fact, the battle of 1398, if located here correctly, was the third battle to take place on this prominent hill-top since ancient and earlier medieval times.   152 Annales Breves Hiberniae, 1397 [recte: 1398]: http://www.ucc.ie/celt/published/L100012/index.html, accessed 9 Mar. 2015. 153 Chronicle of Adam Usk, 1398, pp 40–1; O'Byrne, War, politic and the Irish of Leinster, p. 112.   154 AFM, 1398; Annals of Clonmacnoise, 1398, p. 320.

wife Eleanor Holland, the king's niece, is intended.[155] Art MacMurchadha's absence from the battle of Kells, although many of his sub-chieftains and apparently also the captain of his kerne fought alongside Ó Tuathail and Ó Broin, suggests that MacMurchadha may have been directing the war against the earl of March from behind the scenes. Perhaps in an effort to prevent a complete breach with Richard, Art left command of the actual battle at Kells to Feidhlim Ó Tuathail, who after himself was the most capable military leader among the Leinster Irish. If this was in fact the case the plan failed, owing to Mortimer's death.

155 Annales Breves Hiberniae, 1397 [recte: 1398]; O'Toole, 'The parish of Ballon, County Carlow', 268; Eleanor was the daughter of the king's half-brother, Thomas Holland, the earl of Kent; Beresford, 'Roger Mortimer', p. 709.

CHAPTER 5

Richard's second expedition to Ireland, June–July 1399

Muircheartach Ó Cuindilis inscribed this, two years after the king of the Saxons was dethroned by the earl [recte: duke] of Hereford [*le hiarla darriffed*].[1]

The defeat and death of the earl of March had a substantial impact on the English colony and at court in England. One of Richard's most powerful nobles, Mortimer was a cousin of the king, and he had also been the primogenitary heir to the English throne.[2] As a result, although personally Richard may not have sincerely mourned his cousin's untimely demise, the death of the still young earl at the hands of the Ó Tuathail and Ó Broin chieftains was one

---

1 Note written by Ó Cuindilis in 1401 into a section of the composite Irish manuscript now known as the Yellow Book of Lecan, TCD MS 1318, Col. 320, large note at end of column; there may be a second reference to Richard II below Col. 332, where Ó Cuindilis again gives his name as the scribe of this part of the manuscript. 2 This was through his mother Philippa, who was the daughter of Lionel, duke of Clarence, the most senior son of King Edward III, after Richard's own father, Edward, the Black Prince (C. Given-Wilson (ed.), *Chronicles of the revolution, 1397–1400* (Manchester, 1993), pp 6–7).

of the major catalysts for Richard's second expedition to Ireland in
1399. Richard, regardless of his personal opinion of Roger
Mortimer, may have been compelled by outraged opinion at court
to promptly exact revenge from the Irish of Leinster. The English
king also appears to have been genuinely proud of his achievements
in Ireland in 1394–5. The unravelling of many of the agreements
with the Irish kings in the years since must have been very
frustrating for him. He had also been constrained in how much he
could do to ensure that the royal agreements with the Irish kings
were given the opportunity to settle down and endure because he
was no longer present on the island in person.[3] Richard, due to the
relative ease of his complete victory over Art MacMurchadha and
the Irish of Leinster in late 1394, may have returned to Ireland in
1399 with dangerously erroneous assumptions about the military
capabilities of the Irish kings. He seems to have underestimated
MacMurchadha. It was the Irish king who was to prove that it was
he who had learned the important lessons from the few days of
fighting that had occurred in the early winter of 1394.

The second English expedition to Ireland in 1399 was again
organized on a huge scale, with comparable numbers of great
nobles, household retainers and Cheshire archers from the king's
bodyguard to those in 1394–5.[4] Creton recorded ships at Milford
Haven loading 'bread, wine, cows, and calves, salt meat, and plenty
of water'.[5] Although a great deal of supplies and equipment were
taken to Ireland by Richard's army in 1399, commissariat
arrangements may not have been as well organized as they had
been for the first expedition. Among the important nobles brought
to Ireland on this occasion by the king were many veterans of the

3 Johnston, 'Richard II and Ireland', p. 190.   4 Saul, *Richard II*, p. 289.   5 Creton,
'A French metrical history', 22.

first expedition to the island. These included the king's half-brother, John Holland, the duke of Exeter; Sir Thomas Percy, the earl of Worcester and steward to the king; John Montagu, the earl of Salisbury; and Sir Thomas Despenser, the earl of Gloucester. The king's cousin, Edward, duke of Aumerle, another veteran of the 1394–5 campaign, arrived in Ireland late during the 1399 campaign. The king's nephew, Thomas Holland, the duke of Surrey, was already in Ireland in 1399, along with sizeable numbers of troops, having been appointed lieutenant of Ireland by Richard the previous year. Richard also brought Henry (the future King Henry V, who was only thirteen), the son of the exiled duke of Hereford, with him, as well as Humphrey, the son of his murdered uncle, Thomas of Woodstock, the duke of Gloucester. No doubt this was done by the king to ensure the security of the kingdom of England while he was in Ireland.[6] Many English bishops, assorted clergy, members of the king's household and various hangers-on, such as Creton, looking for an exotic adventure, also accompanied Richard.[7]

Richard had the opportunity to visit Ireland again in 1399 owing to his success in either destroying or exiling his opponents over the preceding few years. As a result, he felt that he could campaign in Ireland, safe in the assumption that he was in complete control of his English kingdom. Richard was soon to discover that his hold over England was not so unassailable as he believed. He apparently intended to spend a long period in Ireland, perhaps even as much as a full year. This might explain the haphazard nature of the early English commissariat measures. Richard and his advisors expected to sort out any early problems over the course of the first weeks. Richard left £40,000 in Holt

6 Ibid.   7 Ibid., 13–22.

castle in the principality of Cheshire to draw on when needed while he was in Ireland. Creton states that 'it contained a hundred thousand marks sterling in gold, and upwards, which King Richard caused to be treasured up there'.[8] He also appears to have taken over £14,000 with him to Ireland, which he put for safe keeping into Trim castle.[9]

The fleet in which Richard II sailed to Ireland was estimated at two hundred ships, which may have been smaller than the fleet of 1394.[10] As a result, the number of troops who accompanied the English king over to Ireland on this occasion may have been smaller than the number that came with the fleet of 1394. Richard, however, had been building up English troop numbers in the lordship of Ireland in the months before he set sail for it, and when all were assembled 'probably produced a total ... army of nine or ten thousand men'.[11] This was equal to or even slightly larger than the estimated size of his army in 1394–5. The compositions of some of the contingents in Richard's army in 1399 raised by his major noblemen have been recorded. John Holland, the duke of Exeter, raised 140 men-at-arms and 500 archers; Sir Thomas Despenser, the earl of Gloucester, raised thirty-five men-at-arms and 100 archers; Sir Thomas Percy, the earl of Worcester, raised thirty-six men-at-arms and 100 archers; Thomas Holland, the duke of Surrey, joined the king with 150 men-at-arms and 800 archers; Edward, the duke of Aumerle, who arrived late, eventually joined Richard with 140 men-at-arms and 800 archers.[12]

8 Ibid., 124.   9 D. Biggs, *Three armies in Britain: the Irish campaign of Richard II and the usurpation of Henry IV, 1397–9* (Leiden, 2006), p. 44.   10 Holinshead, *Chronicles*, The History of Ireland, 3.3, Richard II; Biggs, *Three armies in Britain: the Irish campaign of Richard II*, p. 54; CIHM, 1399.   11 Biggs, *Three armies in Britain: the Irish campaign of Richard II*, p. 46.   12 Ibid., 'Appendix I: Richard II's army, royalist portion', 1399, p. 63.

Richard landed at Waterford on 1 June 1399. As in 1394, his fleet had a smooth sailing over to Ireland. The king wrote that 'we have arrived at our city of Waterford the first day of this present month [June], and have had the weather and the crossing by divine grace so favourable that no one can remember so benign a passage.'[13] According to Creton, Richard spent six days organizing at Waterford before 'He took the field ... with the English, who rode boldly in close order to Kilkenny, eighty miles up the country, in the neighbourhood of the enemy.'[14] Once at Kilkenny, Richard spent a fortnight waiting for the arrival of his cousin, Edward, duke of Aumerle, who was supposed to follow with a substantial part of the army. The duke had business to conclude on the Scottish border and did not land in Ireland while Richard was at Kilkenny.[15]

Nevertheless, the English king decided to strike out into the Leinster mountains to attack Art MacMurchadha. Creton states that 'Every man at the outset had made the best provision that he could of bread, wine, and corn', and that the English army marched out of Kilkenny city on 23 June 1399.[16] Art MacMurchadha 'had with him, according to report, three thousand hardy men. Wilder people I never saw; they did not appear to me to be much dismayed at the English.'[17] Art let it be known to Richard that he:

> would neither submit, nor obey him in any way, but affirmed that he was the rightful king of Ireland, and that he would never cease from war and the defence of his country till his

13 Richard II to Edmund, duke of York, regent of England, 1399, in Curtis, 'Unpublished letters from Richard II in Ireland', 298.   14 Creton, 'A French metrical history', 23.   15 Ibid., 23–4; Johnston, 'Richard II's departure from Ireland, July 1399', 788–9.   16 Creton, 'A French metrical history', 25–7. 17 Ibid., 28.

death; he said that the wish to deprive him of it by conquest was unlawful.[18]

As the English army marched into, 'the entrance of the deep woods', MacMurchadha's warriors disappeared into the forest and, 'the Irish did not shew themselves on this occasion.'[19]

Richard initially thought that his second expedition was going very well. In a letter to his uncle, Edmund of Langley, the duke of York and regent of England, the English king stated that 'We have had a very good beginning, trusting in the Almighty that He will lead us, and that shortly, to a good conclusion of our undertaking.'[20] According to the letter, the king's nephew, Thomas Holland, the duke of Surrey, had taken 'a prey of a great number of beasts', which must have been a severe blow to MacMurchadha.[21] Art again may have made a grave error in the early fighting against Richard, when he allowed a large force he was leading to be caught out in the open. According to the Annals of Connacht, 'MacMurchadha made an expedition, and the foreigners of Leinster and Meath and a large body of the English army came up with him.' The annals continue: 'MacMurchadha's hired troops were slaughtered.'[22] As discussed in Chapter 2, even very large forces of Irish kerne (large numbers of kerne hired from the Irish midlands formed the majority of MacMurchadha's casualties on this occasion), were no match for well-armed and armoured English soldiers. As a result, Art must have known he was in difficulty the moment his opponents caught up with his raiding force. That MacMurchadha successfully managed to escape

18 Ibid., 27.   19 Ibid., 28.   20 Richard II to Edmund, duke of York, regent of England, 1399, in Curtis, 'Unpublished letters from Richard II in Ireland', 298. 21 Ibid.   22 AC, 1398 (recte: 1399); ALC, 1398 (recte: 1399).

suggests that he knew better than to stand and fight on this particular occasion. This major defeat may be the encounter referred to in the letter written by Richard in 1399 that occurred early in the campaign. According to the English king it was Thomas Holland who had surprised MacMurchadha and Ó Broin, 'wherein were killed of them 157 armed men and kernes'.[23] The English king pursued a scorched earth campaign in the Leinster mountains and gave orders 'that everything around should be set fire to: this resolve of burning was to weaken the power of the Irish: many a village and house were then consumed.'[24] Perhaps Richard was attempting to lead a *chevauchée* through MacMurchadha's lands. While encamped in the forests, Richard knighted his thirteen-year-old relative Henry. Creton states that the English king knighted between eight and ten other nobles at the same time in order to give greater dignity to the occasion (see figure 21).[25]

By the time the knighting ceremony took place, Creton states that 'melancholy, uneasiness and care, had ... chosen my heart for their abode.'[26] If these sentiments were representative of the entire royal army, then by this stage in the march through the Leinster mountains, things were not going well for the English. Richard's army appears to have entered difficult terrain and within a very short period was struggling badly.[27] Creton noted the reason for the alarming deterioration in the position of the English army. He states:

23 Richard II to Edmund, duke of York, regent of England, 1399, in Curtis, 'Unpublished letters from Richard II in Ireland', 298; CIHM, 1399.   24 Creton, 'A French metrical history', 28.   25 Ibid., 30–1.   26 Ibid., 31–2.   27 J.F. Lydon wrote that in 1399 Richard 'tried to bulldoze his way through Leinster with the whole army', in Lydon, 'Richard II's expeditions to Ireland', 147.

for there were then no roads, neither could any person, however he might be furnished with bold and valiant men, find a passage, the woods were so dangerous. You must know that it is so deep in many places that, unless you are very careful to observe where you go, you will plunge in up to the middle, or sink in altogether.[28]

According to the Frenchman, however, 'two thousand five hundred of the well affected people resident in the country', suddenly turned up 'to fell the woods great and small' and fortunately freed the king's army. Creton adds 'Thus we passed straight through the woods, for the Irish were much afraid of our arrows.'[29]

MacMurchadha's warriors were getting used to fighting the English soldiers and were becoming more successful in their skirmishing. According to Creton 'Very frequently they assailed the vanguard, and threw their darts with such force that they pierced haubergeon and plates through and through.'[30] The Leinster Irish were using some classic guerrilla tactics that were often used by Irish forces when faced by large English armies. In particular, Art appears to have used his mobile and well-equipped horsemen to isolate Richard's camps:

Many English stragglers they put to death, when parties went out to forage without waiting for the [proper] hour, or the hoisting of the standard. For the horses of the country scour the hills and valleys fleeter than a bounding deer; wherefore they did much mischief to the army of the king.[31]

---

28 Creton, 'A French metrical history', 32.   29 Ibid., 32–3.   30 Ibid., 33–4. 31 Ibid., 34. Although I dislike comparing aspects of medieval history to modern events, there is one good parallel that I can think of for the almost unbelievable deterioration in the position of Richard II's immense army in the forests and

Nevertheless, MacMurchadha did not have it all his own way. Even while the Leinster Irish were gaining the upper hand in the fighting with the English in the forests and mountains, Art's uncle went into the English camp 'afraid of his life ... with a halter about his neck, and a drawn sword in his hand, to throw himself at the feet of the king and sue for mercy'. MacMurchadha's uncle was accompanied by 'a great many others of his retinue naked [unarmoured] and barefoot'.[32] On a personal level Richard II could often be merciful and forgiving, and true to form, he pardoned this group of Irishmen 'upon condition that each of you will swear to be faithful to me for the time to come'.[33] When the king sent word to Art 'that if he would come straight-ways to him, with a rope about his neck, as his uncle had done, he would admit him to mercy, and elsewhere give him castles and lands in abundance', Richard encountered an Irish king who would not be humiliated in such a fashion.[34] According to Creton, Art 'told the king's people that he would do no such thing for all the treasure of the sea, or on this side [of the sea], but would continue to fight and harass him'.[35]

Removing all food supplies from the reach of the English army appears to have been a deliberate and successful tactic used by

mountains of south Leinster in the early summer of 1399. This is a comparison with the destruction of Soviet armoured columns in the forested wildernesses of the Finnish frontier during the Winter War of 1939–40. In 1939 elite divisions of the Red Army could leave Leningrad and be destroyed within a few days, soon after crossing the border into Finland, often by numerically very inferior Finnish forces. The Finns used local knowledge, access to winter shelter and traditional survival skills to first stop Red Army columns with roadblocks on the isolated forest tracks. The Soviet columns were then broken up and finally destroyed piecemeal in the fierce fighting that ensued. In 1939–40 most of the trapped Red Army soldiers froze to death. In 1399 Art MacMurchadha opted to let hunger do this work for him.
32 Creton, 'A French metrical history', 34–5.   33 Ibid., 35.   34 Ibid.   35 Ibid.

MacMurchadha in 1399. Creton recognized this, writing that 'he made them [the English] suffer much pain and grief with hunger.'[36] The French chronicler adds tellingly 'Full well he [Art MacMurchadha] knew that the English had little to eat; nothing was to be got; not even a pennyworth was to be bought by anyone who had not brought it with him.'[37] The Frenchman continued 'I really witnessed that on some days five or six of them [English soldiers] had but a single loaf; some there were, even gentlemen, knights, and squires, who did not eat a morsel for five days together.'[38]

While MacMurchadha appears to have learnt from the mistakes he had made during the fighting with Richard's army in October 1394 – for example, in 1399 he did not allow himself to be cornered in the forests of Co. Carlow – Richard and his advisors seemed to have forgotten many of the measures that had made the 1394–5 expedition to Ireland such a success. In particular, in 1399 Richard does not appear to have set wards about the Leinster mountains as he had in 1394, with the result that MacMurchadha could move about the Wicklow and Blackstairs mountain ranges with ease. The fact that the English army ran out of supplies in 1399 confirms that supply arrangements made for the second expedition were not so good as those made for the first. Creton states that the royal army was blockaded for:

> eleven days, unable to find anything, save only a few green oats for the horses, which being frequently lodged in the open air, [exposed] to rain and wind, were quite faint; and many of them perished of hunger. No one would believe the distress of the men, high and low; nor the evil that the English endured.[39]

36 Ibid.   37 Ibid.   38 Ibid.   39 Ibid.

It must have been very unsettling for the English king and his soldiers to find themselves in the position whereby, having just commenced the campaign and marched into the Leinster mountains, the entire army was suddenly starving and being picked off in small groups as foragers left camp. Richard and his commanders may have realized that they could be in serious difficulty if they were not extremely careful from then on. Perhaps for the first time, Richard may have become aware of the ability of his Irish opponent.

By now Richard and his army were somewhere along the south Leinster coast, possibly near Brittas Bay or one of the other sandy beaches close to Arklow. Creton states that 'The army could on no account have remained there any longer.'[40] Three merchant ships, however, arrived from Dublin to sell supplies to the starving English soldiers (see figure 22). Creton records very unruly scenes on the beach when the English soldiers:

> rushed into the sea, as they would into [their bed of] straw; everyone spent his halfpenny or penny for himself, some in eating, others in drinking ... I believe there were more than a thousand men drunk on that day, seeing that the wine was of Ossey and Spain ... Many a cuff and blow passed between them.[41]

Richard may have watched the discipline of his army disappear on the beach. In any event, he called his campaign off and returned to Dublin the next day.[42]

It was at this moment that Art MacMurchadha sent 'a begging friar' (a Franciscan, perhaps) to Richard:

40 Ibid., p. 36.   41 Ibid., pp 36–7.   42 Ibid., p. 37; CIHM, 1399.

saying that he wished to be friends with him, and with clasped hands to sue for mercy; [requesting] that at least he would send to him some lord who might be relied upon to treat of peace, so that their anger, which had long been cruel, might all be extinguished.[43]

Richard sent Sir Thomas Despenser, the earl of Gloucester, who 'took with him the whole of the rearguard ... they were two hundred lancers, and a thousand archers' to parley with the Irish king.[44] Creton wrote that 'I went with them, as one desirous of seeing the honour, condition, force, and power of Macmore.'[45] Creton's description of the meeting between the earl of Gloucester and Art MacMurchadha (see figure 23) is one of the most famous passages of any text that deals with late-medieval Ireland. It states:

Between two woods, at some distance from the sea, I beheld Macmore and a body of the Irish, more than I can number, descend the mountain. He had a horse without housing or saddle, which was so fine and good, that it had cost him, they said, four hundred cows; ... In coming down it galloped so hard, that, in my opinion, I never, in all my life, saw hare, deer, sheep, or any other animal, I declare to you for a certainty, run with such speed, as it did. In his right hand he bore a great long dart, which he cast with much skill. ... But his people drew up in front of the wood. These two, like an outpost, met near a little brook. There Macmore stopped. He was a fine large man, wondrously active. To look at him, he seemed very stern and savage, and an able man. He and the earl spake of their doing, recounting the evil and injury that Macmore had

43 Creton, 'A French metrical history', 37.   44 Ibid, 37–9.   45 Ibid., 39.

done towards the king at sundry times; and how they all forswore their fidelity, when wrongfully, without judgment or law, they most mischievously put to death the courteous earl of March. Then they exchanged much discourse, but did not come at last to agreement; they took short leave, and hastily parted. Each took his way apart.[46]

Richard was outraged when he was later told MacMurchadha's conditions. According to the earl of Gloucester, Art had asked 'for pardon, truly, upon condition of having peace without reserve, free from any molestation or imprisonment. Otherwise he will never come to agreement as long as he lives.'[47] Creton recorded that:

> This speech was not agreeable to the king; it appeared to me that his face grew pale with anger: he sware in great wrath by Saint Edward, that, no, never would he depart from Ireland, till, alive or dead, he had him [MacMurchadha] in his power.[48]

MacMurchadha had also apparently said 'nothing venture nothing have', as his parley with the earl of Gloucester ended.[49]

Soon after the English army reached Dublin, Richard 'caused three companies of men ... well appointed to go in quest of him [MacMurchadha]'.[50] At the same time Richard put a bounty of 'a hundred marks in pure gold' on Art's head.[51] As Creton noted, 'The king could not forget Macmore.'[52] The English king also appears to have realized, after his march through the Leinster mountains, that he had chosen the wrong time of year to attack MacMurchadha. This can be gleaned from another statement by

46 Ibid., 39–42.   47 Ibid., 43.   48 Ibid., 43–4.   49 Ibid., 43.   50 Ibid., 45.
51 Ibid.   52 Ibid.

the king that Creton overheard while they were in Dublin. Richard is recorded as asking God to give him 'good health, till the season of autumn be gone by, when the trees are stripped and bare of their leaves, [then] he would burn all the woods great and small'.[53] The fighting in the Leinster mountains was now largely over and it was Art MacMurchadha, the Irish king of the region, who had had the best of it. MacMurchadha had learnt from the mistakes he had made during Richard's first campaign in October 1394 and successfully turned the tables on the English king in 1399. It was an outstanding achievement by the standards of late-medieval Irish kingship.

While Richard II was campaigning in Leinster, Niall Óg Ó Néill, the king of Tyrone, remained aloof from any engagement with the English king either militarily or diplomatically. The Annals of the Four Masters record that in early 1399, probably before Richard came to Ireland, Niall Óg Ó Néill led his warriors to attack the surviving English districts of what had been the earldom of Ulster.[54] These annals also record that the sons of Éinrí Aimhréidh Ó Néill made an attack the same year on Dundalk, possibly while Richard was on the island. However, the sons of Éinrí Aimhréidh were heavily defeated and the leading son, Domhnall Bog, captured.[55] The annals add that 'Domhnall [Bog] was sent to Saxony [the word used for England in the text is '*Saxaibh*'] in the following year, after his ransom had been refused.'[56] Elsewhere in Ireland, while Richard was there, the situation was generally quiet. Brian Ó Briain, the king of Thomond, died in 1399. The Annals of Clonmacnoise state that Ó Briain 'numbered amongst the best princes of Ireland'.[57] The

---

53 Ibid.   54 AFM, 1399.   55 Ibid.   56 Ibid.   57 *Annals of Clonmacnoise*, 1399, p. 322; AFM, 1399; AC, 1399; AU, 1400 (recte: 1399).

great warrior, Toirdhealbhach Ó Briain, the son of Murchadh na Raithnighe who was based just over the river Shannon from Thomond, also died in 1399.[58] It was a year of plague in Ireland, perhaps brought to the island by Richard's army.[59] Among the many killed in the outbreak was Cú-Uladh Ruadh Ó Néill, the brother of the king of Tyrone, whom the Annals of Clonmacnoise record as being 'a great benefactor of the professions of Irish poetry and music'.[60]

On the same day that Richard sent his three columns into the Wicklow mountains to hunt for Art MacMurchadha, Edward, duke of Aumerle, finally landed in Ireland with a large force of well-equipped soldiers.[61] Although Creton is most likely mistaken in attributing treacherous motives to Aumerle's actions at this time, according to the French chronicler, 'Many a time did he [Richard] ask him [Aumerle] "Constable, where tarried you so long that you came no sooner to us?"' Creton states that the duke made an excuse that was acceptable to the king.[62] The king's army replenished itself at Dublin, where there was 'such great abundance of merchandise and provisions, that it was said, that neither flesh, nor fish, bread-corn nor wine, nor other store, was any dearer, for all the army of the king'.[63] I am uncertain as to how much store can be put by Creton's ominous statement that:

> full six weeks very pleasantly passed away [at Dublin], without hearing any certain tidings from England; for no peril or pain that could be undergone could bring vessels of any size over in safety; so contrary was the wind in all

---

58 AC, 1399; AFM, 1399; AU, 1400 (recte: 1399).   59 ALC, 1398 (recte: 1399).
60 *Annals of Clonmacnoise*, 1399, p. 322; AFM, 1399; AU, 1400 (recte: 1399).
61 Creton, 'A French metrical history', 45.   62 Ibid., 45.   63 Ibid., 44.

quarters, and so outrageous a tempest on the sea, that, to my thinking, our Lord was wroth with the king.[64]

This sentence appears suspiciously similar to Gerald of Wales' chapter 'De Tempestatibus' or 'Storms', in his *Expugnatio Hibernica* or *The conquest of Ireland*, in which King Henry II appears similarly cut off from news from his other dominions while in Ireland during the winter of 1171–2.[65] Although an impression of a stormy summer in the Irish Sea may be intended, Richard's cousin, the duke of Aumerle, and subsequent intelligence updates from England, do not appear to have been unduly delayed by bad weather.

Around 10 July 1399, a ship crossed the Irish Sea and Richard received unsettling news from England.[66] His cousin Henry, duke of Hereford, the son of the king's recently deceased uncle John of Gaunt, had returned from exile in France and landed at the Humber estuary in Yorkshire.[67] Henry was the closest heir to the English throne by male descent, and, although he landed with only a small group of followers, he was soon joined by large numbers of supporters.[68] (His family had had extensive estates in the Yorkshire region of England.) Richard had exiled the duke of Hereford from the kingdom of England in 1398 for ten years. His exile was caused by a dispute with Richard's former friend and ally, Thomas Mowbray, who had been so effective on the king's first expedition to Ireland. Richard had created Mowbray duke of Norfolk (his previous title had been earl of Nottingham). Relations between the

---

64 Ibid., 45–6; Johnston, 'Richard II's departure from Ireland', 787–90. 65 Scott and Martin (eds), *Expugnatio Hibernica: the conquest of Ireland*, pp 102–3. 66 Creton, 'A French metrical history', 46. 67 Saul, *Richard II*, p. 409; *Chronicle of Adam Usk*, 1399, pp 52–3. 68 Given-Wilson (ed.), *Chronicles of the revolution, 1397–1400*, pp 41–3.

English king and the duke of Norfolk later deteriorated, possibly because of the murky involvement of both in the murder in Calais in 1397 of Richard's uncle, Thomas of Woodstock, the duke of Gloucester, another veteran of the first Irish campaign.[69] The dispute between Henry and Mowbray grew out of Mowbray's growing fear of the king and famously came to a trial by battle held in Coventry on 16 September 1398. The two dukes faced each other across the lists, on horseback, in their finest specially imported European armour, before Richard called the impending duel off in front of a large crowd of spectators (see figure 20).[70] Thomas Mowbray was exiled from England for life and died of the plague in Venice in 1399.[71]

Richard miscalculated in early 1399 following the death of Henry's father, John of Gaunt, the duke of Lancaster.[72] The English king revised Henry's period of exile to one of perpetual banishment and also confiscated the vast Lancastrian estates. Noble opinion in England, which was already sympathetic to the duke of Hereford, swung heavily in his favour due to the perceived injustice of the king's actions towards him. A natural fear for the security of their own estates also arose among these same people, owing to Richard's arbitrary confiscation of the Lancastrian inheritance. As a result, a dangerous climate of support for Henry developed in many parts of England, which the duke of Hereford ably capitalized on once he was back.

Initially, Richard and his close advisors were undaunted by the news from England, and 'Now they agreed on a Saturday, to put to sea on the next Monday, without waiting longer than a day and a

---

69 Saul, *Richard II*, 378–9; Given-Wilson, *Henry IV*, pp 106–15.   70 Saul, *Richard II*, pp 395 and 400; Given-Wilson, *Henry IV*, pp 113–15.   71 Given-Wilson (ed.), *Chronicles of the revolution, 1397–1400*, p. 24.   72 Saul, *Richard II*,

half.'[73] Creton records that the king's cousin, Edward, duke of Aumerle, privately caused the king to change his mind and delay his departure.[74] Richard almost certainly was short of shipping and as a result took the duke of Aumerle's advice.[75] Creton's assertion, however, that the duke deliberately sabotaged the king's early return to England, is probably not correct.[76] The new plan was to send John Montagu, the earl of Salisbury, on ahead to raise north Wales and Cheshire for Richard, while the king himself went to Waterford to gather his army there and then return to his English kingdom. When the earl of Salisbury sailed for Wales, Creton records that Montagu 'had earnestly prayed for me to go over with him, for the sake of merriment and song, and thereto I heartily agreed'.[77] Creton and the earl of Salisbury landed at Conway (see figure 24), which was a well fortified town.[78] Richard promised the earl that he would follow within a week.[79]

The king had to return to his English kingdom quickly. Henry had already seized control of much of it.[80] When the duke captured the city of Bristol on 29 July 1399, he struck a major blow against Richard, as he cut off one of the major routes for the king's return.[81] Henry then advanced on Richard's second possible major point of re-entry into England: the port of Chester, situated near the north-west coast. The principality of Cheshire was also the strongest centre of support for Richard in his entire English kingdom. While marching to Chester, Henry allowed his large army to plunder the principality 'because, siding with the king ... it had, for two years, ceaselessly inflicted murders, adulteries,

---

p. 403; *Chronicle of Adam Usk*, 1399, pp 50–1.   73 Creton, 'A French metrical history', 55.   74 Ibid., 55–6.   75 Saul, *Richard II*, p. 409.   76 Ibid.   77 Creton, 'A French metrical history', 59–61.   78 Ibid., 61.   79 Ibid., 59–60.   80 Ibid., 61. 81 *Chronicle of Adam Usk*, 1399, pp 52–3.

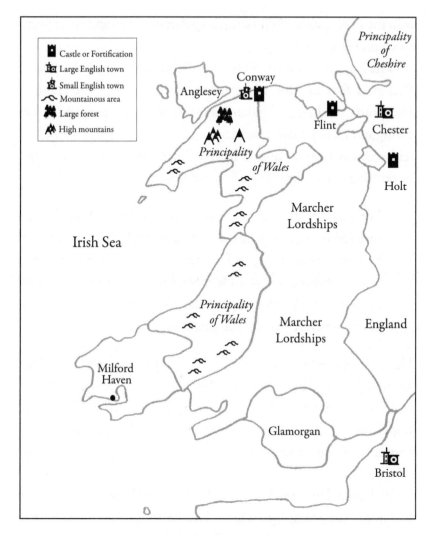

Map 4. Wales 1399.

robberies, assaults, and other insufferable wrongs upon the kingdom; also, because its people had risen up against the aforesaid duke upon his arrival, threatening to destroy him.'[82] Henry moved

82 Ibid., pp 54–7.

into the principality of Cheshire on 9 August 1399 and entered the town on the same day.[83]

The English chronicler Thomas Walsingham states that one of Richard's first actions when he received news of the duke of Hereford's landing in England was to call before him the duke's young son Henry. Henry had accompanied the king to Ireland, and had recently been knighted by him in the Wicklow mountains. According to the chronicler, Richard began:

> Look Henry, at what your own father is doing to me. He has invaded my country and is marching through it in arms as if he were at war, seizing and killing my liegemen without mercy or compassion. It is you I fear for, though, because as a result of your father's unfortunate behaviour you are the one who is likely to be deprived of his patrimony.[84]

Henry is reputed to have replied: 'My gracious king and lord, I too am much grieved by what I hear. Yet it is surely apparent to you, as it is to me, that I am innocent of my father's deeds.'[85] Richard imprisoned Henry along with his cousin, Humphrey, in Trim castle. The king took no further retaliation against his close relatives.[86]

Richard delayed too long in Ireland. The eighteen days recorded by Creton cannot fit into what is known about the chronology of events that occurred at this time.[87] This delay cost the English king his kingdom and ultimately his life. Creton called the long wait 'very great folly' and added 'Accursed be the man by whom this

83 Ibid.   84 'Thomas Walsingham's account of the revolution' in Given-Wilson (ed.), *Chronicles of the revolution, 1397–1400*, p. 121.   85 Ibid.   86 Ibid. 87 Henry Marleburrough records that Richard 'speedily went over into England', CIHM, 1399.

happened.'[88] Richard sailed from Waterford when he left Ireland for the final time. After two days at sea he landed at Milford Haven in south Wales around 24 July 1399 (see figure 25).[89] The return of Richard's supporters and soldiers from Ireland appears to have been chaotic and panicked. The king's ships began arriving at ports as widely dispersed as Plymouth, Dartmouth and Bristol, some of which had already fallen to the duke of Hereford. As a result, much of the treasure and supplies that landed in England from Ireland at this time was seized by the duke's men. Due to a shortage of shipping, Richard was forced to leave valuable military supplies behind in Ireland. These included his 'great tents and pavilions', his almost irreplaceable warhorses, as well as '141 haubercs [coats of mail]; 500 bows; 3,000 sheaves of arrows; 30 gross of cords for bows; 300 lances; 400 heads of lances; 300 large shields; 8 guns with stands for each gun; [and] 200 lb of gunpowder', which were all put into storage in Dublin castle.[90]

By now it was too late. Richard sent Sir Thomas Despenser, the earl of Gloucester, who had so recently parleyed with Art MacMurchadha, to raise troops from Despenser's own lands in Glamorgan, 'but they refused to follow him'.[91] The king was very shocked by this failure and began to make some strange decisions. According to Creton:

> Then he resolved, that without saying a word, he would set out at midnight from his host, attended by a few persons; for he would on no account be discovered. In that place he clad himself in another garb, like a poor priest of the Minors [a

---

88 Creton, 'A French metrical history', 75. 89 Ibid., 75; Saul, *Richard II*, p. 411.
90 Johnson, 'Richard II's departure from Ireland', 794–8. 91 *Chronicle of Adam Usk*, 1399, pp 58–9.

Franciscan friar], for the fear that he had of being known to his foes.[92]

When the king left the English army he had brought over with him to south Wales from Ireland, he took only thirteen followers with him. These included his half-brother, John Holland, the duke of Exeter; his nephew, Thomas Holland, the duke of Surrey; Sir Thomas Despenser, the earl of Gloucester; as well as three bishops and apparently the loyal Gascon soldier Janico Dartas.[93] Put under stress, Richard appears to have begun to doubt the loyalty of the army he had brought back with him from Ireland and, fearing capture, set out to join the army he believed had been raised for him by John Montagu, the earl of Salisbury, in north Wales.[94] Unknown to the English king the earl of Salisbury had failed to recruit an army after the large numbers he did indeed assemble had dispersed following the spread of a false rumour that Richard was dead.[95] When Richard reached Conway and realized there was no northern army, he knew it was all over. The English king probably realized, too, as Adam Usk wrote, that he had taken 'the advice of certain persons who were not, I think, acting in good faith towards him'.[96]

The English troops that Richard had brought with him to south Wales from Ireland were shocked that he had secretly abandoned them.[97] The king's cousin, Edward, duke of Aumerle, apparently spoke aloud: 'Let us begone; since my lord is so careful to secure himself, we are all lost.'[98] Sir Thomas Percy, the earl of Worcester and Richard's steward, gathered the king's household in a hall:

---

92 Creton, 'A French metrical history', 76–8.   93 Ibid., 152–3.   94 Chris Given-Wilson believes he did so 'In the interests of speed', Given-Wilson, *Henry IV*, p. 133.   95 Creton, 'A French metrical history', 70.   96 *Chronicle of Adam Usk*, 1399, pp 58–9.   97 Creton, 'A French metrical history', 99.   98 Ibid.

informed them that the king had fled ... thanked them for their good and long service ... then advised them all to leave this place for the moment and save themselves as best, or in any way that, they could; and, breaking his rod of office, he wept bitterly, for he had never wished to perform such an unwelcome task.[99]

Richard's army in south Wales then began to disband, but not before they plundered his baggage train of 'jewels, fine gold, and pure silver, many a good horse of foreign breed, many a rich and sparkling precious stone, many a good mantle, and whole ermine, good cloth of gold, and stuff of foreign pattern'.[100] Few of Richard's soldiers made it out of Wales with their plunder, however, as they were robbed in turn over the ensuing days by the Welsh.[101]

Richard was now cornered in Conway in north Wales. Once Henry, the duke of Hereford, had secured Chester and the principality of Cheshire, he set about getting control of the king. The duke sent the elderly but experienced Henry Percy, the earl of Northumberland (brother to the earl of Worcester and father of Sir Henry Percy, the famous Hotspur), to secure custody of the king.[102] Percy met Richard at Conway and succeeded in bringing him out of the town to meet with the duke of Hereford. The earl of Northumberland appears to have tricked Richard into leaving the relative security of Conway by making false promises under oath.[103] Richard and his last few followers rode out from Conway

99 'Thomas Walsingham's account of the revolution' in Given-Wilson (ed.), *Chronicles of the revolution, 1397–1400*, p. 122; Boardman, *Hotspur: Henry Percy, medieval rebel*, pp 102–3, 109.   100 Creton, 'A French metrical history', 99–101.
101 Stratford, *Richard II and the English royal treasure*, pp 111–15.
102 Boardman, *Hotspur: Henry Percy, medieval rebel*, pp 1–17, 21–35, 39, 96–110; Hotspur was married to Elizabeth, the sister of Roger Mortimer, the late earl of March and Ulster.   103 Creton, 'A French metrical history', 140–1.

and took the road to Rhuddlan. Four miles into their journey, when the king reached 'the rock', an area of rough terrain through which the road passed, he found himself surrounded by soldiers belonging to the earl of Northumberland, whom the earl had carefully concealed in order to ensure that the king was captured (see figure 26).[104] According to Creton, Richard exclaimed, 'I am betrayed! What can this be? Lord of heaven help me!'[105] When he had recovered his composure somewhat, the king is reputed to have said: 'it is the earl who hath drawn us forth upon his oath'.[106] Richard was taken to Flint castle where he met with the duke of Hereford. He was then taken to Chester, and after a few days, on to London.[107] By 1 September 1399 Richard II, the king of England, was imprisoned in the Tower of London. Could he ever have envizaged returning to his capital under such vastly changed circumstances? In the end it was a shortage of shipping in which to return to England from Ireland that was the greatest factor in King Richard II's dramatic capture in 1399.

THE AFTERMATH TO RICHARD'S SECOND EXPEDITION TO
IRELAND, 1400–17

Richard II was deposed as king of England on 29 September 1399. His first cousin Henry, the duke of Hereford, claimed the crown as King Henry IV the next day. Henry's coronation as king of England took place soon afterwards, on 13 October 1399. The Welsh chronicler Adam Usk visited Richard in the Tower of London on 21 September. During dinner, the imprisoned king is supposed to have exclaimed: 'My God, this is a strange and fickle

104 Ibid., 144–5.   105 Ibid., 146.   106 Ibid.   107 Ibid., 149–81.

land, which has exiled, slain, destroyed, and ruined so many kings, so many rulers, so many great men, and which never ceases to be riven and worn down by dissensions and strife and internecine hatreds.'[108] Once Richard had been imprisoned in the Tower, one of Henry's first actions was to have his son Henry and his cousin Humphrey released from Trim castle and brought over to England. Humphrey, however, died unexpectedly on the island of Anglesey in north Wales on the voyage back.[109] There was an outbreak of plague in Ireland at the time. After Henry IV's coronation, Richard was moved to the great Lancastrian castle of Pontefract in Yorkshire. The deposed king was dead by mid-February 1400.

The defeat of Richard's second expedition to Ireland in 1399 and his ignominious downfall in England had important repercussions for the island. In particular, the collapse of the king's authority ensured that Niall Óg Ó Néill and Art MacMurchadha remained the dominant powers in Ulster and south Leinster respectively for the remainder of their lives. Niall Óg used the opportunity presented by Richard's downfall finally to subjugate the Ó Domhnaill kingdom of Tír Chonaill in west Ulster. In 1401 the annals record that Ó Néill led a large force into Tír Chonaill, which destroyed the crops of the territory, so much so that the next year Toirdhealbhach an Fhiona Ó Domhnaill, the king of Tír Chonaill, made peace and submitted to Niall Óg at Caol Uisce on the river Erne (modern Belleck).[110] This year was probably the high-point of Niall Óg Ó Néill's career, when he truly was high-king of the fifth of Ulster. Niall Óg died the year after, in 1403. According to the Annals of Ulster, he had been:

---

108 *Chronicle of Adam Usk*, 1399, pp 62–5.   109 Ibid., pp 60–1.   110 AU, 1401, 1402.

high-king of Ulster and a courageous, powerful man, and a man who the learned companies and pilgrims of Ireland thought would take the kingship of Ireland on account of the prowess of his hands and the nobility of his blood, to wit, the blood of Niall of the Nine Hostages and of the daughter of the king of the Saxons – and the excellence of his hospitality likewise.[111]

Unfortunately for Niall Óg's immediate family and for the future stability of the kingdom of Tyrone, the heir apparent, Niall Óg's son Brian, who succeeded to the kingship, died very soon after his father, also in 1403.[112] Domhnall Bog Ó Néill, the son of Éinrí Aimhréidh, seized the kingship of Tyrone in 1404, having been set free from captivity by the English in 1402.[113] 1404 was also the year that major damage was finally done to English east Ulster when:

> The foreigners were driven from the whole province [of Ulster] and the north [*Twescard*] was burned, including lay and church property, and the monasteries [of] Downpatrick, Inis Draighin and Coleraine, were despoiled and demolished by MacAonghusa, MacGiolla Mhuire, and by Scotsmen.[114]

In contrast to Niall Óg Ó Néill in Ulster, Art MacMurchadha remained the dominant power in the Leinster mountains for well over a decade and a half following Richard's defeat and deposition. Perhaps due to the intense stress no doubt caused by Richard's two

---

111 Ibid., 1403; ASI, 1403; Niall Óg's wife, Una, the queen of Tyrone, lived until 1417, AFM, 1417.   112 AU, 1403; ASI, 1403; AFM, 1402, [recte: 1403], note e. 113 AU, 1404; ASI, 1402.   114 ASI, 1404; CIHM, 1403, 1404, 1407, 1408, 1409; Simms, 'The Ulster revolt of 1404: an anti-Lancastrian dimension', pp 141–60.

invasions of south Leinster, MacMurchadha separated from his English wife, Baroness Elizabeth de Veel.[115] After some difficulty she appears to have recovered her lands in south Kildare from the English. Throughout the first decade of the fifteenth century Art turned his attentions away from the plains of Kildare to the English liberty of Wexford. English settlement in Wexford was concentrated in the south of the county, with resistance to MacMurchadha led by the 'seneschal of the liberty of Wexford, the sovereign of the towns of New Ross and Wexford', and the heads of the Sutton, Browne, Sinnott and Furlong families.[116] Art enjoyed major success in this war, with victories over the English of Wexford recorded in 1401, 1405, 1408, 1413 and 1414.[117] By 1409 Art had imposed a substantial black rent of 80 marks on the commons of the liberty.[118] In 1416 he won what was perhaps the most impressive victory of his life, when 'Great defeat was inflicted by MacMurchadha, namely Art MacMurchadha, on the foreigners of the County Wexford this year, wherein were slain or captured seven score of them.'[119] The Annals of Connacht record that seventeen score Wexfordmen were killed or taken prisoner.[120]

In 1401 MacMurchadha may have been one of the intended recipients, among 'the lords of Ireland', of a letter sent to the island by the great Welsh rebel leader, Owain Glyn Dŵr. According to the Welsh chronicler Adam Usk, Glyn Dŵr urged the Irish to send 'as many mounted and un-mounted men-at-arms as you can properly and honestly afford', across the Irish Sea to him in North Wales, in order to continue the fight against 'our, and your, mortal

115 Curtis and St John Brooks, 'The barons of Norragh, Co. Kildare', 91. 116 176. 11 July 1409, Patent Roll 10 Henry IV. 117 AC, 1401, 1405, 1413; AFM, 1405, 1408; AU, 1414; CIHM, 1407. 118 176. 11 July 1409, Patent Roll 10 Henry IV. 119 AU, 1416. 120 AC, 1416.

enemies, the Saxons'. Adam Usk records that the messenger carrying the letter was captured in Ireland and executed.[121] Towards the end of his life in 1415 MacMurchadha was in diplomatic contact with the young king of England, Henry V. Art sent an ambassador ('*proctor*'), the Cistercian abbot of Graiguenamanagh, to the English court, who 'acknowledged Arthur to be the king's liege and subject and to owe fealty, subjection and allegiance to the king'.[122] While at the court the abbot also obtained a 'safe-conduct for two years, at the instance of Arthur Makmurgh of Ireland', for his second son, Gearalt Caomhánach to travel to England 'to the king's presence and returning thence and his servants, horses, goods and harness'.[123] Gearalt Caomhánach was Art's second most prominent son and had been captured by the Wexfordmen in 1414.[124] The embassy to Henry V may have been a sophisticated ploy to secure Gearalt's release from English captivity in Ireland.

Art MacMurchadha Caomhánach, the Irish king of the Leinster mountains since 1375, died, according to the Irish annals, in 1416 or very early 1417. The Annals of Ulster, a usually reliable source, record for 1417 that:

> MacMurchadha, namely, king of Leinster, that is, Art, son of Art Caomhánach, to wit, the provincial [king] who was best of hospitality and prowess and charity that was in his own time, died in his own stronghold this year, after victory of Unction and penance.[125]

---

121 *Chronicle of Adam Usk*, 1401, pp 148–53; Davies, *The revolt of Owain Glyn Dŵr*, pp 157–8, 188–9. 122 Safe-conduct for two years, 24 July 1415, Calendar of Patent Rolls Henry V, vol. 1413–16 (London, 1910), p. 328. 123 Ibid. 124 AU, 1414. 125 AU, 1417; AC, 1416; AFM, 1416.

The Irish of the Leinster mountains, however, could not let such a famous king as Art MacMurchadha go so easily. As a result, after recording what was probably the accurate reference to his death for 1416, the Annals of the Four Masters go on to give the well-known account of the murder of Art and his chief brehon, Ó Deoráin, who it states were both killed by a female assassin in New Ross. The full entry, although probably a later legend, states:

> Art, the son of Art, son of Muircheartach, son of Muiris, Lord of Leinster, a man who had defended his own province against the foreigner and the Gael from his sixteenth to his sixtieth year; a man full of hospitality, knowledge, and chivalry; a man full of prosperity and royalty, died (after having been forty-two years in the lordship of Leinster), a week after Christmas. Some assert that it was of a poisonous drink which a woman gave to him, and to Ó Deoráin, chief-brehon of Leinster, at Ros-Mic-Briuin [New Ross], that both died. Donnchadh, his son, assumed his place after him.[126]

---

126 AFM, 1417. Following Art's death his family laid no claim to the lands of his English ex-wife, Baroness Elizabeth de Veel, in south Kildare. She died in 1445. Elizabeth does not appear to have remarried once she left MacMurchadha (Curtis and St John Brooks, 'The barons of Norragh, Co. Kildare', 91 and 99).

CHAPTER 6

'Now for our Irish wars'[1]

Richard II's interest in his lordship of Ireland was concentrated in the period from 1394 to 1399. During these years, the English king only spent around ten months in total on the island. Richard was deposed and killed soon after his return to England. As a result, the long-term and short-term consequences of his two expeditions to Ireland became even more limited. Richard's two appearances in Ireland may have raised the morale of the English population of the island. The king's presence, with a very large army on two occasions, no doubt allowed many of the English nobles to strike back against their Irish enemies. The balance of local power in numerous small localities may have swung back in favour of the English. Richard also personally experienced the plight of many of the small towns in eastern Ireland, which for many years had suffered attacks from their Irish and more gaelicized English neighbours. The king's interventions allowing quite a number of them to retain royal taxation for several years, in order to facilitate

1 W.J. Craig (ed.), 'Richard II' in *William Shakespeare: complete works* (Oxford, 1905), p. 389.

the building or repairing of town walls, may have saved some of them from complete destruction in the ensuing years. Obviously Richard's 1399 Irish expedition had immense repercussions for the kingdom of England. Richard's absence in Ireland with the majority of his most loyal and capable noblemen and soldiers gave his cousin, Henry Bolingbroke, the exiled earl of Derby and duke of Hereford, the opportunity to invade and seize the English throne. On a personal level, Richard II's involvement with Ireland cost him his crown and ultimately his life. If this English king, however, had been able to remain in Ireland in 1399–1400 for the long period that he had apparently intended, then perhaps his 1399 Irish campaign could have been significant for the island.

In the short-term, Richard may have degraded the military and political power of Art MacMurchadha in the Leinster mountains. Certainly the two English campaigns into the mountains and forests of south Leinster caused a great deal of physical damage in the lands of the Leinster Irish. Nevertheless, MacMurchadha succeeded in keeping casualties among his followers to a minimum on both occasions. Art's reign following Richard II's final departure from Ireland was highly successful. MacMurchadha won a series of military engagements (1401, 1405, 1408, 1413, 1414 and 1416), some of them quite large, against the English of south Wexford. Indeed, by the time of Art MacMurchadha's death in early January 1417, he had essentially won the war for overlordship of Co. Wexford. As a result, the real impact that Richard's two expeditions had on Art's power in the Leinster mountains must have been limited and temporary in nature. Perhaps Richard's two campaigns succeeded in preventing MacMurchadha from doing some really serious damage to other surviving areas of the English colony in south Leinster: for example, a conquest of the plains of

Kildare, or the vale of Dublin, or perhaps even Dublin city itself. This is speculation.

Niall Óg Ó Néill, the king of Tyrone and high-king of Ulster, had already reached the limits of his ambitions when Richard II first came to Ireland. An attempt by Niall Óg in the late 1380s to destroy the English settlements on the Cooley peninsula failed. Ó Néill also appears to have had no real designs on the town of Dundalk, except for extorting a lucrative black rent from the townspeople. As a result, during Richard's two expeditions to Ireland, he was concerned with regulating the positions of Ó Néill, the English king and the earl of March and Ulster in the north of Ireland, rather than with repelling any Irish invasion of Co. Louth or Co. Meath. That Niall Óg Ó Néill, with the support of his elderly semi-retired father, Niall Mór, largely preserved Ó Néill hegemony over Ulster in their negotiations with Richard II can be gauged from the outraged reaction of Roger Mortimer. The real long-term consequence of Richard II's two expeditions to the island for the north of Ireland must be that the best opportunity in late-medieval times properly to define the relationship between the Ó Néill kings of Tyrone and the English monarchy was missed. This opportunity did not present itself again until the mid-sixteenth century. By then Tyrone was ruled by lesser, more warlike men than Niall Mór and Niall Óg Ó Néill.

Richard II's first expedition to Ireland was immense and very well supported and organized. The English did very well on the first expedition, owing to their choice of tactics. The placing of wards about the Leinster mountains and the blockading of the south Leinster coastline by some of the fleet succeeded in isolating Art MacMurchadha and the Leinster Irish. The English decision to send multiple columns against MacMurchadha also paid off, with their effectiveness compounded by Art's error in letting himself become trapped in the forests of Carlow. The fact that Richard's second expedition into the Leinster mountains almost turned into a disaster suggests that the success of the first expedition may have owed much to the military skills of someone such as Thomas Mowbray, the duke of Norfolk, rather than of the English king himself. Mowbray played a prominent role in the campaign against MacMurchadha in 1394–5, but was in exile and died abroad in 1399.

Richard was successful in obtaining the submissions of truly impressive numbers of Irish kings and chieftains as well as gaelicized English lords in 1394–5. This success probably owed a great deal to the English king's decision to treat Art MacMurchadha leniently, which appears to have impressed many of the other major Irish kings on the island. The long-term success of these submissions, however, is debatable. While Richard's settlement in parts of Leinster and Munster may have been quite successful and possibly endured into 1396, relations with Art MacMurchadha himself had broken down in 1395, perhaps even before the English king had left the island. War between Roger Mortimer and Niall Óg Ó Néill in Ulster was also looming in 1395 before Richard returned to England. This war finally broke out with a vengeance in 1396. Certainly many Irish kings and English lords personally got to meet the English king and may have been impressed by the experience. Niall Óg Ó Néill, however, appears to have later resented the efforts undertaken on Richard's orders to prepare him for knighthood by training him to become an Englishman.

When Richard II undertook his second expedition to Ireland, he appears to have underestimated both his main adversary, Art

MacMurchadha, and the difficult nature of the terrain in the Leinster mountains. Leading what seems to have been a *chevauchée* into Art's territory, Richard marched his entire army straight into what was probably a carefully prepared trap. Art MacMurchadha had learnt from his costly errors in 1394–5. As a result, he based himself in the wide forests and valleys of the Wicklow mountains rather than allowing himself to become trapped again in Co. Carlow. MacMurchadha also withdrew every possible food source from the reach of Richard's army, and so the English soon ran short of supplies. MacMurchadha may also have prepared defences in the great forests of Shillelagh in south Wicklow where Richard's army quickly got stuck as it marched into the woods unawares. The English army appears to have been completely immobilized for a number of days as MacMurchadha's horsemen cut off and killed many foragers. In the end Richard was fortunate to break out of the trap when the local English woodcutters fortuitously arrived on the scene to cut him a way out through the forest. The destruction of property, livestock and crops must still have been severe for the Irish of the Leinster mountains, but Art MacMurchadha certainly had the better of this second encounter with Richard II.

Art MacMurchadha was the most successful and noteworthy of all the late-medieval Irish kings of Leinster. Determined and able, MacMurchadha had a quite peaceful early reign during his first years as king of the Leinster mountains. Nevertheless, Art could be ruthless. He appears to have been involved in the assassination of his uncle Donnchadh, his predecessor as king of Leinster. Art also went to war without hesitation a number of times before 1394, in order to avenge perceived wrongs or insults perpetrated on both him and his followers by the English of Leinster. On a personal level Art MacMurchadha could also be brave and decisive. This Irish king did not hesitate to offer military resistance to Richard II when the English king first arrived in Ireland in 1394. Although Art made some major errors in the early fighting owing to inexperience and to the immense challenge presented by the very large English forces opposing him, to his credit he immediately recognized this and surrendered. In doing so he probably prevented large-scale loss of life among his followers. Art subsequently gained the upperhand against Richard in the ensuing negotiations. In 1399 MacMurchadha demonstrated that he had the capacity to learn from his mistakes. The manner in which he harassed and isolated Richard's second expedition into the Leinster mountains in the summer of 1399 was very impressive indeed. As previously mentioned, Art MacMurchadha's reign as king of the Irish of the Leinster mountains was extremely successful in the years after Richard II left the island for the last time. When MacMurchadha died, most likely in very early January 1417, he was greatly mourned by his followers. The Leinster Irish were fated never again to have as able or as successful a leader.

Niall Óg and Niall Mór Ó Néill were two highly capable kings of Tyrone and high-kings of Ulster. Great warriors as well as strategic and competent negotiators, their contribution to and significance for late-medieval Irish history have been overlooked. The early peace agreement among the ruling family, Niall Mór's overthrow of English east Ulster in 1374 and the peaceful handover of power to his son Niall Óg in 1387, all indicate that this was a gifted, ambitious and capable family. The negotiations between Niall Mór and Niall Óg with Richard II in Drogheda in early 1395 were probably the greatest challenge that the two Irish kings encountered during their long careers. That they distinguished themselves in these talks and emerged in a strong position is evident from the surviving source material and from the outrage of their greatest rival, Roger Mortimer. Niall Mór Ó Néill died in 1397. Niall Óg Ó Néill had a very successful few years after Richard II left Ireland in 1399. Before his death in 1403, Niall Óg successfully led the subjugation of the Ó Domhnaill kingdom of Tír Chonaill, in west Ulster, which was quite an achievement. Niall Óg's death, followed immediately afterwards by the death of his eldest son and heir Brian Ó Néill, ushered in a period of civil war within the kingdom of Tyrone. This should not detract from the definite achievements of the Ó Néill family and the kingdom of Tyrone, however, under these two Irish kings.

It is striking how many Irish kings and English nobles from this period are later found as major figures in the folklore of the island. Among them were Éinrí Aimhréidh Ó Néill, the son of Niall Mór and the brother of Niall Óg, who dominated the folklore of the Newtown-Stewart area of west Tyrone in the early nineteenth century, Murchadh na Raithnighe Ó Briain, the north Munster raider whose legend was recorded by Sir Edmund Spenser at the end of the sixteenth century, Gearóid Iarla, the third earl of Desmond, who was a dominant figure in Munster folklore, and Art MacMurchadha himself in the south Leinster region. The story of Art's escape from the English ambush in 1395 was the main episode of his life that entered into later Irish folklore.[2] The fact that so many leading figures from this time entered into the folklore of the island suggests that the late fourteenth century was a significant and long remembered period in Irish history.

2 Ó hÓgáin, *Myth, legend and romance*, pp 228–9; D'arcy McGee, *A memoir of the life and conquests of Art MacMurrogh*, pp 41–3.

One wonders whether the one long-term effect of Richard II's two expeditions to Ireland was to make the succeeding late-medieval – and in turn early modern – English kings and queens fear the bad luck that a visit to Ireland might bring to their reign.[3] They certainly had before them the fearsome example of Richard's overthrow, as well as the earlier misfortune of King John, who had been the previous reigning English monarch to visit Ireland, in 1210. Indeed, when cornered in north Wales, Richard cursed his decision to visit Ireland in 1399.[4] Although many of Richard II's successors sent close family relatives to the lordship of Ireland as their lieutenants, this was never sufficient. A reigning English monarch did not set foot in Ireland again until war brought two competing kings, James II and William III, to the island at the close of the seventeenth century.

---

3 Chris Butler and Willy Maley, '"Bringing rebellion broached on sword": Essex and Ireland' in A. Connolly and L. Hopkins (eds), *Essex: the cultural impact of an Elizabethan courtier* (Manchester, 2013), p. 140.   4 Given-Wilson, *Henry IV*, p. 134.

Bibliography

MANUSCRIPTS

Ireland
National Library of Ireland
MS 2656 iii and v
ET D117: Rock and castle of Dunamase
ET A608: Tower of St Mary Magdalene, Drogheda, Co. Louth
ET A837: Carrickfergus castle
ET A667: Trim castle, Co. East Meath
PD 1976 TX21: Castle of Carlow
ET A889: The Seven Churches, Glendalough, Co. Wicklow

Trinity College Dublin
MS 1318: Yellow Book of Lecan
MS 1435: Contains a fifteenth-century tract on the plague

United Kingdom
British Library (BL)
Cotton MS Nero D VI
Cotton MS Titus B XI: Records and papers relating to Ireland, Edward I
    (1272–1307) to Mary I (1553–1558)
Harley MS 1319: Jean Creton, 'La prinse et mort du roy Richart' ('Book of
    the capture and death of king Richard II')

Shropshire Archives
3365/24: Illuminated initial from the Charter of Richard II, 1389.

Electronic
Calendar of Irish Chancery Letters, c.1244–1509 (CIRCLE)
www.chancery.tcd.ie
Edward III Close Roll 48/51
Edward III Patent Roll 48/49
Richard II Close Roll 1/2/3/4/5/6/8/9/12/16/17/18/20/22
Richard II Patent Roll 1/2/4/5/7/9/10/12/13/15/16/17/18/19/20/22
Henry IV Patent Roll 10

PRIMARY SOURCES

Aymot, T., 'An inquiry concerning the death of Richard the Second', *Archaeologia: Miscellaneous Tracts Relating to Antiquity: Published by the Society of Antiquaries of London*, 20: 1 (London, 1823), 424–42.

Berry, H. (ed.), *Statutes and ordinances, and Acts of the parliament of Ireland: King John to Henry V* (Dublin, 1907).

Brereton, G. (ed.), *Jean Froissart: chronicles* (London, 1968).

Butler, R. (ed. and trans.), *Annales Hiberniae: James Grace of Kilkenny, Irish Archaeological Society* (Dublin, 1842).

—The annals of Ireland by Friar John Clyn, of the convent of Friars Minors, Kilkenny, and Thady Dowling, Chancellor of Leighlin: together with the annals of Ross: the Irish Archaeological Society* (Dublin, 1849).

Calendar of the Close Rolls, Richard II, vol. 5, A.D. 1392–96 (London, 1925).

Calendar of the Close Rolls, Richard II, vol. 6, A.D. 1396–99 (London, 1927).

Calendar of Patent Rolls, Richard II, vol. 6, A.D. 1396–99 (London, 1909).

Calendar of the Patent Rolls, Henry V, vol. 1, A.D. 1413–16 (London, 1910).

Carney, J. (ed.), *Topographical poems by Seaán Mór Ó Dubhagáin and Giolla-Na-Naomh Ó hUidhrín* (Dublin, 1943).

Chart, D.A. (ed.), *The register of John Swayne, archbishop of Armagh and primate of Ireland, 1418–39, with some entries of earlier and later archbishops* (Belfast, 1935).

Convery, D. (ed.), *Archduke Ferdinand's visit to Kinsale in Ireland: an extract from Le premier voyage de Charles-Quint en Espagne, de 1517 à 1518*: electronic edition, CELT Project Cork (2012).

Craig, W.J. (ed.), 'Richard II' in *William Shakespeare: complete works* (Oxford, 1905), p. 389.

Curtis, E. (ed.), *Calendar of Ormond deeds, 1350–1413*, vol. 2 (Dublin, 1934).

— 'Letters sent to the King when in Ireland' in Curtis, *Richard II in Ireland 1394–5*, pp 203–25.

— 'The instruments touching Ireland' in Curtis, *Richard II in Ireland 1394–5*, pp 149–201.

— 'Unpublished letters from Richard II in Ireland, 1394–5', *PRIA*, 37C:14 (1927), 276–303.

Dineen, P.S. (ed.), *Foclóir Gaedhilge agus Béarla: an Irish-English dictionary* (Dublin, 1927).

Frame, R., 'A register of lost deeds relating to the earldom of Ulster, c. 1230–1376' in S. Duffy (ed.), *Princes, prelates and poets in medieval Ireland* (Dublin, 2013), 85–106.

Freeman, A.M. (ed.), *Annála Connacht: the annals of Connacht, AD 1224–1544* (Dublin, 1944).

Gilbert, J.T. (ed.), *Calendar of ancient records of Dublin in the possession of the municipal corporation of that city*, vol. 1 (Dublin, 1889).

— *Chartularies of St Mary's abbey, Dublin*, vol. 1 (London, 1884).

— *Facsimiles of national manuscripts of Ireland*, part III (London, 1879).

— *Facsimiles of national manuscripts of Ireland*, part IV.I (London, 1882).

Given-Wilson, C. (ed.), *Chronicles of the revolution, 1397–1400: the reign of Richard II* (Manchester, 1993).

— (ed. and trans.), *The chronicle of Adam Usk, 1377–1421* (Oxford, 1997).

Gleeson, D.F., 'The annals of Nenagh', *Analecta Hibernica*, vol. 12 (1943), pp 155–64.

Griffith, M.C. (ed.), *Irish patent rolls of James I* (Dublin, 1966).

Hardiman, J. (ed.), *A statute of the fortieth year of King Edward III, enacted in a parliament held in Kilkenny, AD 1367, before Lionel duke of Clarence, lord lieutenant of Ireland, in tracts relating to Ireland, Irish Archaeological Society*, 2 vols (Dublin, 1843).

Harris, W. (ed.), *The whole works of Sir James Ware concerning Ireland: revised and improved in three volumes* (Dublin, 1745).

Hayes O'Grady, S. (ed.), *Caithréim Thoirdhealbhaigh by Seán Mac Ruaidhrí MacCraith*, 2 vols (1929).

Hazard, B. and K.W. Nicholls (eds and trans.), *Annales Dominicani de Roscoman, 1163–1314*, electronic edition, CELT Project Cork (2012).

Hennessy, W. (ed.), *Annals of Loch Cé*, 2 vols (London, 1871).

Hennessy, W., and B. Mac Carthy (eds), *Annala Uladh: annals of Ulster, AD 431 to AD 1540* (Dublin, 1887–1901).

Herity, M. (ed.), *Ordnance Survey letters: Londonderry, Fermanagh, Armagh-Monaghan, Louth, Cavan-Leitrim* (Dublin, 2012).

Historical Manuscripts Commission 132: report on the manuscripts of Lord De L'Isle & Dudley, vol. 1 (London, 1925).

Holden, A.J. (ed.), *History of William Marshal*, vol. 1 (London, 2002).

Holinshed, Raphael, *Chronicles of England, Scotland, and Ireland*, 2 vols (1577 edition).

Inquisitionum in officio rotulorum cancellariae Hiberniae asservatarum, repertorium, vol. 2 (Dublin, 1829).

Johnes, T. (trans.), *Chronicles of England, France, Spain, and the adjoining countries, from the latter part of the reign of Edward II, to the coronation of Henry IV by Sir John Froissart*, 2 vols (London, 1839).

Johnston, D. (ed.), *Iolo Goch: poems* (Llandysul, 1993).

Kaeuper, R.W. and Kennedy, E. (eds), *A knight's own book of chivalry: Geoffroi De Charny* (Philadelphia, 2005).

Keating, G., *Foras Feasa ar Éireann le Seathrún Céitinn – The History of Ireland*, ed. P.S. Dineen, vol. 3 (London, 1908).

Lalor, H.J., 'A calendar of the register of Archbishop Sweteman', *PRIA*, C29 (1911/1912), 213–310.

Mhág Craith, C. (ed.), *Dán na mBráthar Mionúr*, vol. 1 (Dublin, 1967); vol. 2 (Dublin, 1980).

McHardy, A.K. (ed.), *The reign of Richard II: from minority to tyranny, 1377–97* (Manchester, 2012).

McKenna, L. (ed.), *Aithdioghluim Dána*, vol. 1 (Dublin, 1939); vol. 2 (Dublin, 1940).

— 'To Art MacMurchadha Caomhánach', *The Irish Monthly*, 56:655 (1928), 98–101.

Manning, C., Gosling, P. and J. Waddell (eds), *New survey of Clare Island: the abbey*, vol. 4 (Dublin, 2005).

Marden, G.H. (ed.), *Knighton's chronicle, 1337–1396* (Oxford, 1995).

Marleburrough: *The chronicle of Ireland by Henry Marleburrough; continued from the collection of Doctor Meredith Hanmer, in the year 1571, in Sir James Ware (ed.), Ancient Irish histories* (Dublin, 1809).

Morrissey, J.F. (ed.), *Statute rolls of the parliament of Ireland: twelfth and thirteenth to the twenty-first and twenty-second years of King Edward IV* (Dublin, 1939).

Murphy, D. (ed.), *The annals of Clonmacnoise: from the earliest period to AD 1408* (Dublin, 1896).

Nicolas, H. (ed.), *Proceedings and ordinances of the privy council of England*, vol. 1, 10 Richard II (1386)–11 Henry IV (1405), (London, 1834).

Ó Donnchadha, T. (ed.), *Leabhar Cloinne Aodha Buidhe* (Dublin, 1931).

Ó Dufaigh, S., 'Cíos Mhic Mhathghamhna', *Clogher Record* (1960–1), 125–33.

Ó hInnse, S. (ed.), *Miscellaneous Irish annals, AD 1114–1437* (Dublin, 1947).

Ó Muraíle, N. (ed.), *Leabhar Mór Na nGenealach: the great book of Irish genealogies*, vol. 1 (Dublin, 2003).

O'Donovan, J. (ed.), 'A narration of the services done by the army employed to Lough Foyle, under the leadings of me Sir Henry Docwra', *Miscellany of the Celtic Society* (Dublin, 1849).

— *Annala Rioghachta Eireann: annals of the kingdom of Ireland by the four masters* (Dublin, 1856).

O'Sullivan, D.C. (ed.), *The natural history of Ireland by Philip O'Sullivan Beare* (Cork, 2009).

Orpen, G.H. (ed. and trans.), *The song of Dermot and the Earl: an Old French poem* (Oxford, 1892).

Perroy, E. (ed.), *The diplomatic correspondence of Richard II*, vol. 48 (London, 1933).

Reeves, W. (ed.), *Acts of archbishop Colton in his metropolitan visitation of the diocese of Derry AD 1397; with a rental of the see estates at that time* (Dublin, 1850).

Renwick, W.L. (ed.), *Edmund Spenser: a view of the present state of Ireland* (Oxford, 1970).

Richardson, H. and G. Sayles (eds), *Parliaments and councils of medieval Ireland*, vol. 1 (Dublin, 1947).

Scott, A.B. and F.X. Martin (eds and trans.), *Expugnatio Hibernica: the conquest of Ireland by Giraldus Cambrensis* (Dublin, 1978).

Shields, H., 'The walling of New Ross: a thirteenth-century poem in French', *Bulletin of the Friends of the Library Trinity College Dublin*, 12 and 13 (1975/76), 24–33.

Simms, K., 'The concordat between primate John Mey and Henry O'Neill (1455)', *Archivium Hibernicum*, 34 (1976/7), 71–82.

Small, J. (ed.), *The image of Irelande with a discoverie of woodkerne by John Derricke, 1581* (Edinburgh, 1883).

Smith, B. (ed.), *The register of Milo Sweteman, archbishop of Armagh, 1361–1380* (Dublin, 1996).

— *The register of Nicholas Fleming, archbishop of Armagh, 1404–1416* (Dublin, 2003).

State papers, King Henry VIII, vol. 3, part III (London, 1834).

Statutes of the realm, vol. 2 (London, 1816).

Walsh, P. (ed.), *Beatha Aodha Ruaidh Uí Dhomhnaill*, vol. 1 (London, 1948); vol. 2 (London, 1957).

Webb, J., 'Translation of a French metrical history of the deposition of King Richard the Second, written by a contemporary', *Archaeologia: Miscellaneous tracts relating to antiquity: published by the Society of Antiquaries of London*, 20: 1 (London, 1823), 1–423.

Williams, B. (ed.), *The annals of Ireland by Friar John Clyn* (Dublin, 2007).

Williams, N.J.A. (ed.), *The poems of Giolla Brighde Mac Con Midhe* (Dublin, 1980).

SECONDARY SOURCES

Allmand, C., *The Hundred Years War: England and France at war, c.1300–c.1450* (Cambridge, 2001).

Andrews, J.H., *A map of the County of Kildare* (Dublin, 1983).

— *The queen's last map-maker: Richard Bartlett in Ireland, 1600–3* (Dublin, 2008).

Bartlett, T. and Jeffery, K. (eds), *A military history of Ireland* (Cambridge, 1996).

Bennett, M.J., 'Richard II and the wider realm' in A. Goodman and J.L. Gillespie (eds), *Richard II: the art of kingship* (Oxford, 1999), pp 187–204.

Biggs, D., *Three armies in Britain: the Irish campaign of Richard II and the usurpation of Henry IV, 1397–99* (Leiden, 2006).

Boardman, A.W., *Hotspur: Henry Percy, medieval rebel* (Stroud, 2003).

Booker, S. and C.N. Peters (eds), *Tales of medieval Dublin* (Dublin, 2014).

Bradbury, J. (ed.), *The Routledge companion to medieval warfare* (Abingdon, 2004).

Bradley, J., A.J. Fletcher and A. Simms (eds), *Dublin in the medieval world: studies in honour of Howard B. Clarke* (Dublin, 2009).

Butler, C. and W. Maley, '"Bringing rebellion broached on his sword": Essex and Ireland' in Connolly, A. and L. Hopkins (eds), *Essex: the cultural impact of an Elizabethan courtier* (Manchester, 2013), pp 133–52.

Caferro, W., *John Hawkwood: an english mercenary in fourteenth-century Italy* (Baltimore, 2006).

Clarke, H.B., *Irish historic towns atlas, no. 11: Dublin, part I, to 1610* (Dublin, 2002).

Clarke, M., 'The abbey, Wicklow', *JRSAI*, 73:1 (1943), 1–14.

— 'The Black Castle, Wicklow', *JRSAI*, 74:1 (1944), 1–22.

Colfer, B., 'Anglo-Norman settlement in County Wexford' in K. Whelan and W. Nolan (eds), *Wexford: history and society* (Dublin, 1987), pp 65–101.

Cosgrove, A., *Late medieval Ireland, 1370–1541* (Dublin, 1981).

— (ed.), *Marriage in Ireland* (Dublin, 1985).

Crouch, D., *William Marshal: knighthood, war and chivalry, 1147–1219* (Harlow, 2002).

Curtis, E., *A history of medieval Ireland from 1086 to 1513* (London, 1923).

— 'Janico Dartas, Richard II's "Gascon squire": his career in Ireland, 1394–1426', *JRSAI*, 63:2 (1933), 182–205.

— *Richard II in Ireland 1394–5 and submissions of the Irish chiefs* (Oxford, 1927).

— 'The "bonnaght" of Ulster', *Hermathena*, 21:46 (1931), 87–105.

Curtis, E. and E. St John Brooks, 'The barons of Norragh, Co. Kildare, 1171–1660', *Journal of the Royal Society of Antiquaries of Ireland*, seventh series, 5:1 (1935), 84–101.

D'arcy McGee, T., *A memoir of the life and conquests of Art MacMurrogh, king of Leinster* (Dublin, 1847).

Davies, R.R., *The revolt of Owain Glyn Dŵr* (Oxford, 1995).

De hÓir, S., 'Guns in medieval and Tudor Ireland', *The Irish Sword*, 15 (1982–3), 76–89.

De Paor, M. (ed.), *Saint Moling Luachra: a pilgrimage from Sliabh Luachra to Rinn Ros Broic above the stream-pools of the Barrow* (Dublin, 2001).

Develin, J.C., *The O'Develins of Tyrone: the story of an Irish sept* (Rutland, 1938).

Dillon, C., and H.A. Jefferies (eds), *Tyrone: history and society* (Dublin, 2000).

Duffy, S. (ed.), *Medieval Ireland: an encyclopedia* (New York, 2005).

— *Princes, prelates and poets in Medieval Ireland* (Dublin, 2013).

— *Robert the Bruce's Irish wars: the invasions of Ireland, 1306–1329* (Stroud, 2002).

— *The world of the galloglass: kings, warlords and warriors in Ireland and Scotland, 1200–1600* (Dublin, 2007).

— 'The Bruce invasion of Ireland: a revised itinerary and chronology' in S. Duffy (ed.) *Robert the Bruce's Irish wars: the invasions of Ireland, 1306–1329* (Stroud, 2002).

Everett, N., *The woods of Ireland: a history, 700–1800* (Dublin, 2014).

Falls, C., *Elizabeth's Irish wars* (London, 1950).

Fitzgerald, W., 'Norraghmore and the barons of Norragh', *Journal of the Kildare Archaeological Society*, 7 (1913), 242–72.

Fitzpatrick, E., *Royal inauguration in Gaelic Ireland, c.1100–1600: a cultural landscape study* (Woodbridge, 2004).

Flanagan, D., 'Three settlement names in County Down: the Turters of Inishargy, Dunsfort, Tullumgrange', *Dinnseanchas*, 5:3, 65–70.

Flanders, S., *De Courcy: Anglo-Normans in Ireland, England and France in the eleventh and twelfth centuries* (Dublin, 2008).

Foster, R.F. (ed.), *The Oxford illustrated history of Ireland* (Oxford, 1991).

Frame, R., *Colonial Ireland, 1169–1369* (Dublin, 1981).

— 'The defence of the English lordship, 1250–1450' in T. Bartlett and K. Jeffery (eds), *A military history of Ireland* (Cambridge, 1996), pp 76–98.

— 'The justiciar and the murder of the MacMurroughs in 1282' in R. Frame (ed.), *Ireland and Britain, 1170–1450* (London, 1998), pp 241–8.

— 'Two kings in Leinster: the crown and the MicMhurchadha in the fourteenth century' in T.B. Barry, R. Frame and K. Simms (eds), *Colony and frontier in medieval Ireland* (London, 1995), pp 155–76.

Gilbert, J.T. (ed.), *Account of facsimiles of national manuscripts of Ireland* (London, 1884).

Gillingham, J., 'Killing and mutilating political enemies in the British Isles from the late twelfth to the early fourteenth century: a comparative study' in B. Smith (ed.), *Britain and Ireland, 900–1300: Insular responses to medieval European change* (Cambridge, 1999), pp 114–34.

— *The Angevin Empire* (London, 2001).

Given-Wilson, C., *Henry IV* (London, 2016).

— 'Richard II and the higher nobility' in A. Goodman and J.L. Gillespie (eds), *Richard II: the art of kingship* (Oxford, 1999), pp 107–128.

Goodman, A., *John of Gaunt: the exercise of princely power in fourteenth-century Europe* (Harlow, 1992).

Goodman, A. and J.L. Gillespie (eds), *Richard II: the art of kingship* (Oxford, 1999).

Gordon, D., Monnas, L. and C. Elam (eds), *The regal image of Richard II and the Wilton Diptych* (London, 1997).

Grogan, E. and A. Kilfeather (eds), *Archaeological inventory of County Wicklow* (Dublin, 1997).

Gwynn, A. and R.N. Hadcock, *Medieval religious houses: Ireland* (Dublin, 1970).

Hannigan, K. and W. Nolan (eds), *Wicklow: history and society* (Dublin, 1994).

Harbison, P., 'Native Irish arms and armour in medieval Gaelic literature, 1170–1600', *The Irish Sword*, 12:48 (1976), part I, 173–99; *The Irish Sword*, 12:49 (1976), part II, 270–84.

Haren, M. and Y. de Pontfarcy (eds), *The medieval pilgrimage to St Patrick's Purgatory: Lough Derg and the European tradition* (Monaghan, 1988).

Hayes-McCoy, G.A., *Irish battles: a military history of Ireland* (Belfast, 1969).

— 'The making of an O'Neill: a view of the ceremony at Tullaghoge, Co. Tyrone', *Ulster Journal of Archaeology*, 33 (1970), 89–94.

Hickey, K., *Wolves in Ireland: a natural and cultural history* (Dublin, 2011).

Hogan, J., 'The Irish law of kingship, with special reference to Ailech and Cenél Eoghain', *PRIA*, 40C (1931–32), 186–254.

Hughes, S., *Illustrating the past: archaeological discoveries on Irish road schemes* (Dublin, 2015).

Hunt, J., *Irish medieval figure sculpture, 1200–1600: a study of Irish tombs with notes on costume and armour*, 2 vols (Dublin, 1974).

Jefferies, H.A., 'The visitation of the parishes of Armagh *inter Hibernicos* in 1546' in Dillon and Jefferies (eds), *Tyrone: history and society*, pp 163–80.

Johnston, Dafydd, *Iolo Goch* (Caernarfon, 1989).

— 'Iolo Goch and the English: Welsh poetry and politics in the fourteenth century', *Cambridge Medieval Celtic Studies*, 12 (1986), 73–98.

Johnston, Dorothy, 'Richard II and the submissions of Gaelic Ireland', *IHS*, 22:85 (1980), 1–20.

— 'Richard II's departure from Ireland, July 1399', *English Historical Review*, 98: 389 (1983), 785–805.

— 'The interim years: Richard II and Ireland, 1395–99' in J. Lydon (ed.), *England and Ireland in the later Middle Ages* (Blackrock, 1981), pp 175–95.

Jope, E.M., Jope, H.M. and E.A. Johnson, 'Harry Avery's castle, Newtownstewart, Co. Tyrone: excavations in 1950', *Ulster Journal of Archaeology*, third series, 13, parts I and II (1950), 81–92.

Joyce, E., *Borris House, Co. Carlow, and elite regency patronage* (Dublin, 2013).

Kelly, M., *A history of the Black Death in Ireland* (Stroud, 2001).

Kewes, P., Archer, I.W. and F. Heal (eds), *The Oxford handbook of Holinshed's chronicles* (Oxford, 2013).

Kildare, Marquis of, *The earls of Kildare and their ancestors, from 1057 to 1773* (Dublin, 1857).

Lydon, J.F., 'Select documents XXIV: Edward II and the revenues of Ireland in 1311–12', *IHS*, 14 (1964–5), 39–57.

— 'Medieval Wicklow – "a land of war"' in K. Hannigan and W. Nolan (eds), *Wicklow: history and society* (Dublin, 1994), pp 151–89.

— 'Richard II's expeditions to Ireland', *JRSAI*, 93 (1963), 135–50.

— 'The Bruce invasion of Ireland: an examination of some problems' in S. Duffy (ed.), *Robert the Bruce's Irish wars: the invasions of Ireland, 1306–1329* (Stroud, 2002), pp 71–88.

McCone, K.R., 'Werewolves, cyclopes, *díberga*, and *fianna*: juvenile delinquency in early Ireland', *Cambridge Medieval Celtic Studies*, 12 (1986), 1–22.

McCullough, C. and W.H. Crawford, *Irish historic town atlas, no. 18: Armagh* (Dublin, 2007).

McDowell, H., *Irish family treasures* (Dublin, 1985).

McGuire, J. and J. Quinn (eds), *Dictionary of Irish biography*, vols 1–9 (Cambridge, 2009).

McNeill, T.E., 'County Down in the later Middle Ages' in L. Proudfoot (ed.), *Down: history and society* (Dublin, 1997), pp 103–22.

— *Anglo-Norman Ulster: the history and archaeology of an Irish barony, 1177–1400* (Edinburgh, 1980).

Maginn, C., 'English marcher lineages in south Dublin in the late Middle Ages', *IHS*, 34:134 (2004), 113–36.

Matthew, H.C.G. and B. Harrison (eds), *Oxford dictionary of national biography*, 60 vols (Oxford, 2004).

Moody, T., F.X. Martin and F.J. Byrne (eds), *New history of Ireland: a chronology of Irish history to 1976*, vol. 8 (Oxford, 1982).

Mullin, T. and J. Mullan, *The Ulster clans: O'Mullan, O'Kane and O'Mellan* (Belfast, 1966).

Nicholls, K., 'Scottish mercenary kindreds in Ireland, 1250–1600' in S. Duffy (ed.), *The world of the galloglass: kings, warlords and warriors in Ireland and Scotland, 1200–1600* (Dublin, 2007), pp 86–105.

Ó Dufaigh, S., 'The MacCathmhaoils of Clogher', *Clogher Record*, 2:1 (1957), 25–49.

Ó hÓgáin, D., *Myth, legend amd romance: an encyclopædia of the Irish folk tradition* (London, 1990).

Ó Murchadha, D., 'Select documents XXXVI: is the O'Neill–MacCarthy letter of 1317 a forgery?', *IHS*, 23:89 (1982), 61–7.

— 'The battle of Callan, AD 1261', *JCHAS*, 66:204 (1961), 105–16.

Ó Murchú, L.P. (ed.), *Caithréim Thoirdhealbhaigh: reasssessments* (Dublin, 2012).

Ó Riain, P., *A dictionary of Irish saints* (Dublin, 2011).

— *Four Tipperary saints* (Dublin, 2014).

O'Brien, G. (ed.), *Derry and Londonderry: history and society* (Dublin, 1999).

O'Byrne, E. and J. Ní Ghrádaigh (eds), *The march in the islands of the medieval west* (Leiden, 2012).

O'Byrne, E., *War, politics and the Irish of Leinster, 1156–1606* (Dublin, 2003).

O'Neill, T., *Merchants and mariners in medieval Ireland* (Dublin, 1987).

— *The Irish hand: scribes and their manuscripts from the earliest times to the seventeenth century with an exemplar of scripts* (Portlaoise, 1984).

O'Toole, E., 'A miscellany of north Carlow folklore', *Béaloideas*, 1:4 (1928), 316–28.

— 'The parish of Ballon, County Carlow', *Journal of the County Kildare Archaeological Society*, 11:4 (1933), 201–310.

Orpen, G.H., 'The earldom of Ulster', *JRSAI*, 43:1 (1913), 30–46; 43:2, 133–43; 44:1 (1914), 51–66; 45:2 (1915), 123–42.

Packe, M. and L.C.B. Seaman (ed.), *King Edward III* (London, 1983).

Phillips, S., *Edward II* (London, 2010).

— 'Royal authority and its limits: the dominions of the English crown in the early fourteenth century' in E. O'Byrne and J. Ní Ghrádaigh (eds), *The march in the islands of the medieval west* (Leiden, 2012), pp 251–60.

— 'The Irish remonstrance of 1317: an international perspective', *IHS*, 27:106 (1990), 112–29.

Phillips, J.J., *The annals and archaeology of Dundrum, County Down* (Hollywood, 1883).

Power, C., 'The town wall of Waterford', *JRSAI*, 73:4 (1943), 118–36.

Price, L., *The place names of Co. Wicklow V: the barony of Rathdown* (Dublin, 1957).

Reeves, W., 'The seal of Hugh O'Neill', *Ulster Journal of Archaeology*, 1 (1853), 255–58.

Richardson, H.G. and G.O. Sayles, *The administration of Ireland, 1172–1377* (Dublin, 1963).

Rogers, E., *Memoir of the Armagh cathedral, with an account of the ancient city* (Belfast, 1886?).

Ronan, M., 'Killadreenan and Newcastle', *JRSAI*, 63:2 (1938), 172–81.

Roskell, J.S. (ed.), *The house of commons, 1386–1421*, vols 1–4 (Stroud, 1992).

Rynne, E., 'Three Irish knife-daggers', *JRSAI*, 99:2 (1969), 137–43.

Saul, N., *Richard II* (London, 1997).

— 'The kingship of Richard II' in A. Goodman and J.L. Gillespie (eds), *Richard II: the art of kingship* (Oxford, 1999), pp 37–58.

— *The three Richards: Richard I, Richard II and Richard III* (London, 2005).

Scheifele, E., 'Richard II and the visual arts' in A. Goodman and J.L. Gillespie (eds), *Richard II: the art of kingship* (Oxford, 1999), pp 255–72.

Simms, K., *From kings to warlords: the changing political structure of Gaelic Ireland in the later Middle Ages* (Woodbridge, 1987).

— 'Gaelic warfare in the Middle Ages' in T. Bartlett and K. Jeffery (eds), *A military history of Ireland* (Cambridge, 1996), pp 99–115.

— 'Guesting and feasting in Gaelic Ireland', *JRSAI*, 108 (1978), pp 67–100.

— 'Late medieval Tír Eoghain: the kingdom of "the Great Ó Néill"' in C. Dillon and H.A. Jefferies (eds), *Tyrone: history and society* (Dublin, 2000), pp 127–62.

— 'Niall Garbh II O'Donnell, king of Tír Conaill, 1422–39', *Donegal Annual*, 12:1 (1977), 7–21.

— 'Propaganda use of the Táin in the later Middle Ages', *Celtica*, 15 (1983), 142–9.

— 'The archbishop of Armagh and the O'Neills, 1347–1471', *IHS*, vol. 19:73 (1974), 38–55.

— 'The barefoot kings: literary image and reality in later medieval Ireland', *Proceedings of the Harvard Celtic Colloquium*, 30 (2010), 1–21.
— '"The king's friend": Ó Néill, the crown and the earldom of Ulster' in J. Lydon (ed.), *England and Ireland in the later Middle Ages: essays in honour of Jocelyn Otway-Ruthven* (Dublin, 1981), pp 214–36.
— 'The medieval kingdom of Lough Erne', *Clogher Record*, 9:2 (1977), 126–41.
— 'The Ulster revolt of 1404: an anti-Lancastrian dimension?' in B. Smith (ed.), *Ireland and the English world in the late Middle Ages: essays in honour of Robin Frame* (Basingstoke, 2009), pp 141–60.
— 'Tír Eoghain "North of the Mountain"' in G. O'Brien (ed.), *Derry and Londonderry: history and society* (Dublin, 1999), pp 149–74.
— 'Warfare in the medieval Gaelic lordships', *The Irish Sword*, 12 (1975/6), 98–108.
Simpson, L., 'Anglo-Norman settlement in Uí Briúin Cualann, 1169–1350' in K. Hannigan and W. Nolan (eds), *Wicklow: history and society* (Dublin, 1994), pp 191–235.
Smith, B. (ed.), *Ireland and the English world in the late Middle Ages* (Basingstoke, 2009).
— 'The murder of John Dowdall, sheriff of Louth, 1402' in S. Duffy (ed.), *Princes, prelates and poets in medieval Ireland* (Dublin, 2013), pp 185–95.
Stratford, J., *Richard II and the English royal treasure* (Woodbridge, 2012).
Taylor, J., 'Richard II in the chronicles' in A. Goodman and J.L. Gillespie (eds), *Richard II: the art of kingship* (Oxford, 1999), pp 15–36.
Wallace, P.F. and R. Ó Floinn (eds), *Treasures of the National Museum of Ireland: Irish antiquities* (Dublin, 2002).
Weir, A., *Katharine Swynford: the story of John of Gaunt and his scandalous duchess* (London, 2007).
Williams, G.A., 'Cywydd Iolo Goch I Rosier Mortimer: Cefndir a Chyd-Destun', *Llên Cymru*, 22 (1999), 57–79.
Ziegler, P., *The Black Death* (London, 1969).
Zophy, J.W. (ed.), *The Holy Roman Empire: a dictionary handbook* (Westport, 1980).

Index

Abberbury, Richard the Younger,
117
Adam Usk (d. 1430), 162–3, 186,
191–2; visits Richard in the
Tower of London, 28–9, 188–9
An Dúdalach (the Dowdall?), 137
Anglo-Normans, 47, 57, 119;
twelfth-century invasion of
Ireland, 42, 67
Annales Breves Hiberniae, 25, 163
Annales Hiberniae, 25, 59
Annals of Clonmacnoise, 24, 96, 178
Annals of Connacht, 24, 56, 126,
161, 191
Annals of Ireland by Friar John Clyn,
25
Annals of Loch Cé, 24
Annals of Saints' Island, 24–5, 96,
98, 106, 111–13, 155
Annals of the Four Masters, 24, 56,
66, 113, 155–6, 158, 193
Annals of Ulster, 24, 46, 102, 126,
160–1, 189–90, 192
Anne of Bohemia (d. 1394), queen of
England, 34–5

Antrim, Co., 57, 59–60, 129; battle
in (1374), 127–8
Aoife, daughter of Diarmait
MacMurchadha, marries
Strongbow, 48
archbishop of Armagh, 67, 131–2
Archbold family, 151
Ards peninsula, 60, 129
Arklow, 47, 49, 151; sandy beaches
close to, 175
Armagh, Co., 61, 63
Armagh monastery, 66–7, 131–2,
142–3, 160; cathedral, 67, 131,
160
Arundel, Sir William, 155
Assaroe abbey, Tír Chonaill
(Cistercian), 161
Ath an Imuricc, battle of (1366), 126
Athenry, 45; battle of (1316), 55
Augher crannog and palace
(Fraochmhagh?), 62–3, 77

Bagenalstown, 68
Bann (river), 57–8, 60, 63, 77;
bridge, 133

Barbary, land of the sultan, 78
bardic poets, 24, 63, 65–6, 83, 101–3,
    113, 124, 130, 134, 179
Barrett family, 52
Barrow (river), 68
Bath and Wells, cathedrals, 42
Beaumont, Sir John, 96, 108, 148;
    granted vast estates in Co.
    Wexford, 151
Belfast, 58
Bermingham (MacFheorais) family,
    55–6
Bermingham, Walter, 154–5
Bigod family, earls of Norfolk, 49
Bigod, Roger, earl of Norfolk
    (d. 1306), 49
Black Death (plague outbreaks in
    Ireland), 54, 133, 179, 189; great
    plague of 1348–50, 25, 39, 41, 58
black rent, 99–101, 191, 197
Blackstairs mountains, 68, 110, 174
Blackwater (river in Tyrone), 131,
    138
Blackwater (Avoca river in Wicklow
    mountains), 151
Bocksa family, 127
bonnacht of Ulster, 136, 139
Book of St Mulling, book shrine
    (cumdach), repaired by Art
    MacMurchadha, 103
Bordeaux, birthplace of Richard, 18,
    31
Brin Costerec, 19
Bristol, 19, 94, 155, 182, 185
Browne family, 191
Bruce, Edward (d. 1318), 57
Bruce, Robert, king of Scotland
    (1306–29), 40, 57
Bruce invasion of Ireland (1315–18),
    40, 57

Butler, James, second earl of Ormond
    (1338–82), 19
Butler, James, third earl of Ormond
    (1382–1405), 46–7, 71–2, 151,
    160; spoke Irish 147
Buttevant, 55

Callan, 157
Carlingford, 130
Carlow, Co., 42, 50, 68, 77, 148, 153,
    199; forests of, 27, 48, 69, 174,
    198; liberty of, 49
Carlow castle, 100, 115
Carlow town, 99–100, 115, 148
Carrickfergus castle, 57, 60; repaired
    by Edmund Mortimer, 133
Carrickfergus town, 35; destroyed by
    Irish, 129
Castledermot, 148
Cattle, vast herds possessed by Irish,
    79, 81, 109–110, 170, 176;
    blood puddings, 80; ox meat, 80,
    82; used by Irish in lieu of
    currency, 79
Ceann Eich, 103
Cenél nEógain population group, 65,
    126
Charles IV, Holy Roman emperor
    (1346–78), 34
Charles VI (d. 1422), king of France,
    21–22
Cheshire, principality of, 34, 168,
    182
Cheshire archers, 95, 166
Chester, 182–4, 187–8
chevauchée (English military tactic),
    16, 107, 134, 171
Chronicle of Adam Usk, 28, 155
Chronicle of Ireland by Henry
    Marleburrough, 25

Cinnsealach family, 69
CIRCLE (Calendar of Irish Chancery Letters), 27
Clann-Cuilen (MacConmara family), 53
Clare castle, 54
Clement VII, Avignon antipope, 35
Clogher cathedral, 134
Clogher valley, 65
Clontarf, 44
Clyn, Friar John (d. 1349), 25
Cnoc an Bhogha (Knockboy, Co. Carlow?), 68
Coleraine, 35–6, 57, 60, 133–4, 190
Colton, John, archbishop of Armagh (1381–1404), 21, 141–2, 146
Conchobhar mac Neasa, mythological king of Ulster, 123, 130
Connacht, 54, 56, 72, 87, 132, 148, 152
Conway (Welsh town), 182, 186, 187
Cooley peninsula, 130, 135, 197
Cork, Co., 45–6
Cork town, 41, 45, 52
Courtenay, Sir Philip, lord lieutenant of Ireland, 100
Coventry, 42; site of famous trial by combat, 181
Creton, Jean, (fl. 1386–1420), Burgundian chronicler, 21–22, 42, 72–3, 84; importance, 22; accompanies second expedition to Ireland, 167; records plight of English army, 171–5; witnesses famous parley between Art MacMurchadha and the earl of Gloucester, 16, 21, 81, 176–7; suspects duke of Aumerle of treachery, 22, 179, 182, 184–5;

accompanies earl of Salisbury to Wales, 22, 182; eyewitness to capture of Richard, 188
Cristall (Crystede), Henry, captured by Irish, 19; interpreter for first expedition, 19; trains Irish kings, 20, 82–3, 143–4; his assessments of the Irish, 83, 86, 89–90; family, 19
Cú Chulainn, mythological Irish warrior, 123
Curtis, Edmund (modern historian), 27, 105

Dalkey, 44
Dartas, Janico, 27, 110, 151–2, 186
de Bellemonte, John, constable of Dover and warden of the Cinque Ports, 94
de Búrca of Mayo, 56
de Burgh (de Búrca) family, 55, 57, 72, 128
de Burgh of Caimlinn, 128
de Burgh, Elizabeth, countess of Ulster, 132
de Burgh, William, earl of Ulster (1326–33), 58
de Burgh, Sir William (d. 1423) ('Uilleag an Fhíona'), 154–5
de Clare, Isabel, 47
de Clare, Richard (Strongbow), 47–8
de Courcey, John, 57, 128
de La Hyde, Sir James (d. 1374), 128
de Lacy family, 57
de Lisle, Sir William, 18
de Mortimer family; see also Mortimer family
de Peréllos, Raymon (d. c.1419), first viscount Peréllos and second viscount of Roda, 20, 42, 72–4,

76, 78–81, 84–5, 87; friend to
King John I of Aragon, 20;
de Peréllos, Raymon (*continued*)
   meets Richard, 20; visits St
   Patrick's Purgatory, 17, 21;
   spends Christmas at court of
   Ó Néill, 21, 73, 82, 144
de Veel, Elizabeth (d. 1445), baroness
   of Norragh, 105–6, 109, 116, 191
de Veel, Sir Robert (d. *c.*1378), baron
   of Norragh, 105
de Vere, Robert, earl of Oxford and
   marquis of Ireland, lord
   lieutenant of Ireland, 100–1
Derg (river), 66
Derg valley, 134
Derry, 134
Derry, Co., 61
Despenser, Sir Thomas (d. 1400),
   earl of Gloucester, 16–17, 96,
   167–8, 176–7, 185–6
Dingle, 45–6
Donaghmore church, 134
Down, Co., 57, 60, 133
Downpatrick, English town, 36, 60,
   190; battle of (1374), 128
Drogheda, 21, 41–2, 117, 142–4,
   157, 200
Drumarg (episcopal palace), 67
Drummond Missal, 162
Drumtarcy castle, 133
Dublin castle, 44, 185
Dublin city, 16, 21, 35, 42, 51,
   112–13, 117, 135, 144, 147–8,
   197; bridge falls down, 44;
   Christ Church cathedral, 42; St
   Patrick's cathedral, 42–3;
   merchant ships supply English
   army (1399), 175; plentiful
   supplies in, 179

Dublin, Co., 41–2, 153
Duffry forest, 110
Dunamase castle, 50
Dundalk, 21, 35, 42, 57, 130, 142,
   146, 153, 178, 197
Dungannon castle, 63
Dungarvan, royal manor, 114

Eamhain Mhacha, 124, 130–1, 134
Edward I (d. 1307), king of England,
   40
Edward II, king of England
   (1307–27), 40
Edward III, king of England
   (1327–77), 31, 44, 99
England, kingdom of, 32, 38, 93,
   117, 162, 167, 182
English expeditions to Ireland, first
   expedition (1394–5), 18, 26–7,
   93–119, 121–57; second
   expedition (1399), 72, 165–85
English language, 38
English law in Ireland, 38
English of Ireland, 36–8, 42, 67, 119,
   153, 155, 159, 195–6; becoming
   increasingly gaelicized, 38, 45–6,
   55–6
English of earldom of Ulster, 56–60,
   127–9, 190, 199; of lordship of
   Leinster, 50, 100–1, 105, 113,
   148, 152, 158, 161, 191, 196–7,
   199–200; of Louth, 42; of
   Limerick, 53; of Cork, 52–3; of
   Connacht, 55; of Munster, 42,
   45, 47, 52–4, 113, 148; of
   Meath, 135; of Cooley
   peninsula, 135
English soldiers, 51, 85, 88, 93, 175,
   185–7; excellent reputation,
   106; tactics, 107, 110–11, 131,

197; wear plate armour, 86, 108–9, 172; ransom prisoners, 90; numbers on first expedition, 95, 108; numbers on second expedition, 166–8, 176; men-at-arms, 106, 108, 168; mounted archers, 107, 108–9, 111, 168

Errigal-Keeroge church, 134

Faughart, battle of (1318), 57

fish, 80

Fitzgerald, Gerald, third earl of Desmond (1357–98), known as Gearóid Iarla, 45–6, 52–3, 114, 147; later prominence in Irish folklore, 201

Fitzgerald, Gerald fitzMaurice (d. 1432), fifth earl of Kildare, 160

Fitzgerald, Maurice (d. 1390), fourth earl of Kildare, 49–50

Flint castle, 188

Fotharta territory, 110

Foyle (river), 63

France, 35, 95

Franciscan friars, 24, 175, 185–6; friary at Armagh, 67

Freyne, James, 105

Freyne, Leonard, 105

Froissart, Jean (c.1337–c.1410), Burgundian chronicler, 18–19, 73, 82, 84, 86, 89; story of the knighting of the Irish kings, 143–4

Furlong family, 191

Gaelic revival, 35, 50–1, 54–60

gall (foreigners – the English of Ireland), 84, 133, 160–1, 190

Gaelic Scotland, 86–7

galloglasses (gallóglaigh – foreign warriors), 86; weaponry and armour, 87

Galway, Co., 45

Galway town, 45, 157

Garryhill forest (An Gharbhchoill), 68, 77, 106–7, 109, 152

Garryhill palace, 68, 77, 108, 163

Gascony, 31

Gleann Concadhain forest, 61–2

Glendalough monastery, 70, 161–2

Glenmalure valley and forest, 69

Glen of Imaal, 69

gold, 104, 177, 187

Graiguenamanagh, abbot of (Cistercian), 192

Great Connell (Newbridge), 148

Greencastle (Co. Down), 57, 133

Gregory, bishop of Kilmacduagh (Gregorious Ó Leaáin), 149

Harold family, 151

Harry Avery's castle, 78; see also Éinrí Aimhréidh Ó Néill

Henry II (d. 1189), king of England, 156, 180

Henry III (d. 1272), king of England, 39

Henry IV (1399–1413), king of England; see also Plantagenet, Henry Bolingbroke

Henry V (1413–22), king of England; see also Plantagenet, Henry of Monmouth

Holland, Eleanor, countess of March and Ulster, 21, 164

Holland, John (d. 1400), earl of Huntingdon and duke of Exeter, 95, 167–8, 186

Holland, Sir Thomas (d. 1400), duke of Surrey, 95, 109, 163, 167–8, 170–1, 186
Holt castle, 167–8
Holyhead, 20
Holy Trinity priory, Irishtown, Kilkenny (Dominican), 148
Howth, 44
Hy Kinsella, Irish of, 158

Iolo Goch (Welsh poet), 121
Ireland, 36, 40–1, 60–1, 79, 93, 96, 119, 140, 156, 161, 163, 166–8, 179, 184–5, 196–7, 198, 201–2; Gaelic Ireland, 36; forests of, 39; hawks from, 39; severe weather events in, 40–1; famine in, 40–1
Ireland, lordship of, 34, 36–8, 40–1, 47, 51–3, 195; neglected by English kings, 39, 44
Irish (native people of the island), 35, 38–9, 47, 49–52, 54–6, 59–60, 83–4, 114, 118, 141–2, 149, 161, 163, 166, 169, 193; viewed as savages by Europeans, 36, 72–3, 119, 176; description of women, 74–5; clothes and customs, 73–77, 82, 136; food and drink, 79–80
Irish exchequer, 115
Irish horses (hobbies), 16, 81, 176
Irish horsemen (*marcach*), 16, 84–6, 128, 172, 176; equipment and weaponry, 84–6; training, 86
Irish language, 24–5, 88, 139
Irish PRO, destroyed 1922, 28
Irish Sea, 180, 191
Irish warriors, 84–91, 129, 141, 163–4, 178; tactics, 89–91, 170, 172; behead prisoners, 90, 158

Irish whiskey (*uisce beatha/aqua vitae*), 80
Isle of Man, 21

Jerpoint, 106
Joan of Kent (d. 1385), 31
John (d. 1216), king of England, 34, 40, 202
John I, king of Aragon (1387–96), 20

Kavanagh Charter Horn, 103
Kells (Kellistown), battle of (1398), 163–4
kerne (*ceatharnaigh*), 16, 88–9, 170
Kerry, Co., 45
Kildare, Co., 42, 50, 105, 148, 153; plains of, 196–7; liberty of, 153
Kilkenny, Co., 25, 41, 45–6, 50, 68, 105, 152
Kilkenny castle, 47
Kilkenny town, 25, 41, 45, 148–9, 169
Killaloe, 55
Kilmallock, 45
Kinsale, 36, 45, 52
Knighton's Chronicle, 28

Lagan (river), 57
Laois, Co., 50; forests of, 70
Latin, 25–6, 140
Laveroc forest, 68, 108–9, 152; palace, 68, 110
Lecale, 129
Leighlin bridge, 148, 153
Leinster, lordship of, 26, 47–8, 198
Leinster, new Irish kingdom of, 16, 20, 50, 68–72, 97, 116–17, 158, 193
Leinster, old kingdom (pre-Anglo-Norman), 47, 70

Leinster mountains, 16, 151, 169–75, 178, 196–7
Liffey (river), 42, 44–5
Limerick, Co., 45–6
Limerick town, 35, 45, 53
Lollards, 155
London, 20, 22, 32
Lough Gur, 46
Lough Neagh, 58, 65, 122, 160
Lough Ree, 24
Loundres, Edmund, 36
Louth, Co., 42, 65, 67, 197

MacAonghusa family, kings of Iveagh, 58, 190
MacAonghusa, Art, king of Iveagh, 132–3, 138
MacAonghusa, Muircheartach, king of Iveagh, 146
MacArtáin family, 58
MacCába, galloglass chieftain, 146
MacCana family, 65
MacCarthaigh Mór, Tadhg (na Mainistreach), king of Desmond (1391–1428), 76, 141, 147, 149
MacCathmhaoil family, 65
MacCon Mídhe family (bardic poets to Ó Néill), 65
MacConmara, Síoda Óg (d. 1370), warden of Limerick, 53
MacCraith, Eoghan, bardic poet, poem for Art MacMurchadha, 101, 103–4
MacDaibhéid Mór family, 69; chieftain fights in battle of Kells, 163–4
MacDiarmada family, 149
MacDomhnaill galloglass family (Clann Alasdair), Hebridean mercenary dynasty, constables of

Ulster, 65, 87, 128; fight in Ó Néill civil war, 125–6
MacDomhnaill, Eoin Maol (fl. 1395–97), constable of Ulster, 21, 87–88, 146
MacDonnchadha family, 149
MacEochaidh Eolach (d. 1399), *ollamh* to the house of Caomhánach in poetry, 102
MacGiolla Mhuire family, 58, 190
MacGiolla Mhuire, Adam, 146
MacLochlainn, Muircheartach, captain of Art MacMurchadha's kerne, fights in battle of Kells, 163–4
MacMathghamhna, Seán, king of Oriel, 146
MacMathghamhna family, kings of Oriel, 113
MacMhadóc family, 69
MacMurchadha, Art (d. 1282), 49
MacMurchadha, Diarmait (d. 1171), king of Leinster, 48
MacMurchadha, Enna (son of Diarmait), 69
MacMurchadha, Muircheartach (d. 1282), 49
MacMurchadha, Murchadh (brother of Diarmait), 69
MacMurchadha family, 48–9, 69
MacMurchadha Caomhánach family, 50–1
MacMurchadha Caomhánach, Art, Art Mór's father, king of Irish Leinster (1354–61; d. 1362), 98–9
MacMurchadha Caomhánach, Art Mór, king of Irish Leinster (1375–1416/17), 26, 71, 77, 90–1, 98, 156, 166, 196–8;

MacMurchadha Caomhánach, Art
  Mór (continued)
  birth, 98; becomes king of Irish
  Leinster, 99; levies black rents,
  99–101; bardic poetry for,
  101–2; hires mercenaries, 88,
  99–100, 170; personal military
  skills, 16–17, 86; depicted
  wearing spurs on his bare feet,
  17, 73, 85–6; marries Elizabeth
  de Veel, 105–6; resistance to
  Richard (1394), 107–8; almost
  captured, 109–10; surrenders,
  111–12; negotiations with
  Thomas Mowbray, 116, 118;
  alleged to be at knighting
  ceremony of four Irish kings,
  143–4; fails to keep agreement
  with Richard, 152; rebuilds
  power, 157–8; escapes English
  trap, 158, 201; absent from
  battle of Kells, 164; commands
  3,000 warriors (1399), 169; loses
  force of kerne, 170–1; success
  against Richard's army, 178;
  removes all food supplies,
  173–5; famous parley with the
  earl of Gloucester, 16, 21, 81,
  175–7; bounty of gold placed
  on his head, 177; great victory
  over the English of Wexford
  (1416), 191; sends embassy to
  Henry V, 192; death of, 192–3,
  200; speeches preserved, 17,
  169, 173, 177; legend surrounding his death, 193; a capable and
  successful Irish king, 15, 161,
  178, 189–90, 196, 199–200
MacMurchadha Caomhánach,
  Donnchadh (d. 1375),

(Art Mór's uncle), king of Irish
  Leinster, 99, 199
MacMurchadha Caomhánch,
  Donnchadh (d. 1478), king of
  Irish Leinster, Art Mór's son and
  heir, 193
MacMurchadha Caomhánach,
  Gearalt (d. 1431), Art Mór's
  son, 192
MacMurchadha Caomhánach,
  Muircheartach (Art Mór's
  grandfather), king of Irish
  Leinster (c.1346/7–1354), 98
MacMurchadha Caomhánach,
  Tomás Carrach (d. 1402),
  brother of Art Mór, 102
MacDonald, lord of the isles, 88
MacQuillan, Johnock, 147
Mag Oirc (coarb) family, 66
Mag Uidhir family, kings of
  Fermanagh, 156
Magraidhin, Canon Aughuistín
  (d. 1405), 24
Marshal, Matilda, countess of
  Warren, 48
Marshal, William, lord of Leinster, 47
Marshal family, 48
mead (miodh/mil-fion), 80
Meath, Co., 41–2, 197
Michel, Le (ship), 94
Milford Haven, 22, 96, 185
Mitford, Richard, bishop of
  Chichester, 154–5
Monasteranenagh, battle of (1370),
  46, 53
Montagu, John (d. 1400), third earl
  of Salisbury, 22, 167, 182, 186
Mortimer, Edmund, third earl of
  March and Ulster (1368–81),
  132–4, 138

Mortimer, Roger, fourth earl of
March and Ulster (1381–98),
lord lieutenant of Ireland, 21,
72, 95, 112–13, 136, 138, 140,
159, 161–2, 197; praised in
Welsh poetry, 121; Richard's
cousin (once removed), 165;
argues with Niall Mór Ó Néill,
139; unhappy with Richard's
agreement with Niall Óg Ó
Néill, 143, 153, 197; attacks
Niall Óg, 160, 198; burns
Armagh cathedral, 160; killed at
battle of Kells, 163–4; impact of
his death, 165–6
Mortimer, Roger, lord of Laois, 50
Mortimer, Sir Thomas, 162
Mortimer family, 28, 60
Mourne mountains, 60
Mowbray, Thomas (d. 1399), earl of
Nottingham, duke of Norfolk,
marshal of England, 95, 108;
almost captures Art
MacMurchadha, 109–10;
negotiates with MacMurchadha,
116, 118, 152; brings Ó Briain
to Richard, 147; granted Carlow
castle, 151; involved in murder
of duke of Gloucester, 181;
begins to fear Richard, 181;
dispute with Henry
Bolingbroke, 180–1; trial by
combat cancelled, 181; exiled
for life, 181; dies of the plague
in Venice, 181; his military
skills, 180, 198
Moyola (river), 61
Munster, 50, 54, 87, 152, 198
Murroes territory, 69
Myshall village, 68, 163

New Ross, 35, 41, 45, 71–2, 107, 114;
sovereign of, 191; legend Art
MacMurchadha poisoned in, 193
Norragh, barony of, 105–6, 116

Ó Beirn family, 149
Ó Briain of Ara family, 100
Ó Briain, Brian, king of Thomond
(1369–99), 141, 147; victor of
battle of Monasteranenagh, 46;
captures Limerick, 53; submits
to Richard, 76, 144; knighted by
Richard, 143–4; probably at
ceremony of knighting of Irish
kings, 143–4; death of, 178–9
Ó Briain, Murchadh na Raithnighe
(d. 1383), lord of Ara, 47, 54–5,
201
Ó Briain, Toirdhealbhach, (d. 1399),
lord of Ara, son of Murchadh na
Raithnighe, 47, 113, 149, 161,
179
Ó Broin, Gearalt, 76
Ó Broin family, 52, 69; chieftains of,
69, 111–12, 171; chieftain fights
in battle of Kells, 163–5
Ó Catháin, Maghnus, king of
Oireacht Uí Chatháin, 146–7
Ó Catháin family, kings of Oireacht
Uí Chatháin, 63
Ó Ceallaigh, Muircheartach (d. 1407),
archbishop of Tuam, 147–8
Ó Ceallaigh family, 149
Ó Cearbhaill family, 100
Ó Conchobhair Faly family, kings of
Offaly, 70
Ó Conchobhair, Cathal Óg, sons of,
56
Ó Conchobhair, Feidhlim (d. 1316),
king of Connacht, 55

Ó Conchobhair, Muircheartaigh, king of Offaly, 76

Ó Conchobhair Donn, Toirdhealbhach (1384–1406), 76, 141, 143–5, 149–51, 154

Ó Conchobhair family, kings of Connacht, 127

Ó Conchobhair Ruadh, Toirdhealbhach (1384–1425/6), 150–1

Ó Cuindilis, Muircheartach, 165

Ó Cuinn family, 64

Ó Dálaigh, Cúchonnacht, family of, 66

Ó Dálaigh, Tadhg Camchosach, poetry in praise of Niall Mór Ó Néill, 130

Ó Deoráin, chief brehon of Leinster, according to legend poisoned alongside Art MacMurchadha, 193

Ó Deoráin, Ulliam (d. 1404/5), law *ollamh* to the house of Caomhánach, 102

Ó Díomasaigh family, kings of Clanmalier, 112

Ó Díomasaigh, Tomaltach, 112

Ó Domhnaill family, kings of Tír Chonaill, 122, 156

Ó Domhnaill, Toirdhealbhach, king of Tír Chonaill (1380–1422; d. 1423), 56, 161, 189

Ó Doibhlín family, 64

Ó Donnghaile family, 64

Ó Dubhagáin, Cam Cluana, *ollamh* in history and poetry, 113

Ó Dubhda, Domhnall, 56

Ó Dubhda family, 56, 149

Ó Fearghail family, kings of Annaly, 113, 159

Ó Flaithbheartaigh family, kings of Iar-Connacht, 156

Ó Flannagáin family, 149

Ó Floinn, Muircheartach (d. 1356), 58

Ó Floinn, Tomás (d. 1368), king of Uí Tuirtre, 58

Ó Floinn family, kings of Uí Tuirtre, 58, 60

Ó Gadhra family, 149

Ó Goirmleadhaigh family, 65

Ó hAgáin family, 64

Ó hÁinle family, 149

Ó hAnluain family, kings of Orior, 65, 133, 146

Ó hEachaidhéin, Tadhg (d. 1394), bardic poet, 66

Ó hEaghra family, 149

Ó Luchráin, Master Tomás, secretary to Niall Óg Ó Néill, 142

Ó Madáin family, 149

Ó Maoilriain family, 149

Ó Mealláin family, 64

Ó Mongáin family, 66

Ó Mórdha, Laoighseach (d. 1342), chieftain, overthrows English of Laois, 50

Ó Mórdha family, kings of Laois, 50, 70, 111

Ó Murchadha family, 69

Ó Néill, Aodh Reamhar, king of Tyrone (*c*.1345–64), successful Irish king, 63, 122–5; death-bed advice to his sons, 124–5

Ó Néill, Aodh of Clann Aodha Buidhe, 58

Ó Néill, Brian, king of Tyrone (d. 1403), son of Niall Óg, 136, 159, 190, 201

Ó Néill, Cú-Uladh Ruadh (d. 1399), son of Niall Mór and brother of Niall Óg, 63, 131–2, 146, 179

Ó Néill, Domhnall, son of Aodh Reamhar, 63, 74, 125–7

Ó Néill, Domhnall Bog, king of Tyrone (1404–10 dep.; 1414–19 dep.; 1421–32), son of Éinrí Aimhéidh, 159, 178, 190

Ó Néill, Éinrí Aimhréidh (d. 1392), *ríoghdhamhna*, 63, 78, 126, 131–2, 201; his sons, 178

Ó Néill, Feidhlimidh, son of Niall Óg, 160

Ó Néill, Niall Mór, king of Tyrone (1364–97), high-king of Ulster (1374–97), 88, 90–1, 121–2, 125–34, 157, 197; in bardic poetry, 24, 130; personal skills as a warrior, 86, 161; relations with archbishop of Armagh, 131–2; peace agreement with his brother Domhnall, 126; defeats the English of Ulster, 127–9, 135; becomes high-king of Ulster, 130; plan to build *longphort* (fortress) at Eamhain Mhacha, 130–1, 134–5; compared to a pope or emperor, 131; negotiates with Edmund Mortimer, 132; attacked by Mortimer, 133–4; abdicates into semi-retirement, 134; secures Niall Óg's release, 136; prince of the Irish of Ulster, 137; negotiates with Richard, 26, 63, 138–40; argues with Roger Mortimer, 139; submits to Richard, 140; death of, 160–1; a capable and successful Irish king, 15, 161, 200–1

Ó Néill, Niall Óg, king of Tyrone (1387–1403), high-king of Ulster (1387–1403), son of Niall Mór, 88, 90–1, 122, 134–7, 146, 157, 197; skills as a warrior, 86, 137; household cavalry, 85; marries Una Ó Néill, 126–7; Raymon de Peréllos at his Christmas court, 17, 73, 79, 81–2, 87, 144; enquires about kings of France and Spain, 82; castle at Dungannon, 63; very large horse stud, 81; becomes king, 134–5; captured by English, 135–6; son surrendered as a hostage, 136–7; negotiates with Richard, 26, 138; governor of the Irish of Ulster, 140; calls provincial gathering, 141–2; submits to Richard, 76, 142; knighted by Richard, 19, 143–4; central role at knighting of the four kings, 143; resents training by Henry Cristall, 82, 144, 198; complains about English of Dundalk, 153; fears attack by Roger Mortimer, 153–4, 159–60; saves kingdom of Tyrone, 157, 197; ransoms son Brian, 160; subjugates Tír Chonaill, 161, 189, 201; invited to England by Richard, 162; remains aloof from Richard 1399, 178; at the height of his power, 189; death of, 189–90; a successful and capable Irish king, 15, 159, 189, 200–1

Ní Néill, Una (d. 1417), queen of Tyrone, 74, 126–7, 159

Ó Néill of Clann Aodha Buidhe family, 58, 60, 77

Ó Néill of Tyrone family, kings of Tyrone, 58, 62, 67, 73, 87, 145; lucht tighe lands, 63–4; *lucht tighe* families, 64; *ollamh*-ship in poetry, 65–6

Ó Nualláin family, right to inaugurate MacMurchadha, 68; lands plundered by English, 110; chieftain surrenders to Richard, 111; chieftain fights in battle of Kells, 163

Ó Raghilligh family, kings of East Breifne, 113, 159

Ó Riain family, 69

Ó Ruairc family, 149

Ó Tuathail, Feidhlim (d. 1404), king of Imaal, 157–8; victory over English (1396), 158; commands Irish army at battle of Kells (1398), 163–5

Ó Tuathail family, kings of Imaal, 52, 69

O'Brennan's cross, 152

O'Donovan, John, nineteenth-century Irish historian and antiquarian, 80

O'Sullivan Beare, Philip, early modern author and historian, 61–2, 81

Offaly, Co., 50; boglands of, 70

Oriel, kingdom of, 140

Otway-Ruthven, Jocelyn, modern historian, 28

Owain Glyn Dŵr, sends letter to the Irish kings, 191–2

Oxford, 20

Oxford University, Bodleian Library, 24; All Souls' College, 27

Oxmantown, 42

papacy (Roman), Irish kings' allegiance to, 83; Irish kings bound to pay large sums to, 118, 143, 147

parliament of the lordship of Ireland, meets 1394, 114

Patrick, bishop of Kilfenora, 149

Peasants' Revolt (1381), 31–2

Percy, Henry (d. 1408), first earl of Northumberland, sent by Henry Bolingbroke to secure custody of Richard, 187–8

Percy, Sir Henry ('Hotspur') (d. 1403), 155(?), 187

Percy, Sir Thomas, earl of Worcester (d. 1403), steward of the king's household, 95, 109, 167–8, 186; breaks his rod of office, 187

Philip the Bold, duke of Burgundy, 24

Philippa, countess of Ulster (d. 1378), 132, 163

Philippa of Hainault (d. 1369), queen of England, 18

Plantagenet, Edmund of Langley, duke of York (d. 1402), uncle to Richard, regent of England (1399), 118–19, 170

Plantagenet, Edward of Aumerle (d. 1415), earl of Rutland, duke of Aumerle, cousin to Richard, admiral of the fleet, 95, 108, 110; brings MacCarthaigh Mór to Richard, 149; gift to Richard, 145; arrives late during second expedition, 167–9, 179; suspected of treachery towards Richard, 22, 182 shocked by Richard's departure, 186

Plantagenet, Edward of Woodstock (d. 1376), prince of Wales, known as the Black Prince, Richard's father, 31

Plantagenet, Henry Bolingbroke (d. 1413), duke of Hereford, cousin to Richard, dispute with Thomas Mowbray, 181; trial by combat cancelled, 181; exiled from England for ten years, 180; death of father John of Gaunt, 180–1; Lancastrian inheritance confiscated by Richard, 181; news of his landing in England arrives at Dublin, 180; captures Bristol, 182; captures Chester, 184, 187; secures custody of Richard, 187–8; deposes Richard, 22, 29, 165, 188; crowned king of England as Henry IV, 188–9, 196; imprisons Richard, 188–9

Plantagenet, Henry of Monmouth (d. 1422), son of Henry Bolingbroke, future King Henry V, 167, 184, 189, 192; knighted by Richard in Wicklow mountains, 171

Plantagenet, Humphrey (d. 1399), son of Thomas of Woodstock, cousin to Richard, 167, 184, 189

Plantagenet, John of Gaunt (d. 1399), duke of Lancaster, uncle to Richard, father of Henry Bolingbroke, 32

Plantagenet, Lionel (d. 1368), duke of Clarence and earl of Ulster, uncle to Richard, lord lieutenant of Ireland, 18–19, 98–99, 115, 132

Plantagenet, Thomas of Woodstock, duke of Gloucester (d. 1397),

uncle to Richard, 95, 106; murdered in Calais, 33, 181

Plantagenet, Richard of Bordeaux: see Richard II

Poddle (river), 44

Pontefract castle, Richard imprisoned in, 189

Priory of St John the Baptist, Kilmainham (Knights Hospitaller), 43

Rede, Robert, bishop of Lismore, 154

Ribenuzo (Ryvenys), Nicholas, 117

Richard II, king of England (1377–99; d. 1400), 27, 44, 76, 82, 90, 106, 118–19, 132, 136, 157–8, 164; birth, 18, 31; Peasants' Revolt, 31–2; interest in art, 32; marriage to Anne of Bohemia, 34; first expedition to Ireland (1394–5), 93–7; death of his queen, 35; lays siege to Garryhill, 98, 106–8, 111, 113; dealings with Art MacMurchadha, 111–13, 116–17; calls an Irish parliament, 113, 115–16; negotiations with the Ó Néill kings, 121–2, 137, 143, 145–6; knights Irish kings, 143–5; orders their training, 82–3, 144; receives submission of minor Ulster kings, 146; receives submission of southern and western Irish kings, 147, 149; knights Ó Conchobhair Donn, 154; grants estates in Leinster mountains, 151–2, 156; his agreements begin to unravel, 152–4, 166, 198; returns to England (1395), 155, 157; Irish annals view his first expedition with favour, 155–6; invites Niall Óg Ó Néill to England, 162; falls out with Mortimers, 162; exiles his English enemies, 167; second expedition to Ireland (1399), 166–85; leads army against Art MacMurchadha, 169–77, 199; his army starving, 173–5; sends earl of Gloucester to parley with MacMurchadha, 175–7; outraged by Art's conditions, 177; returns with army to Dublin, 175, 177; places bounty on MacMurchadha's head, 177; hears of Henry Bolingbroke's landing in England, 180; miscalculates own return, 181–2, 184; imprisons relatives in Trim castle, 184; chaotic return of his fleet, 185; abandons his army for north Wales, 185–6; rumour he is dead, 186; royal baggage plundered by own soldiers, 187; captured by the earl of Northumberland, 188; imprisoned in the Tower of London, 188; deposed by Henry Bolingbroke, 22, 29, 165, 188; death of, 189, 196; his speeches, 17, 177–8, 184, 188; consequences of his expeditions to Ireland, 188–9, 195–6, 198, 202; reasons for success of first expedition, 197–8; under-estimated Art MacMurchadha, 199; curses decision to visit Ireland, 202

Richard II (Shakespearean play), 15–16, 195

Rither, Henry, 94
Roche, the knight, 127
Rower forest, 68
Rupert, Count Palatine of the Rhine, 117
Rynaux, John, chamberlain of the liberty of Ulster, 129

St Mary Magdalene priory, Drogheda (Dominican), 139, 142, 146
St Mary's abbey, Dublin (Cistercian), 43; Latin annals of, 25
St Mary's priory, Coleraine (Dominican), 60
St Mullins monastery, 70, 103
St Patrick, 66, 160
St Patrick's Bell (relic), 64
St Patrick's Purgatory, Lough Derg, 17–18, 20–1, 72
St Patrick's staff (relic), 112
SS Peter and Paul abbey, Armagh (Augustinian), 67
St Thomas the Martyr Abbey, Dublin (Augustinian), 43, 147
Saints' Island (Oileán na Naomh), 24
Sandal family, 127
Saul, Nigel, modern historian, 34
Savage, Edmund, 146–7
Savage, Sir Robert (d. 1360), 59–60
Savage family, 60
Saxons (Englishmen from the kingdom of England), 84, 156, 158, 192
Saxony (England), 178
Scotland, 125
Scottish border, 35, 169
Scottish wars of independence, 40, 86–7
Scots, 57, 190

Scrope, Richard (d. 1405),
    archbishop of York and
    chancellor of England, 117
Scrope, Sir William, 96
Shannon (river), 54, 179
Shillelagh woods, 172, 199
Simms, Katharine, modern historian,
    73–4
Sinnott family, 191
Slieve Gallion mountain, 61
Sligo, Co. (Lower Connacht), 56
Sligo town, destroyed by Irish, 56
Spenser, Sir Edmund, 54–5, 201
Sperrin mountains, 61–3, 80
Statute of Kilkenny (1366), 37, 105
Staunton, Anastasia, 105
Staunton, Margaret, 105
Staunton, Sir John, lord of Otymy,
    105
Straw, Jack, 32
Sutton family, 191
Sweteman (Sweetman), Milo,
    archbishop of Armagh
    (1361–80), 131–2; allegations
    against Niall Mór Ó Néill, 131

Táin, 123
Temple of the Relics (Temple na
    Ferta), Armagh (Augustinian
    nunnery), 67
Templebreed (Temple Brigid),
    Armagh, (Augustinian
    nunnery), 67
Termonamongan, 66
Termonmaguirk, 66
Thomond, kingdom of, 53–4
Thurles, 55
Tipperary, Co., 41, 45–6
Tír Chonaill, kingdom of, 122, 161,
    189

Tower of London, Richard
    imprisoned in, 29, 188–9
Tralee, 45
Trim castle, 72, 133; Richard places
    £14,000 in, 168; used by
    Richard as prison for
    Plantagenet kinsmen, 184
Trinite, La (ship), 148–9, 154
Tullaghoge (rath), 64, 77; Ó Néill
    kings inaugurated at, 62
Twescard (the North), 60, 129, 190
Tyler, Wat (d. 1381), 32
Typhayne, La (ship), 94
Tyrone, kingdom of, 17, 61–7, 123,
    126–7, 129, 133, 138, 190, 201

Ulaid population group, 123, 160
Ulster (fifth/province), 87, 121, 123,
    126–7, 130–2, 159, 161
Ulster Cycle of mythological tales,
    123, 130–1
Ulster, earldom of, 26, 56–7, 60, 72,
    123, 133, 135, 137, 152, 178,
    190
Urney church, 134

vale of Dublin, 52, 151, 197
View of the present state of Ireland,
    54–5
Viking fleets, 97

Wade, Richard, 99
Wales, 21, 34–5, 37, 182, 185–8, 202
Walsingham, Thomas, English
    chronicler, 184
Waltham, John, bishop of Salisbury
    (1388–95), treasurer of
    England, 26–7, 152
Walworth, Sir William, mayor of
    London, 32

wardrobe account for first
  expedition, 28, 95
Waterford, Co., 45–6, 153
Waterford town, 41, 45, 71, 96–7,
  149, 154–5, 169, 182, 185
Webb, John, 24
Welsh (native population), 34, 187,
  191–2
Wenzel, king of the Romans, 34
Westmeath, Co., 42
Wexford, Co., 45, 68, 100, 153, 191;
  liberty of, 191; seneschal of, 191

Wexford town, 45; sovereign of, 191
White, Geoffrey (Seifin), 137
Wicklow, Co., 16, 50
Wicklow mountains, 48, 68–70, 76,
  157–8, 174, 179, 184, 199;
  severe weather event in, 49
William of Baile-Dalat, 127
wine, 80, 169, 175, 179
wolves, 20, 39

Yorkshire, 180
Youghal, 41, 157